BABY BULL

*From Hardball to
Hard Time and Back*

BABY BULL

◆ ◆ ◆

FROM HARDBALL TO HARD TIME AND BACK

Orlando Cepeda

with
Herb Fagen

TAYLOR PUBLISHING COMPANY
Dallas, Texas

Published by Taylor Publishing Company
1550 West Mockingbird Lane
Dallas, Texas 75235
www.taylorpub.com

Library of Congress Cataloging-in-Publication Data

Cepeda, Orlando.
Baby Bull : from hardball to hard time and back / Orlando Cepeda with Herb Fagen.
p.   cm.
ISBN 0-87833-212-X
1. Cepeda, Orlando. 2. Baseball players—United States—Biography.
3. Puerto Ricans—Biography. 4. Marijuana. I. Fagen, Herb. II. Title.
GV865.C37   A3   1998
796.357'092—dc21
[B]
98-31068
CIP

Printed in the United States of America
10 9 8 7 6 5 4 3 2 1

This book has been printed on acid-free recycled paper.

To the memory of my parents,
Perucho and Carmen Cepeda

I am not here on earth for strife,
Love is the mission of my life.
YUNUS EMRE

Contents

Foreword

Orlando Cepeda represents the San Francisco Giants as our community-relations ambassador. Anyone who meets him is struck by his personality. If you're a little kid you pay attention to what he says. There's something behind that magnetic personality that makes you concentrate on him. He works so well with the Giants in countless ways.

I've been with him at some of the appearances he's made in the Mission District of San Francisco. What I really admire about Orlando is his ability to openly confront the problems that he had and his candor in telling kids about them. He shows how we can all own up and learn from our mistakes.

The first time I really got to know him was a few years ago when we had a celebration at Union Square. We were celebrating our victory in keeping the Giants in San Francisco. Orlando was in the audience. It was clear to me then, as it is now, that part of the reason the Giants were able to stay in San Francisco was people such as Orlando Cepeda, who has been an important part of the Giants' tradition for so long.

I first saw him play in 1958. I was sixteen years old at the time and went to Seals Stadium every time I could. I had a job bagging groceries at Safeway, and I must have seen twenty-five games that summer. He was my favorite player.

From that first season, the city embraced him. He was the most popular player here, not Willie Mays. I think that's because

Willie was considered part of the New York Giants and Orlando came up as part of an exciting group of young rookies in 1958.

Like Willie Mays, Orlando always looked like he wanted to play ball. That he enjoyed it. He got a lot of love from the fans, and what he got he always gave back. If you go to a game with Orlando and sit down with him today, he roots with the same enthusiasm as when he played. He keeps the rest of us optimistic. He makes you forget your own problems.

The entire Giants organization feels he belongs in the Hall of Fame. During his last year of eligibility in 1993, we put together a good packet of material to help convince others. We met with people who were on the committee at the time. We did numerous interviews with newspaper writers across the country. We flew Orlando to St. Louis, where he was also a big star and the National League Most Valuable Player in 1967. We tried hard to get his story out. To lose by only seven votes was devastating. I admired the grace with which he handled it.

I think some writers hold his problem against him and won't vote for him for that reason. He's got the statistics. I think if any of these people had seen Orlando play, they would have voted for him. He played baseball with so much flair and style. He was a flashy player at first base, an acrobatic first baseman. He was an excellent base runner, and daring—he'd slide beautifully into a base. He was exciting to watch.

As I said, I think he was always our most popular player. That comes across when people see him. They love Orlando Cepeda. He's got a wonderful smile for everybody, from any walk of life or any age, from old ladies to young boys. When he smiles he just lights up a room. And he has the personality to go with that smile. He appreciates the good things now. He's a special person, and the Giants could not be better represented.

Peter A. Magowan
President and Managing General Partner
San Francisco Giants

Introduction

Orlando Cepeda was far and away the National League's most dominant player in 1967. No one was even close. He was the National League's Most Valuable Player, and he won by a landslide.

Acquiring Orlando was the first major piece in solving the puzzle that allowed us to be pennant winners in 1967 and 1968. The second piece, of course, was Roger Maris. Bob Howsam made both these shrewd deals. We gave up Ray Sadecki and Charlie Smith, but when you consider what we got in return it was an extraordinary exchange.

Orlando was traded to the St. Louis Cardinals in May of 1966. What I remember more than anything was that our team physician made sure to find out if Orlando was healthy. We had his knees checked before we allowed the deal to go through.

At the time of the trade Orlando had been living in the shadow of Mays and McCovey in San Francisco, although arguably he was as popular as the other two. But when you talk about group dynamics, it's very hard to put your finger on exactly how something happens. In St. Louis, for whatever reason, Orlando became one of the leaders on our ballclub.

Bob Gibson was the dominant force. Mike Shannon was a force in his own way, especially when he had the courage and guts to move from right field to third base. Roger Maris in his quiet way had a real influence on us winning two pennants and one World Series title. But it was Cepeda whose combined enthusiasm and charisma brought us that "we are a very good team" attitude.

His enthusiasm and the strength of his personality was so dominant, he blended in perfectly with the rest of us. Even the nicest and smartest guy around has to have baseball ability. Orlando's was extraordinary. I learned a great deal hitting behind him in the days when we were teammates.

Just his approach to hitting impressed me greatly. He'd set pitchers up beautifully. He'd intentionally take the first pitch or two, then BOOM. He'd unload when the pitcher thought he'd be taking again. The cat-and-mouse game he played with different pitchers was remarkable. A lot of people think he did it just on ability alone. He was a very smart hitter, an extremely smart hitter. In fact, he was one of the smartest hitters I have ever seen.

Few grant him that. They look only at his size and at his strength. But Orlando's intelligence and his approach to the plate was just as impressive as his physical strength and his uncanny ability to hit the ball the other way.

His leadership tools were extraordinary, and we were smart enough to let him take over. That's why we were named *"El Birdos."* He had a great second half in 1966, and when we realized that we would have Cepeda for the whole year in 1967 . . . why, we couldn't wait for the next season.

We hated to go to New York because of the long, boring bus rides. In New York the bus had to leave earlier because of all the traffic. One day Orlando wasn't on time for the bus. We had an 8:00 game, and we were leaving at 4:15. Usually, the bus pulled out right on the mark. If you were not on it, then you'd have to find your own way to the ballpark.

Orlando wasn't there, and everyone knew that he always rode the bus. Manager Red Schoendienst said, "I guess we ought to go." Gibson was pitching that night. Bob yelled, "We're not going. Bussee, we're not going anywhere until Cepeda's here. 'Cause I'm not going out there tonight unless Cepeda's there." He meant it, too.

In the clubhouse after a win Orlando would get up on a trunk and spout something in Spanish. He was so funny. I don't know if I ever understood any of it, but everybody would laugh and cheer. It was so much fun to go to the ballpark with him there.

I think I was one of the first guys to make him feel at home. "Orlando, you've really made a difference. You're one of the leaders here." What I was implying was that he shouldn't feel shy. He should take over.

We had this fight in Cincinnati in 1967. It started when Don Nottebart hit Lou Brock in the leg. Lou had singled in the first inning, then tried to steal with a six-run lead.

Now it was our turn. Tony Perez was leading off the next inning for the Reds. Bob Gibson was on the mound. Bob threw tight at Tony. He didn't hit him but teased him with a brushback pitch. Tony made an out and as he was coming back in front of the mound he said something to Gibson. Bob came off the mound, but no punches were thrown. Things were all right.

Orlando and I moved to the mound to protect Bob. That's when a Reds pitcher named Bob Lee, a big guy who had played winter ball against Orlando, ran in to where we were standing and said, "Cepeda! I want you, Cepeda!"

Orlando was standing to Bob's side looking around. Then Orlando smoked him. This ignited the worst fight I was ever in. The bullpens emptied, the whole bit. Everyone was throwing punches.

A policeman named Casey, an older cop who had been around the ballpark for years, came on the field. Reds manager Dave Bristol threw a punch and broke Casey's jaw. I'm sure that in this day and age there would be a lawsuit. But Bob Lee sure got more than he wanted when he went after Orlando.

I've been one of the leading proponents in getting him into the Hall of Fame. He and Tony Perez belong there. Orlando spread out his numbers, which are very impressive, over a long period of time. I think that initially his prison sentence on marijuana charges affected his chances for admission. The drug incident was still fresh in the minds of the voters. But I think he'll eventually get in. I just hope it doesn't drag on. I hope he has time to enjoy it. Check his numbers. There are guys in the Hall of Fame without anywhere near the numbers Cha Cha has. And all his teammates loved him. He was smart, and he came to play.

But what particularly impressed me about Orlando was the extreme love and affection he had for his father. Before the days when blacks could get into the major leagues, his father was one of the great players in Puerto Rican history. And Orlando was proud of that. Orlando Cepeda is as good as they get.

Tim McCarver

Preface

October 7, 1989

A capacity crowd of 62,056 filled San Francisco's Candlestick Park for the third game of the National League Championship Series between the Chicago Cubs and the San Francisco Giants. The series was tied at a game apiece. Manager Roger Craig's Giants were battling for their first National League flag since 1962.

A fifty-two-year-old-man walked slowly to the mound to throw out the ceremonial first pitch. When the Giants last played in a World Series in 1962, Orlando Cepeda had been one of baseball's frontline stars, the inimitable "Baby Bull," San Francisco's very own, who just a year earlier had paced the National League with 46 home runs and a still-standing team record of 142 runs batted in.

Since then the vagaries of life had led him through the best of times and the worst of times. He had known wealth and fame, a celebrity status only few attain. He had also known disgrace and degradation as a fallen baseball hero, a tarnished idol.

From the late 1950s through the 1960s he was one of baseball's very best, the only man in the game's history to be unanimously chosen both Rookie of the Year and League MVP. But by the late 1970s and into much of the 1980s, he was an outcast here at home and a pariah in his native Puerto Rico. His life had come full circle, from hardball on the baseball diamond to hard time in a minimum-security prison. He had lost everything: money, pride, family, dignity. He said publicly that he hated baseball, that he wanted no part of it anymore. But privately, it meant everything to him. It always had and always would.

Now, on this night, the cheers from the stands brought tears to his eyes. The Baby Bull was back, and the partisan crowd of more than 60,000 welcomed him home in thunderous ovation. He thought about many things: his mother, Carmen, whom he had so adored; his father, Perucho, his hero and perhaps the greatest Puerto Rican baseball player of them all; his wife, Miriam, who stuck with him through the hard times with love and devotion; and his Buddhist faith, the spiritual force that helped soothe his pain.

When he'd begun practicing Buddhism in 1985, his friend and mentor Al Albergate told him that some day it would all turn around, that he'd be back in baseball and he'd hear those cheers once again.

He could hear them now.

♦ ♦ ♦

Today Orlando Cepeda is a contented man, at peace with himself and the world. His work as community-relations ambassador for the San Francisco Giants has earned him respect and admiration throughout the Bay Area of Northern California and in schools, communities, and neighborhoods the country over.

In this book he will shoot straight—no punches pulled, he insists: "For the first time, here's the *real* story of my life—the struggles, the pain, the glories, the triumphs, the good, the bad. This book is the real thing. I will talk about everything. My story is controversial, sure. But it is truthful, and it is honest."

His stories and commentaries run from the scathing to the heartwarming: from his unsettling and dubious relationship with Willie Mays to his deep-felt friendship and respect for Roger Maris; from his painful encounters with Alvin Dark and Herman Franks to the kindly mentoring of Ty Cobb and Bill Rigney; from the racially torn 1962 National League Champion San Francisco Giants to the blissful harmony of the 1967 World Champion St. Louis Cardinals.

So this is the story of baseball's Baby Bull. But it is more than a baseball book. It is the complete story of a man nature blessed with the capacity to play a remarkable game of baseball. It's a story of courage and love, of frailty and conquest, of optimism and learning. It's a story about life and the human condition—a story that needs to be told.

Herb Fagen

Perucho

The sun shines brightly over our native island. The temperature hovers at a balmy 73 degrees. Travel agents like to call Puerto Rico the shining star of the Caribbean. "Spain moved to a tropical island" is how they often describe it. The beaches are pale and golden, and baseball is as Puerto Rican as *madre* and *pasteles*, the islanders tell you. Baseball fans there are devoted and sincere. They take the game seriously, and they have long memories.

My father, "Perucho", was born Pedro Anibal Cepeda in San Juan, Puerto Rico, and was one of the greatest baseball players the island has ever produced. At 5'11" and 200 pounds, he was mainly a shortstop, but he played first base and in the outfield as well. He was fast for a big man and was a dangerous line-drive hitter who could also hit the long ball, primarily to the power alleys for extra bases. Two decades before his youngest son was among the first wave of Latin players to hit the mainland in the 1950s, Perucho Cepeda was being hailed as the Babe Ruth of Puerto Rico—a baseball legend in his own time.

In 1938 and 1939 Perucho won successive batting titles in Puerto Rico. Twice he hit over .400. The first time was in 1941 when he hit .423 and led the league in RBIs. He bettered that mark the following year with an average of .454.

He once went 4 for 4 in an exhibition game against the New York Yankees. His base hits came off Allie Reynolds and Vic Raschi, two of the major leagues' toughest pitchers in the late 1940s and early 1950s.

Perucho Cepeda had all the tools to have been a major league superstar had the timing been right and the era been different. But two obstacles loomed.

My father was a Latin superstar. But Puerto Rican big leaguers were a scarcity back then. More than 150 native-born Puerto Ricans have played Major League Baseball. But no Puerto Rican star even appeared in a big league uniform until Hi Bithorn suited up for the Chicago Cubs in 1942, and Luis Olmo signed with the Brooklyn Dodgers in 1943. Both were white. Not until the 1950s, after the color barrier was finally broken, would Puerto Rican players play again on big league diamonds.

Pride was the second factor. My father was a proud man, maybe too proud. As a black man he had neither the inclination to endure segregation nor the temperament to buck racism in the United States. He was aware of this. Puerto Rican society he knew and understood. Anything else he could never abide or tolerate.

He was nicknamed the "Bull" by Puerto Rican fans. Alex Pompez, the owner of the New York Cubans in the Negro Leagues, pursued him regularly. My father was listed on the Cubans' roster in 1941 but changed his mind before the season. Had he decided to play there he would have been a big Negro League star.

My father's temper was as legendary as his baseball skills. One writer called him "The Babe Cobb of Puerto Rico." He could not only hit a baseball, but he was a fury on the bases as well. A former ballplayer and president of the Puerto Rican Winter League once recalled having to deal with my father on the basepaths.

"One day we had him [Perucho] trapped between the bases, and he put his head down and flew at me with his spikes. Ssst! He cut off my pants from the waist down."

Playing for Santurce at age forty-four—just five years before he died—Perucho cracked out a pinch-hit double in a game against Caguas. A fan in the third-base seats shouted that my father was an "old man." Perucho bolted from the field, socked the fan with a terrific blow, and was hauled off to jail.

"Ah, Perucho," cried the desk sergeant and the lieutenant

in charge. As usual they slapped him on the back and sent him home.

My father's Puerto Rico bore little resemblance to the appealing brochures tempting today's tourists and travelers. We proudly boast 272 miles of beaches and coastline, an array of barren canyons, and forest-clad mountains. But there are also miles upon miles of sordid slums and thousands upon thousands of people living in poverty. For us, Puerto Rico was no island paradise. Being poor in Puerto Rico was no blessing, and being hungry was no honor.

Although Perucho Cepeda attained baseball fame in his native land, fortune never followed. To the contrary, baseball players didn't make much money in Puerto Rico. My father was limited by a fifth-grade education and had few skills other than being a superb athlete. He knew baseball and little else. He lived most of his life poor or on the edge of poverty. He traveled a lot, often more than a week at a time. But he never made more than $60 a week playing baseball.

The Latin experience in baseball has been underexamined and long ignored. That's too bad. Ken Burns's highly touted PBS baseball miniseries a few years ago all but ignored the complexities and contributions of the Latin heritage to the game of baseball. Only recently, with the enormous influx of top-flight Latin stars on the big league scene, have we been getting the attention we have long deserved.

Most Americans have little knowledge of our history and culture, our triumphs and travails. So my story can only unfold and be understood against a backdrop of the Latin culture in general and the Puerto Rican experience in particular. Ours is a Spanish heritage, not an Anglo heritage. There's a big difference. And it presents a unique addition to the landscape of our national pastime.

My father was born in 1906, eight years after Puerto Rico was ceded to the United States by the treaty ending the Spanish-American War. Spanish culture is pervasive and reflects the language and the customs of the Latin people. Many of us who first came to the United States to play baseball had a double obstacle to endure. We were black. But even worse, we could not speak the language. It wasn't easy.

The name Puerto Rico comes from the Spanish words for "rich port." During his second voyage to the Western Hemisphere, Christopher Columbus sailed to Puerto Rico. Before long it became Spain's most important military outpost in the Caribbean.

The Spanish settlers—many of whom were seeking gold—did not bring women on the ships with them. So when the Spanish colonists began building settlements in 1508, they took Indian women to help populate the country. The arrival of African slaves resulted in a historic mingling of the races. The result is an island without the serious racial problems of the United States, and some other Latin countries as well.

We were made United States citizens in 1917, and Puerto Rico soon evolved from a US territory to commonwealth status within the United States. Puerto Ricans are allowed total access to the mainland without immigration restrictions, but we don't vote in presidential elections, nor do we pay federal income taxes while living in Puerto Rico. The United States provides for our common defense, but the Puerto Rican government has authority in many local matters.

My ancestry on both sides dates back to the arrival of African slaves to the island. Although race itself is not a big problem per se, nor is segregation a major issue, most black Puerto Ricans are born poor and remain poor.

Pedro "Perucho" Cepeda was a handsome man, strong and virile, with chiseled, finely defined features. He had a God-given talent to play baseball, and he was a star among stars. He met my mother when he went to Juncos to play baseball for the local team. A young woman named Carmen Pennes noticed him in the town square and fell in love with the handsome baseball star. He was as stunned by her green eyes and petite beauty as she was by his masculine good looks and manly presence.

My mother was a truly beautiful woman. At 4'11" she was small and dainty. But in matters of the heart and human decency, she was an absolute giant. I could not have been more blessed. She was also very smart and very wise. Today I'm able to utilize her wisdom. I only wish I would have done so earlier. I might have avoided some bad mistakes in life.

If my father was my hero, my mother was my inspiration.

There was always love in our house; even the debilitating effects of illness and poverty never changed that. My mother reminded me of one thing always: Environment is very hard to conquer. "Orlando," she'd say, "a person's shadow follows him wherever he goes. Please be careful."

I have never revealed the full extent of our poverty, nor the shackles of the Puerto Rican slums where I grew up and hung out. The best of times were tough. Like army brats who follow their fathers from post to post, we would follow my father from city to city: Juncos, Ponce, Guayama, Santurce, anywhere he might be playing ball.

Our living conditions were never good. For example, in Guayama there were no paved roads, only dirt roads lined with rocks. The houses were built of wood. We never had a refrigerator or a telephone anywhere we lived. Toilet facilities were outside the house. In the evening, when nature called, a fifty-foot walk into the night seemed more like a mile.

It took half a day for my mother to visit her family in nearby Juncos. Today you can make the trip from Guayama to Juncos in forty-five minutes. We'd get up at four in the morning, wait for the little bus to pick us up, and arrive in Juncos at noon. Each time my mother went there her brother gave her money to take back home. Sometimes when things were bad there was barely enough money to put food on the table.

Once when she was in Juncos a violent storm prevented her from returning home for two days. We had no food in the house, and the severity of the storm made it impossible to leave. For two days all we had to eat and drink was bread, sugar, and water. A kindly neighbor took pity and gave my father two goat sandwiches for my brother and me.

My father was a gambler and often gambled away his paycheck. When his eyesight started to fail, he was a perfect target for the local sharks, professional gamblers who could steal his money from right under his eyes. A city worker when his ballplaying days were over, his job was to go to the different rivers and check the water. He contracted malaria, and the disease lingered and worsened toward the end of his life. Things became rough on my mother, and tougher and tougher for all of us as illness consumed my father.

Living conditions went from bad to worse. We moved from

Guayama to Juncos, where my father coached an amateur team. A fifteen-year-old named Roberto Clemente tried out for the team but did not make it. Roberto was a shortstop then and grew up playing softball. As good as he was, he was still too young and inexperienced to make the team.

Our living conditions deteriorated further. We moved to Santurce and lived in three of the worst ghettos in the San Juan area: Barrio Hoare, Barrio Obrero, and finally Trastalleres, which was as bad you could get.

Our wooden dwelling was virtually in a mushy creek. The neighbor's latrine was a stone's throw from our kitchen. As my mother cooked meals, the stench drifting into our kitchen became unbearable.

Perucho received his paycheck on the last day of each month. He'd usually gamble it away. There wasn't enough money for food. I loved ketchup as a kid, and I recall one day there wasn't even enough money to buy a bottle of ketchup at the grocery store. So my mother cooked white rice and french fries for me, then put tomato sauce and sugar on it to make me happy.

There were no supermarkets. My mother walked long distances to the grocery store just to buy the necessities. When there was no money she'd promise to pay the grocer in a week or two, which she always managed to do by working odd jobs. We never ate staples like meat or chicken.

My father became increasingly bitter. He'd return home from a gambling binge an angry man. It was pure hell. He'd lash out at my mother and threaten to hit her. One time, when I was thirteen or fourteen, I came home from school and couldn't find my mother. She had left the house because my father was out of control.

But Perucho was a loving father, believe me. He was a good man who just couldn't shake his environment—his shadow, as my mother would say. When I was a little boy I was hit by a car. My brother, Pedro, thought I was dead and ran to tell my father. Perucho dropped everything and ran full steam to where I was. Finding me alive, he cradled me in his arms and hugged and kissed me. There were tears in his eyes. I've never forgotten that moment.

Latin men are a proud breed. Our culture is very macho. If a man is stripped of his dignity, or even thinks he is, he is sensitive to the extreme. A man cannot be humiliated. We were a patriarchal society, more so then than we are today. Women were secondary except in their roles as wives and mothers.

It was not unusual for Latin men to have a "second wife." Not a wife in the true sense of the term but a girlfriend, even many girlfriends. Because I was young and naive, my mother tried to hide the fact that Perucho had other women and other children. So I have sisters by women other than my mother, sisters I am close to today.

As a boy I couldn't understand this. It hurt me when I found out. But as I grew older I followed a similar route. There were other women during my first two marriages. And years later, when I hit the skids, I battled the same demons as Perucho: anger, bitterness, domestic battles, the whole works. The acorn never falls too far from the tree, as they say.

Eventually Buddhism saved me and helped me gain the tools to turn pain and poison into medicine. But before Buddhism turned my life around, that shadow of which my mother had always warned, lured me straight back to the slums of my boyhood and the ghettos of my youth. It was a one-way ticket back to the world I once knew and a life I thought I left behind for good.

It was rough, believe me. My boyhood pals were a bad lot— and I had been one of them. Most became dope addicts, thieves, or killers. Many went to jail, where they stayed, or were killed. For recreation we'd go downtown, stake out department stores, and steal as much as we could. If we fought, we fought with anything we could lay our hands on. We smoked marijuana long before it became part of today's mainstream culture.

I grew up in a world of poverty and an environment of deprivation. Buddhism helped me escape that shadow. My father was not as fortunate. But what saved me as a youngster was baseball—and the talent I inherited from my father. There is no question about that in my mind. Had it not been for baseball and the legacy of Perucho Cepeda, I could have followed my boyhood pals into a world of crime, violence, and hate.

Looking back, I am even more sure of this today. My best

boyhood friend is serving a thirty-year jail sentence, and he has served time before. Others have already died of disease or been killed. I didn't care about school, and we didn't have money for me to go to college.

Baseball saved my life. It gave me a great career and a future. It provided me with celebrity and wealth. And until I got in trouble, it gave my mother some wonderful years as well.

Baseball was my destiny. I am blessed that I was able to play Major League Baseball and that I am still in baseball today, back with the San Francisco Giants, where my career started forty years ago. It's been an incredible journey.

Heroes Great and Small

It's fair to say that baseball was in my blood from the start. How could it have been otherwise? My father was a great baseball player in Puerto Rico, and right from the beginning I wanted to be a ballplayer like my father.

I was born in Ponce, Puerto Rico, on September 17, 1937, four years after my brother Pedro. Because my father was a great baseball player, I grew up around baseball people. The only way my parents could get me to take a shower—or to stay home if that's what they wanted—was to tell me an important ballplayer was coming to our house. Many of the great Negro League stars would play winter ball in Puerto Rico and in the other Latin countries. My father played alongside and against many all-time greats: Satchel Paige, Josh Gibson, Leon Day, Silvio Garcia, and Roy Campanella, just to name a few.

It was a special treat whenever Satchel Paige paid us a visit, which he did quite often. Satchel Paige stories can fill up entire volumes depending on who is telling them. It's no secret, though, that Satchel Paige was a genuine ladies' man. One of his favorite ladies was our neighbor, a woman named Tommie. After visiting Tommie he'd stop at our house to talk with my father and enjoy a good cup of coffee, which my mother always had waiting for him.

My father told me that when Satchel Paige was warming up, his control was so great that he could put fifty-cent coins to the left and right of the plate and pinpoint each pitch. During one game Satchel loaded the bases. He calmly motioned to his three outfielders and told them to sit down. The outfielders were bewildered, not knowing what to expect. It didn't take long for Satchel to put them at ease, dispatching the next three batters quickly by striking out the side. No one touched the ball.

A similar thing happened in 1969 when I was with the Atlanta Braves. We were playing an exhibition game in Savannah, Georgia. Ole Satch was up there in years, but he was pitching some innings for the Braves as a public-relations stunt.

The Baseball Encyclopedia lists Satchel as being sixty-three years old then. The bases were loaded, and I was playing first base. It looked like trouble, so I walked to the mound to see what I could do. He told me to relax, to just wait and see. Then he did it again: BOOM, BOOM, BOOM. He struck out the side. He was a nice man and a marvelous baseball player—one of the greatest pitchers ever.

Then there was Josh Gibson. When I was a seventeen year old, Peter Zorilla, the owner of the Santurce club in Puerto Rico, compared me to a young Josh Gibson. True or not, it was a great compliment. As everyone familiar with baseball should know, Josh Gibson was a superb hitter.

The first time I ever saw my father play baseball was in 1946. Josh Gibson was the catcher, and Perucho was playing second base. The game went sixteen innings. My father had 12 assists that game, and the pitcher struck out 18 batters. That's when I really became hooked on baseball.

It's been said that nobody ever swung a baseball bat better than Josh Gibson. He was one of the greatest hitters, black or white, who ever played the game. I only met Josh Gibson once, that day in the clubhouse in 1946. He scared me, too.

Josh was drinking heavily at the time and suffering bouts of mental illness. They played on Sunday, and on Monday Josh was caught walking naked in the hotel across the street from the ballpark. From that point on I was afraid of him. He died shortly after, suffering from a fatal stroke on January 20, 1947, three months after his thirty-fifth birthday and just months before Jackie Robinson broke Major League Baseball's long-standing color line.

Peter Zorilla, the Santurce owner who brought me to the

attention of the New York Giants, brought these great Negro stars to Puerto Rico during the winter months. Pete later told me that Gibson was drinking so much because he was angry and hurt at being passed over by Branch Rickey. Josh wanted to be the first Negro baseball star in the major leagues.

For three years there had been a push to bring black baseball players to the major leagues. Branch Rickey interviewed many high-quality black players, including Josh Gibson and Silvio Garcia. Whatever the reason—maybe it was just age—Josh was turned down.

Instead Rickey went with Jackie Robinson. Jackie had been a four-letter athlete at UCLA and an Army officer during World War II. Rickey was an intelligent man, and he well understood that baseball talent alone was not enough. Jackie had the talent, but he also had the stamina and the grit to deal with the abuse and name-calling sure to come his way. If he failed, then the whole cause could be set back for years.

Recently I was visiting with Silvio Garcia's daughter, and we were talking about that very subject. Silvio had enormous talent, some say even more talent than Jackie had. Silvio's daughter said that when Branch Rickey interviewed her father, he asked him what he'd do if another player called him a "nigger." Silvio answered that he would kick the guy's butt, or something to that effect. That was not the answer that Rickey was looking for.

Early in 1947 the Brooklyn Dodgers played an exhibition game in Puerto Rico. Luis Olmo, who led the National League in triples and drove in 110 runs for the Dodgers in 1945, was one of our native sons and a big star in Puerto Rico.

I saw Jackie Robinson as he arrived at the ballpark in a car. He played first base for the Dodgers then. In 1947 Gil Hodges was reserve catcher and Eddie Stanky was the Dodgers' scrappy second baseman. When Roy Campanella came up in 1948, Hodges moved to first base, Stanky was traded to the Boston Braves, and Jackie moved to second base.

Because I was young and it was getting late, I didn't stay for the game. But I did get to shake Jackie's hand. Remember, my father never wanted to play in the United States because of the racial strife. But he pointed to Jackie and said to me, "That man there will make it possible for others like us to play in the major leagues. If you play in the majors one day, it will be because of him."

I never forgot that lesson. Jackie's courage helped me hurdle the racism and bigotry I encountered, particularly in the early years of my career. Last year, to commemorate the fiftieth anniversary of Jackie Robinson's historic major league debut, I was honored to participate in many tributes.

A special one was held in New York with many of Jackie's former teammates participating: Pee Wee Reese, Al Gionfriddo, Spider Jorgensen, and Gene Hermanski, all members of the 1947 Brooklyn Dodgers. They were joined by Preacher Roe, Carl Erskine, and Don Newcombe, each of whom came to the Dodgers just a year or two later and had the honor of playing with Jackie.

Of the great Negro League players my father observed, he insisted that Leon Day was the best of the lot. Leon played ball in Puerto Rico in 1947 and 1948 and is a member of the Puerto Rican Baseball Hall of Fame. He was recently elected to the Hall of Fame in Cooperstown by the Veterans Committee.

Leon was a second baseman and pitcher. In the morning he might play second and go 4 for 4. Then in the evening he'd throw a no-hitter. I met Leon Day at a card show in New Jersey shortly before his death. He remembered my father well. He died just a short time before his Hall of Fame selection and was honored posthumously.

I recall the first game I ever listened to on the radio. It was 1944, and I was seven years old. It was an All-Star Game between Puerto Rico and Cuba, and my father was on the Puerto Rican squad.

I had heard about the Cuban All-Stars and a nineteen-year-old third baseman in particular who was born and raised on a sugar plantation. His name was Orestes Minoso. No one called him Minnie at that time.

He was so fast and played with such intensity that he had the old-timers talking in superlatives. Before the game began, they broadcast a foot race between Minnie and the great Puerto Rican speedster Luis Marquez. I don't remember who won the race, but I do remember becoming a devout Minnie Minoso fan by the tender age of seven.

Minnie became a hero in the best sense of the word. I followed his career in the Caribbean with the Mariano Tigers in the Cuban League, with the New York Cubans in the Negro Leagues, and finally in the major leagues when he became one of the most exciting and productive ballplayers of the 1950s, a seven-time American League All-Star.

Signed originally by the Cleveland Indians and traded to the Chicago White Sox in 1951, Minnie enjoyed one of the finest rookie seasons ever. In his first turn at bat in a White Sox uniform, Minnie leveled Vic Raschi's second pitch into the left center-field bullpen for a two-run homer. He was the first black to play Major League Baseball in the Windy City.

Believe me when I say that Minnie Minoso is to Latin ballplayers what Jackie Robinson is to black ballplayers. As much as I loved Roberto Clemente and cherish his memory, Minnie is the one who made it possible for all us Latins. Before Roberto Clemente, before Vic Power, before Orlando Cepeda, there was Minnie Minoso. Younger players should know this and offer their thanks. He was the first Latin player to become a superstar.

I was eighteen years old and playing minor league ball when I saw Minnie at a hotel in Miami Beach. I was so excited I fainted. He was like a god to me. The next year Minnie came to Puerto Rico. I was glad to be his private chauffeur. I drove him all over in my new car. He could party with the best, and he can still light up any room. He's a thorough original, and I love him dearly.

There was another boyhood hero of mine on that same White Sox team. Shortstop Chico Carrasquel hailed from Venezuela. His uncle Alejandro (Alex) Carrasquel pitched eight seasons with the Washington Senators, winning 11 games in 1943.

Chico was the third Venezuelan player to play in the major leagues, breaking in with the White Sox in 1950. Many old-timers will tell you that there has never been a better shortstop than Chico Carresquel in his prime. In 1951 Chico was the first

Latin player to start an All-Star Game. He started in three more All-Star Games—1953, 1954, and 1955. He led the American League in fielding three times. One magazine called him the best since Honus Wagner. Casey Stengel said he had not seen anyone better, not his own Phil Rizzuto, not anyone.

When Chico was traded to the Cleveland Indians in 1956, it was because the White Sox were sure they had a worthy successor, a twenty-two-year-old shortstop also from Venezuela by the name of Luis Aparicio. By then Chico had put on weight and his best years were behind him. Luis, of course, went on to have a Hall of Fame career. Many years later we would be teammates with the Boston Red Sox.

When I reported to Phoenix, Arizona, for spring training in 1958, Chico and Minnie were both with the Cleveland Indians. We played three games against the Indians early in the exhibition season, and I did quite well. But try to imagine what it felt like seeing two boyhood heroes and Latin greats in the opposite dugout. Distracting, to say the least.

Chico Carrasquel still lives in the Chicago area. Until recently he did color commentary for the White Sox games in Spanish. Chico is another great Latin pioneer whose enormous contributions to the major league scene have been largely forgotten.

Being the son of a baseball legend in Puerto Rico was not always easy. On the contrary, being Perucho's son was often difficult. My older brother, Pedro, was a hell of an athlete and a promising baseball player. But he gave up the game early on because the pressure of being constantly compared to Perucho finally got to him.

By the time I was ten or eleven there was nothing I wanted more than to play baseball. I started selling newspapers because there was a tournament for the boys who sold papers. I wanted to play for Hi Bithorn, the Puerto Rican pitching star who once won 18 games for the Chicago Cubs.

Like all kids we managed to play baseball wherever we could. We'd play by the tracks, using a stick and a ball. My father would bring new baseballs home with him. But we rarely used them to play or practice. When we needed money my mother would sell baseballs for seventy-five cents apiece.

Wherever I went people began comparing me to Perucho. If I'd strike out I'd hear taunts like, "Perucho's son can't hit. You'll never be as good as your father."

At thirteen I suffered a blow to my youthful pride. There was a team I hoped to play for. It required fifty cents for the ID card and registration fee. It would be my first real team, but we didn't have the fifty cents to spend. I was so inconsolable the tears were running down my cheeks. My mother came to the rescue. She did some extra work and managed to scrape together the fifty cents I needed.

I bought a picture for the ID card and paid for the registration. How excited I was. Then, after practicing with the team for three months, I realized one day that everyone seemed to have a uniform but me. I just stood there waiting. Then I discovered I hadn't made the team. I was good, but not good enough.

So I forgot about baseball and concentrated instead on basketball. I played more basketball than baseball and became very good. Pedro would want to play baseball, so we'd walk twenty blocks to the ball fields, where there were three different baseball diamonds. But as soon as I'd see someone shooting baskets, away I'd go. Pedro would call me back. "We came here to play baseball," he'd scream. But I wouldn't listen. I was now determined to be a basketball player.

I was on a full concrete court one day when I jumped for a rebound and came down on my right knee, tearing the cartilage. It was the first of many knee injuries that would plague my entire career.

I had the first operation on my knee when I was fifteen. The doctors told my dad there was a good chance that I'd never play ball again. A wonderful young doctor named Dr. Roquenido operated on me. He was a resident then. Today he is seventy-eight years old. On my last visit to Puerto Rico I had dinner with him. The knee he operated on is the same knee I hurt in 1962, then again in 1965, and once more in 1970.

In 1950 a group of the guys got together to watch the All-Star Game. It was televised in the big square in downtown San Juan. It was the first baseball game I ever saw on TV and my first major league game ever.

We were very excited. This was Major League Baseball at its

best. Chicago's Comiskey Park seemed worlds away from San Juan. But we could see it all on television. What a treat. Here were such great major leaguers as Robin Roberts, Allie Reynolds, George Kell, Stan Musial, and Ted Williams performing right before our eyes through the magic of television. Four black players were on the All-Star squads in 1950: Jackie Robinson, Roy Campanella, and Don Newcombe of the Dodgers for the National League and Larry Doby of the Cleveland Indians for the American League. We were pulling heavily for these players.

Funny, how I still remember that All-Star Game so clearly. It was one of the most thrilling ever played. Ted Williams made an off-the-wall catch in the 1st inning, then learned later that he had broken his left shoulder.

It was the first All-Star Game to go into extra innings. In the top of the 9th Ralph Kiner of the National League hit a game-tying home run. After four scoreless innings, the Cardinals' Red Schoendienst hit the first pitch of the 14th inning in to the seats for a home run that secured a 4–3 win for the National League. At the time I could never have guessed that seventeen years later, in 1967, I would be a unanimous choice for the National League MVP honors and that Red would be my manager—with both the 1967 World Champion St. Louis Cardinals and the 1968 National League Champion St. Louis Cardinals.

My bout with knee surgery is a remarkable story and a puzzling one. At the time of the surgery I was fifteen years old, 5'6" tall, and weighed 130 pounds. When I left the hospital a month and a half later, I had grown almost six inches and gained fifty pounds.

It was amazing. I had been wearing a size-seven shoe, so my father brought home that size. They didn't come close to fitting. We went back to the store to get measured and quickly found out why. My shoe size was now ten. I was almost six feet tall and weighed 180 pounds. People were stunned.

The injury kept me inactive for almost a year. Absolutely no sports. But soon after I had thrown away the crutches and began walking again, a friend asked me to watch a baseball game with him. We knew someone who was playing. I was in jeans and wearing tennis shoes. I hadn't picked up a bat for two years.

Because they needed a third baseman, they asked me to play. I refused. My father did not want me playing ball anymore, at least not this soon. But they pleaded with me because they needed another player for a full team, so I agreed to go to third.

My first time at bat, BOOM! I knocked the stuffing out of the ball. I said to myself, "What is this? What's happened?" I hadn't picked up a bat in two years, and there I was hitting the ball a long, long way. I couldn't believe it. Kids were standing around with their mouths wide open.

A few weeks later I played ball again, this time in a park where I'd never gotten near the fence. Suddenly I was hitting balls over the fence left and right. My brother was there, and he was shocked when he saw me hit the tar out of the ball. He ran and told our father that I was knocking baseball after baseball over the fence. Perucho came by and watched me closely. For the first time he saw all the tools.

Perched in the stands was a star player from one of the top amateur teams in Puerto Rico. After watching me play, he asked me to join his club. He said I could be a real asset. I hit 2 home runs and drove in 5 runs in my first game with them. I was on my way.

My father always told me that baseball talent was something you were born with. If you had true talent then somehow, some way, it would come out. That's why he had never pressured me to be a ballplayer.

Perucho was fully convinced now that I had all the tools. I could hit with power, throw, and run. He examined my swing carefully. Then he simply said, "I don't need to teach you anything. You have a natural swing. Just keep doing it."

Our team went on to win the Puerto Rican Amateur Championship. Two weeks later our amateur All-Star team flew to the Dominican Republic to play a team of Dominican Republic All-Stars. On that Dominican Republic All-Star team were two talented teenage stars who later became good friends of mine and great teammates: Julian Javier and Felipe Alou.

Watching the game from the stands was a very smart and

distinguished-looking gentleman. He appeared to be about sixty, and success was written all over him. His hair was streaked with gray. He looked like an important politician, maybe the president of the country. His name was Pedro (Pete) Zorilla, and he would become one of the most important people in my life.

Pete Zorilla was the owner of the Santurce Crabbers, one of Puerto Rico's more prominent professional baseball teams. He had close ties to New York Giants owner Horace Stoneham and Brooklyn Dodgers owner Walter O'Malley.

That day Pete was checking out Jose Pagan, then the boyhood baseball rage of the islands. Jose played for the other team. Pete may have come to see Jose, but that particular night belonged to me. I was 4 for 5, including a long home run over the left-field fence. Pete, who had just recently helped sign Roberto Clemente to a Brooklyn Dodger contract, liked what he saw.

"Who is that kid?" he wanted to know. Someone told him I was Orlando Cepeda, Perucho Cepeda's son. Because I was just sixteen years old, Pete asked my father if it would be okay for me to join Santurce as its batboy and start working with the club.

So in the winter of 1953 I started working out with the Santurce Crabbers. Here I was, a kid, working out with Willie Mays and Roberto Clemente, two of the many major and minor leaguers who played winter ball in Puerto Rico. Roberto had just finished a Triple A season in Montreal. He had been drafted by the Pittsburgh Pirates, and in March he would be heading to Florida for spring training.

It was Horace Stoneham who personally "delivered" Willie Mays to Santurce that winter. He was paying back Pete Zorilla for tipping him off to Ruben Gomez, the Puerto Rican righthander who pitched so well for the New York Giants in 1953 and 1954.

Willie, it should be remembered, was the National League's Most Valuable Player in 1954, and he had led the Giants to the National League flag and an upset World Series sweep of the Cleveland Indians.

Willie was very helpful to Roberto. Herman Franks was our manager. Each day he'd fungo line drives and long fly balls to Willie and Roberto in the outfield. Under Willie's watchful eye, Roberto would charge in and throw shots on the run with that rifle arm of his. Remember, Roberto had originally been a short-stop. And there I was taking throws from Willie Mays and Roberto Clemente.

Herman Franks had been a catcher before becoming a suc-cessful major league coach and manager. He would manage me for two and a half years with the San Francisco Giants before the Giants traded me to the St. Louis Cardinals in May 1966.

The Santurce Crabbers were a great team. I was just a kid working out with ballplayers, who were like gods to me. In addition to Mays and Clemente there was George Crow of the Milwaukee Braves at first; Don Zimmer, a scrappy young short-stop and second baseman with the Brooklyn Dodgers; catcher Harry Chiti of the Chicago Cubs; and Bob Thurman, a veteran of the Negro Leagues who had joined the Cincinnati Reds in 1955.

The pitching staff was anchored by my boyhood hero, Ruben Gomez. Ruben still remains the winningest pitcher in Puerto Rican history, recording 174 winter league victories over twenty-nine seasons; and Sad Sam Jones, soon to become the strikeout king of the National League. He had one of the most wicked curveballs I ever saw, though I learned to hit him rather well.

I was Perucho Cepeda's son, and I was learning from some of the best in the business. For three months my father followed me from game to game. He made sure I went to school, and before every game he'd meet me at the ballpark with my uniform.

Pete had taken me under his wing. A mentor and sponsor in the best sense, he convinced my parents that he could arrange for me to have a tryout with the New York Giants along with four other promising Puerto Rico youngsters. He would enclose a letter to the Giants promising each of us $500 if the Giants signed us. If we weren't signed, we would return home.

Five hundred dollars doesn't seem like much in today's millionaire market. But for a seventeen-year-old from the Puerto Rican slums, it seemed like a million dollars. Perucho agreed to let me go, somewhat reluctantly at first. He knew I had ability and the necessary baseball tools. But perhaps I had his temper, too. I would be playing baseball, but the culture and the language were different. How would I handle the racism and bigotry that was certain to come my way?

One thing was uppermost in his mind. If I could cut it, professional baseball in the United States offered me an opportunity to escape the slums and poverty of the Puerto Rican ghetto.

My father's health was failing. The malaria had taken a huge toll on him. He was stubborn and didn't take his medicine regularly. He was a strong man, he reasoned, and he could survive without medication. He had always survived the toughest of times.

Perucho had never been able to shake his shadow. He was caught in a trap. I watched as my father grew old before his time. But maybe I could escape. Perucho gave me his blessing. I hugged and kissed my parents goodbye at the San Juan Airport. Many things were on my mind. But not once did I imagine that the next time I would see my father he'd be in a deep coma and very near death.

·3·

The Blossoming Baby Bull

In today's world of jet airliners and supersonic travel, a flight from San Juan, Puerto Rico, to Miami would hardly merit a mention. So it might be difficult to imagine what it was like for a group of five kids whose only world had been the Puerto Rican slums and barrios.

I was not the only young player to make the pilgrimage to Miami in the spring of 1955. Pete Zorilla had also sent Julio Navarro, the father of major league pitcher Jaime Navarro; Jose Pagan; a shortstop named Al Rodriguez; and a pitcher named Francisco Sayas. Pete Zorilla's letter accompanied the five of us. Because we were all underage, Pete anointed Roberto Clemente as our official "baby-sitter" until we arrived in camp. Roberto was all of twenty-one years old that spring.

The flight to Miami seemed to take forever, though it was just a four-hour flight then. I was frightened. There would be language and cultural barriers to tackle. My father's fears of racism now seemed very real to me. How would I handle it? But the plane ride went well, and we arrived in Miami on time.

Then the fun started. We missed our bus. Roberto had to report immediately to Fort Myers to join the Pirates' training camp. So five wide-eyed Puerto Rican kids were left to fend for themselves. We asked a guy to phone the Giants' minor league camp in Melbourne, but he refused. Finally, someone at the Greyhound station called the police. This was the segregated South, and civil rights legislation was still a decade away. A few black officers arrived to escort us to the spring training barracks.

We arrived in Melbourne at 4:30 in the morning, dead tired from lack of sleep. We managed to close our eyes for two hours. Then we were suddenly shaken out of our beds. It seems that we were deposited in the white section of the barracks in the early morning hours. We were told to move promptly to the black quarters on the second floor and far to the corner.

The Giants' rookie camp was stockpiled with talent. Most of us were there to try out before the regulars arrived in camp. Standing next to me as we were checked in the following morning was a tall, lanky lad with a blue fedora hat. He had been brought to the Giants camp from his home in Alabama by a bird-dog scout named Jesse Thomas, who, like Pete Zorilla, had close ties with Horace Stoneham.

Because of the language barrier, we nodded and grinned at each other. We were both ill at ease. The Melbourne camp had four diamonds where we practiced and worked out. An hour later I happened to gaze across to the next diamond and saw this same kid hitting rockets all over the place. He was at least 6'4" and probably weighed no more than 150 pounds. Wow, I said to myself, can this kid hit! And this kid can run! Like me he was seventeen years old, and like me he was an unsigned, non-rostered kid hoping to make it in professional baseball. His name was Willie McCovey, and in time we would become good friends and teammates.

My biggest obstacle was language. When I arrived in the States, I knew only one word that could pass for English, and that one word was *beisbol*. I don't think people can really grasp the difficulty of coming from a Latin country to play baseball in the United States back then. Today it's a lot easier. Then it was close to impossible. But if you made it, you would have more than you could ever have at home.

A person appeared out of nowhere to help me over some big hurdles. He was Dave Garcia. Born in East St. Louis, Illinois, Dave later enjoyed a successful and substantial coaching and managerial career in the major leagues. He knew every aspect of the game, but best of all he spoke fluent Spanish. He and Al Lopez were probably the only two people from the coaching and managing ranks who spoke Spanish then. Dave was managing the Giants' Mayfield club in the Kitty League that year.

Willie McCovey and I had both been assigned to Sandersville, a Class D club—Willie as a first baseman and me as a third baseman, along with a kid named Crosby.

Of course, we never knew what was going on behind the scenes. But there were meetings every night. I had no idea how close I came to being cut loose. According to Dave Garcia, each night the various managers and coaches had meetings to evaluate the talent pool. Remember, there was a lot of talent to evaluate. A group of scouts were told to look at the five of us sent by Pete Zorilla. It was actually on the advice of these scouts that a decision was reached to give each of us our $500.

An American Cuban named Alex Pompez owned the New York Cubans in the Negro Leagues, and he had close ties to Major League Baseball. Because he spoke Spanish, his job was to see that we all signed contracts with as little confusion as possible. He would come to our rooms to mediate our contract negotiations and to see that everything went smoothly.

Pete Pavlick was the young manager of the Sandersville club. At one meeting he made it clear that he preferred Crosby over me as a third baseman. Giants farm director Jack Schwarz asked if anybody could speak on my behalf before the Giants released me. Nobody said a word. So Schwarz suggested that Dave Garcia take me to the Mayfield club with him to look me over. Here is how he remembers it:

> I had yet to see Cepeda play, but to say the least he was surprised to see that I spoke Spanish. He was such a nice kid with so much talent. I was very surprised that Pavlick made the decision he did. The first day that Orlando played an intersquad game with my ballclub he hit 2 home runs. I went over and took a look at the other fellow, Crosby. He was a pretty good ballplayer, but there was no comparison.
>
> In these meetings they would ask the same question. They'd ask you, "What happened?" You'd answer by saying, "He's all right for now." That was in case you decided to keep him and didn't want to blow your hand. These were the most

frequently used words at a minor league meeting: "He's all right for now."

At one particular meeting I told Pavlick that I had taken a look at Crosby, and he should put Cepeda at third base instead. I told him Cepeda had hit 5 home runs for me in 2 games. I'd been managing for eight years and was a pretty good judge of talent. But Pavlick insisted he liked Crosby better, and that was that.

Richie Klaus was the manager of another D ballclub in Oklahoma. He had about the same managing experience as me, and I asked him to put Cepeda anywhere he could, just hit him cleanup. "The kid can really hit," I told him. But he had Sonny Robertson at third base and was satisfied with Sonny.

Dave and Alex Pompez were the only people who spoke fluent Spanish in the entire camp. Dave was in my corner all the way, and he helped all the Latin ballplayers. When we'd get down or lonely, he'd come up to our rooms and do card tricks, anything to take our minds off our problems. I hoped that Dave would take me to Mayfield with him. What I didn't know was that black ballplayers were not allowed to play in the Kitty League.

As I understand it, Dave even suggested to Jack Schwarz that because Dave spoke fluent Spanish and I had a Latin name, maybe Orlando could then be a dark-skinned Spaniard. It didn't work. Instead, Schwarz told Dave that there was an independent club in Salem, Virginia, that he was talking to about me and that he should keep me for a few days until something might be arranged. Dave told the manager at Salem, John Crosswhite, that I could play, that I could run, hit, and throw. Crosswhite told him to send me up to him. Here's how Dave tells the story:

> Jack Schwarz told me to go to Cepeda's room and tell him that he was going to Salem. The tears just poured out of his eyes. He had no idea why he wasn't going with me. I didn't want to tell him that blacks weren't allowed in the Kitty League.
>
> The same thing happened with Felipe Alou. When he came up he was sent to Lake Charles, Louisiana. They found out he

was black, and he had to go elsewhere. He was given twelve hours to get out of town.

Traveling from Melbourne to Salem, Virginia, was a nightmare. Charlie Weatherspoon, Frank Lee, and I went by Greyhound bus. We were all blacks. Charlie was supposed to look out for me because of my language barrier, but he became so confused by everything that I ended up looking out for him. The blind leading the blind, as they say.

We changed buses in Jacksonville, Florida, then made stops in Birmingham, Alabama, and Jackson, Mississippi. It was a full house, and the back of the bus was packed. I could barely move or sleep. One morning I saw an empty seat and sat next to a white girl. She started talking to me. She asked where I was from and what I was doing.

The driver got so mad that he pulled over and stopped the bus. He yelled so hard at the girl that she began crying. He let her off the bus right in the middle of downtown Birmingham.

We pushed on to Virginia, where the driver managed to miss the Salem stop. He let us out in the next town, and we had to wait for another bus to take us back to Salem. We arrived at noon on Sunday. In the confusion I lost my suitcase. I was dead tired and had worn the same clothes for three days. The first game I played in for Salem I struck out three times.

Everything there was black and white. I wasn't used to this. I went out to walk around that night about 8:00. I was looking through the store windows, gazing at all the merchandise and imagining what I would buy first once I became a rich baseball star. All of a sudden the police grabbed me and said that blacks had to be with their own people.

Perucho had worried and warned me about such incidents. Later, we took our first road trip by bus, out to West Virginia. Each time we stopped I couldn't get out. I couldn't communicate, and I didn't understand. Nothing made any sense at this point. The other black players could at least speak English. We arrived in West Virginia and waited for the black driver to take us to a guest house. The Jim Crow laws were on the books, so we were not allowed to stay at a "white" hotel with the rest of the team.

But the guest house was full, and we couldn't find a hotel with available rooms. So we headed to the ballpark, played the game, and headed right back. We managed to find a small motel with rooms located on top of the bar that we could stay in. There was one room left—with one bed for the three of us. Charlie and Frank Lee were older than me. They went out on the town. I just fell on the bed exhausted. The song "Blue Velvet" was being played continually in the bar room below.

As soon as we returned to Salem, Pete Zorilla called me long distance. He had tracked me down to tell me that my mother wanted me to come home. Perucho was very sick. I caught the first flight I could. When I arrived, he was in a coma. He died a short time later.

My father's death hit me hard. I remembered that the last time he saw me play baseball I hit a home run. It made him so proud. But his death devastated me. He was only forty-nine years old. I used the $500 I had received when I signed my contract to pay for my father's funeral.

Pedro had joined the army, and my mother was all alone. I gave serious thought to quitting baseball, about giving it all up. I didn't want to leave my mother alone and return to Salem, not for baseball, not for anything. But my mother wouldn't hear such talk. She insisted that there was nothing for me in Puerto Rico except poverty. It had been Perucho's dream to see me play professional baseball. I knew she was right. I stayed three or four days, then returned to Salem to resume my baseball career.

It was one of the saddest times of my life. In the evenings and on Sundays I'd sit alone in a room in the black section of town, listening to the sounds of gospel music from the church across the street. When I'd think about my father, my eyes would swell with tears and I would sob.

Looking back, I don't know how I did it. I couldn't hit anything. My father was on my mind. Every time we made a road trip, I'd be by myself. I never knew such loneliness. Once in Bristol, Tennessee, I was walking down the street and I saw three or four girls, white girls, speaking Spanish. They were Cuban, I could tell. I wanted to talk to them so badly. I hadn't spoken Spanish for two months. But they ignored me completely. They wouldn't give me the time of day. That's how entrenched segregation was in the South back then. How little I really knew, and how little I understood.

We returned from that road trip on Sunday. Monday morning Salem released me. It's no wonder. In 26 games I hit .247 with just 1 home run. That afternoon Pete Zorilla called me. He told me not to give up. I said, "Pete, I want to go home. I've had it!" He said to hold on. A friend of his had a team in Kokomo, Indiana, and the third baseman was hurt. Pete suggested that I go there for ten days, make $100, take the money, and return home. I needed the money so I agreed to go.

Dave Garcia was working behind the scenes on my behalf. The contact man was Jim Tobin, a former major league pitcher who umpired in the Caribbean during the winter months. Jim owned the Kokomo club in the Mississippi-Ohio Valley League. Dave told me later how he had helped me:

> There were three players we were going to recommend to Jim Tobin: Orlando Cepeda; Charlie Weatherspoon, a right-handed catcher; and a little shortstop named Al Rodriguez. Tobin said, "You can send them to me, but only if they're not black or Catholic." I didn't understand. Then Jim reminded me that Kokomo, Indiana, was Ku Klux Klan country.
>
> I told him I didn't know anything about that nonsense, but these boys had three things in common: They were black, at least two were Catholic, and all were good ballplayers. Jim agreed to take them.

So I caught the noon train to Kokomo. That, too, was an ordeal. Nobody had told me where to go exactly. There'd be no one to pick me up when I arrived as far as I knew. I spent all day, all night, and all morning awake on the train. My bags had been lost on the way to Salem. I was afraid someone might steal them if I went to sleep. I told the conductor who clipped the tickets to let me know when we got to Kokomo. Each time the train stopped, I'd yell, "Kokomo?" And he'd yell back, "No Kokomo. I'll let you know!"

I arrived there at five in the morning. Believe it or not, my bags managed to get lost once again. My father always told me to carry my baseball glove and shoes with me at all times because those were the two things you always needed to play ball. I was lucky. At least I still had my mitt and my spikes.

It was pitch dark when I got off the train. I tried to ask somebody where the Kokomo Giants were located, but the man I asked didn't know. So I started walking. I was tired, and I finally saw a hotel and walked into the lobby. I can still picture it vividly. People were drinking their early morning coffee. I said, "Please, could I get a room?" I was told it was too early and I would have to wait for the manager to arrive.

I waited and waited. Finally the manager, a woman, came in. "No, no," she told the desk clerk. "We don't have rooms for these types of people." So they kicked me out. This time I finally got the message.

So I began walking through town. A police officer drove by and saw me. He stopped and in my broken English I said something like, "Me a baseball player!" The officer made a phone call to Jim Tobin. Then he told me everything was all right and that he'd drop me off in the black part of town. Another black player, a Cuban named Chico Cardenas, was there. I had met him briefly in spring training, and we'd clicked as friends. That made me feel a lot better.

The Kokomo ballclub couldn't have been any nicer to me. They made me feel welcome from the start, especially manager Walt Dixon. A person like Walt restores your faith in humanity. From the very start Walt made me feel at home. He told me not to worry about a thing, that I was going to be a hell of a baseball player. I'd be playing third base and would hit in the cleanup slot. This was no mere ten-day visit, Walt assured me. The club really wanted me. Walt and his wife took good care of me the entire year, and my teammates were a good bunch of guys. I only wish I could see them today, just to tell them after all these years how much they really meant to me.

Walt Dixon was a player/manager. I played third and he played first. Chico Cardenas and I became good pals. Each time a player hit a home run, a popular restaurant in town gave him a free steak dinner. Since I hit 21 home runs for Kokomo that year, I had plenty of steak dinners. Nobody seemed to mind that I was black. In fact, I was treated like a king. Since I had more than my share of steak dinners, one night I took Chico Cardenas with me. I wanted him to have my steak that night. I guess being a big star made a difference after all, because suddenly no one was eager to serve us. I felt bad for Chico. Obviously I was okay, but they wouldn't serve him. So I got up, left with Chico, and never set foot in that restaurant again.

Everything was a novelty, a new experience. It was exciting. The way Walt treated me—just like any other ballplayer—was enough. I didn't care too much about any thing but playing baseball.

Walt kept reminding me that I was a hell of a ballplayer with a real shot at the major leagues. "Don't let the small things bother you," he'd say. "Just concentrate on playing baseball." I used to stay home, go to the ballpark, play ball, and come back home. At seventeen years old I was 6'2" and 205 pounds, but I was still a kid.

Kokomo was the turning point of my career. I put some strong numbers on the board. I hit a robust .393 to lead the league, with 21 homers and 91 RBIs in just 347 at-bats. Actually, I was hitting .415, but I got homesick and went 0 for 25 at one stretch. But I knew my destiny. When I returned to Puerto Rico I told my mother not to worry about anything. I would be a Major League Baseball player soon, and when that happened I'd buy her a house with my first few paychecks.

What I did not know at the time was that I had technically become the property of Jim Tobin. As owner of the Kokomo ballclub, Jim had full rights to my contract. He could have kept me and made a lot of money in a year or two by selling me to another club. But Jim was an honest man and concerned about my future. So instead of holding on to me further, he sold me back to the New York Giants for just $100.

In 1956 the Giants sent me to Class C with St. Cloud, in Minnesota. I wasn't the only third baseman in spring camp. In fact, there were two or three others. So manager Charlie Fox gave me a first baseman's glove and sent me to first. I adapted quickly and became a full-time first baseman.

I had a great year with St. Cloud in 1956, winning the Northern League Triple Crown. I hit .355 with 26 home runs and 112 RBIs. But Jack Schwarz wanted to move me up just one notch to Class B. This time I put my foot down. Willie McCovey was going to Double A. Bill White, who'd had a good rookie year with the Giants in 1956 with 22 home runs, would be returning from a two-year Army stint in 1958. What was becoming more and more obvious to me was that as farm director, Jack Schwarz was not particularly anxious to push Latin prospects up the organizational ladder.

Felipe Alou and I were talking about this at a recent game between the Expos and the Giants at Candlestick. Felipe recalled how he was hitting over .380 for Cocoa in the Florida State League and Jack never even knew who he was. So with two great seasons behind me, my only bonus was to move up to Class B.

I talked things over with Pete Zorilla and my brother, Pedro, that same winter. Pete, in fact, had just told Jack that I was ready for a shot at the majors. Schwarz's answer to that one was an emphatic "No!" But I made up my mind. McCovey and I both had strong seasons in 1956, and there was no way I was going to let myself go to a level under him.

That winter I had a hell of a season at Santurce. I hit .310 and ranked near the top of the league with 11 home runs and 40 RBIs facing major league and Triple A pitchers. After two outstanding minor league seasons and a strong winter in Puerto Rico, I was brimming with confidence. I asked the Giants to send me to the Minneapolis Millers, the Giants' top Triple A club.

Pete Zorilla pleaded my case to Jack Schwarz. Again Jack responded with a flat-out refusal. I gave in and signed a contract with Springfield in Class A, but with the provision that I could go to spring training early on with the Minneapolis Millers.

Felipe Alou was also with the Millers that spring. Felipe had started his professional career in 1956 at Lake Charles, Louisiana. But a Louisiana law prohibited blacks from playing on the same field with whites. The Giants sent him to Cocoa, where his .380 average led the Florida State League. We had already become good friends a few years earlier when our respective amateur league All-Star teams had played each other in the Dominican Republic. Felipe was one of the best-looking ballplayers I'd ever seen. At 6', 195 pounds, he had a great arm and could run like hell. In addition to leading the Florida State League in hitting, he belted 21 homers and drove in 99 runs for Cocoa.

Luck was with me that spring. The regular first baseman was in the Army Reserve doing his two weeks of training. BOOM, BOOM, BOOM, I started hitting like crazy. They had to play me. Felipe and I stole the show that spring. He hit about .370 and stole something like 15 bases. I hit around .350. Eventually he was sent down to Springfield, and rumor had it that I would be next.

I didn't do well once the season started. I believe I went 0 for 11 and had only 1 hit in my first 18 at-bats. The manager of the Millers, Red Davis, went on record saying that I never had hit too well in early months, which was true to a point.

The problem was, I missed Felipe a lot. We'd lived together and done everything together. We were friends and we were both Latin. He was the link to my culture and my heritage. The day they sent him down, I went to my room and started crying. I wouldn't have minded being sent down with him right then. Besides, the general manager of the Millers, Rosy Ryan, was not particularly keen on Latin players.

But the very day I was to be sent down I went 4 for 4. Soon base hits were flying off my bat left and right. I was on a roll. After 18 games my average shot up to .328, and I was leading the club with 19 RBIs. Thoughts of sending me down vanished. Suddenly I was a big star with the Minneapolis Millers. This was my ticket to the major leagues.

The press took notice. I became a local poster boy. "Millers' Cepeda Following in Footsteps of His Famed Dad" blazed across the sports page of one of the leading papers. I was called "The Socking First Sacker" and "The Millers' Puerto Rican Rookie."

"If he ever learns the strike zone, he'll be murder up there. He's tough enough now," Red Davis told the press.

The Minneapolis Millers included future San Francisco Giants teammates Jim Davenport, shortstop Ed Bressound, and catcher Bob Schmidt. Davenport was like a human vacuum at third base, and a gem of a big league prospect. I liked him from the start.

The Millers were one step from the major leagues. I was close, and I knew it. I did well, hitting .309 with 25 home runs and 108 RBIs. In one year I'd made the successful jump from Class C at St. Cloud to Triple A at Minneapolis.

I was sure I had earned the opportunity to be called up in September, when rosters are expanded and major league clubs take a good look at their future prospects. The Giants were a sixth-place club and going nowhere, but despite my outstanding 1957 season they did not call me up at the end of the year. It would have at least given me a chance to show them what I could do against major league pitching. *The Sporting News* thought so, too. Early in 1958 it picked Albie Pearson and me to be the year's top rookies. It was right on both counts. Albie and I would be named the American and National League Rookies of the Year by the Baseball Writers of America.

In August 1957 owner Horace Stoneham announced that the New York Giants were moving to San Francisco for the 1958 season. After more than fifty years in New York, the Giants were heading west. History was soon to be made, and I would be there to see it all happen.

·4·

San Francisco, Here I Come

It was a good time to be young and to be chasing a baseball dream. I went to spring training in 1958 as a nonrostered player without a contract. I ended the season as the National League Rookie of the Year and was named the San Francisco Giants' most popular player and club MVP. I fell in love with San Francisco, and the city embraced me like a native son.

In *The Sporting News,* Jack MacDonald related that Giants manager Bill Rigney, in sizing up his chances for an improved 1958 season, said, "We've got a kid in Minneapolis who might do the job at first base until Bill White gets out of the Army but danged if I can't remember his name. I think it starts with a C."

During the winter months, however, Bill Rigney, Horace Stoneham, and chief scout Tom Sheehan paid a visit to Puerto Rico. Tom had been in my corner since 1955. A friend of Pete Zorilla's, he'd spent many winters in Puerto Rico sizing up the potential talent. Now, three years later, he'd brought Bill and Horace along. They watched me play a few games, and Bill was impressed by what he saw. To make things even better, I was enjoying another banner season with Santurce.

Bill White had taken over the first base chores in 1956, but now he was in the Army. Thirteen-year veteran Whitey Lockman, a member of the Giants' 1951 and 1954 championship teams, was slated for first. Whitey's average had dipped to a career-low .248 in 1957, and Bill knew I was waiting in the wings. He was ready to see what I could do in Arizona that spring.

The Giants' spring training camp was swarming with talented rookies in 1958: Felipe Alou, Willie McCovey, Jim Davenport, Bob Schmidt, Leon Wagner, and Jose Pagan. It was the most talented rookie class to appear anywhere in years. But it was Willie Kirkland, a 6'2", 206-pound slugger from Siluria, Alabama, who was considered the best of the lot and the one rookie the most likely to make the Giants a factor in 1958.

At age twenty-four, Willie Kirkland had all the tools. He was fast and he was quick; he had a great arm and he was smart; and he was a nice fellow with great looks. He was also a terror with the bat, hitting 37 home runs and driving in 120 runs in Triple A in 1956. To this day, I'm amazed that he never made it really big. He had a decent career, but his numbers never were what they should have been. I've heard that Lefty O'Doul tampered with his swing in spring training and Willie was never the same after that.

From the day we first arrived at spring camp, Bill Rigney began playing his rookies. We were not only the future, we were the present, too. Since they had swept the Cleveland Indians in the 1954 World Series, the Giants had been in decline, dropping from 97 wins and a World Championship in 1954 to 80 wins and a third-place finish in 1955. Then they'd plummeted even farther in 1956 and 1957, with losing records and sixth-place finishes both years.

Attendance had also dropped steadily, from over a million paid in 1954 to less than 654,000 in 1957. The Giants were getting old. Willie Mays, Ruben Gomez, and Johnny Antonelli were still frontline players. But Marv Grissom, a fine relief pitcher who starred in the 1954 World Championship team, was forty years old and at the end of his career. Then there was Hank Sauer, the former Chicago Cub slugger and National League MVP who, at forty, had worthy numbers. One of the game's truly nice guys, Hank had hit 26 home runs and driven in 79 runs in under 400 at-bats. He'd been named National League Comeback Player of the Year in 1957. Hank became my mentor and friend. If I was hurting or starting to sulk, I could always count on him to be there to listen and advise.

I was lucky from the start. Bill Rigney was a great manager, clearly the Giants' best and most deserving skipper during my eight and a half years with the team. Bill built that ballclub from the ground up. He would be fired after two winning seasons and a winning record through 55 games. No reason at all, they just let him go. Some things are just hard to figure.

Bill had been a second baseman, and he'd played his entire eight-year career with the New York Giants, retiring in 1953. He was a member of the 1947 Giants, the team that hammered a major league record 221 home runs, and a member of the National League All-Star team in 1948.

When Leo Durocher retired after finishing a distant third in 1955, Bill became the Giants' skipper. When the Giants let him go in 1960, Gene Autry quickly named him manager of the Los Angeles Angels, the American League's first expansion team. In 1962 the Angels under Bill finished in third place with an 82–72 record, a remarkable feat considering there was no free agency or multiyear contracts back then to lure established stars into the expansion market.

After that, with the help of such Latin stars as Tony Oliva, Leo Cardenas, Cesar Tovar, and Rob Carew, Bill took the Minnesota Twins to 98 wins and a division title in 1970. All told, Bill managed for eighteen big league seasons. Now eighty years old, he lives in Northern California where he's still in baseball as an assistant to Sandy Alderson, president of the Oakland Athletics.

Here's how Bill Rigney remembers that 1958 spring training camp:

> The bell had tolled. We suffered in New York the last two years. We finished sixth and sixth. But we knew what there was in the farm system. There was Cepeda. There was Alou. There was Jimmy Davenport. There was Bob Schmidt. We had definitely decided we were going with the young players when we got to San Francisco. It was going to be a new look.
>
> I remember when the Dodgers brought the old guard over from Brooklyn: Pee Wee Reese, Duke Snider, Gil Hodges—they brought them all. I was later told that they had to do that since they were going to LA, where the fans expected all the big names.

We didn't feel that way. We had Willie Mays. That made up for a lot of New York players. I definitely wanted to go with the young players out in San Francisco because it looked like the pendulum was swinging back and there was going to be a lot of good things going on.

During batting practice one day, I saw [Whitey] Lockman and Cepeda at first base. I was behind the cage and kind of watching. I couldn't figure out what was going on, but I could see that Whitey was telling him how on close plays to go and get the ball. You cheat a little. You go off the bag and usually get the play called in your favor.

I was kind of a nosy manager, so I walked over there and started listening. Someone was hitting ground balls, and Orlando was making the play. He took to it in a minute. At any rate, it was time for batting practice and time for Lockman to hit. I said to Whitey, "What do you think?" Now, if Cepeda made the club, there would be a chance that Whitey wouldn't be there or he would be an extra player.

Well, Whitey turns around and says to me, "Too bad he's a year away." "A year away from what?" I asked. "The Hall of Fame," Whitey answered.

I don't think I ever saw a player who could hit a curveball as well as Orlando from the moment he came up, with the possible exception of Tony Oliva. Orlando had a great attitude, and he was so full of the sheer joy of baseball. It was a pleasure managing him.

Back then you paid full dues before becoming a major league ballplayer. Remember, there were just sixteen major league teams and twenty-five positions on each to be filled. It was also one of the best baseball eras ever. Many great stars, including some whose careers had been interrupted because of World War II or the Korean War, were pursuing Hall of Fame careers: Stan Musial, Ted Williams, Robin Roberts, Warren Spahn, Mickey Mantle, Duke Snider, and Yogi Berra, to name a few.

So were the black stars who had achieved major league stardom once the color line was broken, men such as Willie

Mays, Hank Aaron, Frank Robinson, Roberto Clemente, and Ernie Banks.

How can I ever forget that spring of 1958? It was special. The flight from San Juan to New York took four hours, then another twelve hours from New York to Phoenix. I was traveling with Ruben Gomez, one of my boyhood heroes. Ruben had won 17 games for the Giants in 1954 and 15 games in 1957. He was a big Puerto Rican star whom I had admired for years.

Many things crossed my mind during that flight. I remembered my father and thought how nice it would be if he could see me play now. I knew he'd be proud. I thought of my mother, alone now, living in slumlike conditions. I was excited at the thought of playing alongside and against the greatest baseball players in the world—and being paid for it! I had followed a dream, and it was about to come true.

Yet I knew that there were people out there who weren't exactly wishing me well. Surprisingly, some of them were in Puerto Rico, people who had revered my father and thought I was trying to upstage him. One writer, a man who had played with Perucho, said publicly that I would never make it in the major leagues.

Many people in the United States had a negative impression of Latin players, thinking that we were lazy, moody, and difficult to work with. And this showed up everywhere. I won the Triple Crown for St. Cloud in 1956 and led the league in almost every department, but I wasn't even named my team's most valuable player that year. Jack Schwarz, the Giants' farm director, was slow to promote me even with the strong numbers I put on the board every year.

When Felipe Alou signed for $200 in 1956 and was given twelve hours to leave Lake Charles, Louisiana, he went to the Florida State League and led the league in hitting. But he didn't see his $200 until the end of the season. When I was at St. Cloud, there was a fellow from Colombia named Ino Rodreguez who was one of the best ballplayers I'd seen anywhere. He got so fed up with being overlooked that he went to Mexico to play and eventually returned to Colombia.

Ruben Gomez and I arrived in Phoenix on February 28, 1958,

and went to the Adams Hotel. I checked in and returned to the lobby. I wanted to see Willie Mays. Willie was my hero, my idol. He was the Say Hey Kid who could do it all—and even more. As a sixteen-year-old kid, I'd taken his throws when he was tutoring Clemente in Santurce four years earlier. Now I was going to be his teammate.

Willie had been twenty years old when he went to the Giants in 1951, full of pure baseball talent. That was the year that Bobby Thomson hit that dramatic home run off Ralph Branca in the postseason playoffs, the shot that sent the Dodgers packing for home and the Giants to square off against the New York Yankees in the World Series. Willie was chosen National League Rookie of the Year by a comfortable margin over Chet Nichols and Clem Labine.

Willie spent most of the next two years in the service. He returned in 1954 with a flurry and a fury. In a staggering MVP season, Willie hit .345 to lead the majors while slamming 41 home runs and driving in 110 runs. In 1955, Willie pounded out 51 home runs, joining Hack Wilson, Johnny Mize, and Ralph Kiner (twice) as the only National Leaguers till then to hit 50 or more home runs in a season. In 1965 he topped that with 52 homers. Willie was an idol to kids everywhere, black and white.

When I saw Willie in the lobby, I went up to him and talked about the Santurce days. I don't think he remembered me, although he went through the motions. I didn't care. I was too excited.

During spring training I played every day. Rigney put me at first base. We played a number of intersquad games, and I did well, popping 1 home run. When we opened against the Cleveland Indians, I went 3 for 4. I hit into a double play my first time at bat, but the next time I dug in and singled up the middle off Bud Daley. Then I hit a double off a fellow named Dick Brodowski and followed up with a home run my last at-bat. It was a nice spring debut: 3 hits and 4 RBIs as we beat Cleveland 5–1 in Tucson.

A few days later we played Boston and Ted Williams, another living god to me. In Puerto Rico we had some hard throwers, lots of veterans and kids coming up. But I was really impressed by major league pitching. There were so many fine pitchers, real craftsmen who could pitch as well as throw, and do it with great control—high and inside, low and outside.

I had quite a spring. Over the first sixteen exhibition games in the Arizona desert, I was hitting .353. I banged out 8 home runs and drove in 22 runs. Frank Lane, the great Chicago White Sox GM who built the Go Go White Sox of the 1950s and took Minnie Minoso to Chicago, was the general manager of the Cleveland Indians in 1958. After seeing the way I hit and ran, he said, "That kid can't miss" and called me the best rookie he had seen in years. Bill Rigney was saying for the record that I hit a curveball better than any young player he'd seen.

On March 22 Hank Sauer and I hit 2 home runs apiece and Willie Mays hit 1 as we combined to drive in 11 runs and beat the Chicago Cubs 18–12 in a battle of longball. Four days later, Willie and I each homered twice in defeating the Orioles 7–5.

Once *The Sporting News* proclaimed me as the National League Rookie of the Year front-runner, the writers flocked to me. I was hitting the ball well, and hitting with power. Many of my hits whistled to the right side of second base, but I was hitting well to all fields.

It was great to be reunited with Minnie during the spring. Over the winter he had been traded to the Indians in a deal that took Al Smith and Early Wynn to the White Sox. Despite the fact that Minnie had one of his best seasons in 1957, the White Sox wanted Wynn's right arm to bolster their staff. Minnie would enjoy two excellent years with the Indians before returning to the White Sox in 1960, unfortunately missing out on the White Sox championship season in 1959.

My main sidekick with the Giants in the spring was Felipe. Just as I had been recommended to the Giants by Pete Zorilla, Felipe was recommended by a man outside the organization— a fellow named Horatio Martinez who advised Alex Pompez about him in 1956 when Felipe was twenty.

Felipe and I were roommates. I loved him like a brother. I still do. During the winter months, Felipe would hunt sharks in the Dominican Republic. His trusty knife was his main hunting tool. When we would go to sleep at night, he'd put that knife on the table between our beds. Each night before I fell asleep, I'd hope that Felipe would not have a bad dream and think I was a shark.

One day at the start of spring training, Felipe and I were playing pepper. I'll never forget that day. A couple of gray-haired guys were in uniform. They looked pretty old to us. Felipe was convinced one was actually Horace Stoneham. Maybe the other fellow was a major stockholder or someone equally important. Felipe said we should be very quiet and very careful. We wouldn't want to give these two important gentlemen a bad impression. We almost did back flips when we discovered that these two "gentlemen" were our teammates Hank Sauer and Marv Grissom, ages forty-one and forty respectively.

As I said earlier, Hank Sauer took to me immediately. He's the man I turned to when things got rough. He liked the way I hit and was amazed by the way I ran. Like Bill Rigney, he was impressed with the intensity in my eyes, the way I followed the ball when I came to the plate. He liked the way I hit a curveball and how I could go to all fields. When he became batting coach of the Giants in 1959, he helped me a lot. He'd throw lots and lots of batting practice to me.

Johnny Antonelli was another teammate who stands out in my mind. A fine left-hander who came up with the Braves when he was just eighteen years old, Johnny was the National League's best pitcher in 1954, when he won 21 games for the Giants and led the league in earned run average. He won 20 games with the Giants again in 1956, then won 16 more in 1957.

In 1956, when I had visited my sister (from a relationship Perucho had prior to marrying my mother) in New York, I'd gone to the Polo Grounds to see my first major league game. It was between the Giants and the Milwaukee Braves. It was a battle of southpaws with Johnny pitching for the Giants and Warren Spahn for the Braves. The next year, when I had a brief workout with the Giants in New York, Johnny and I got to talking. When I joined the club in 1958 we became friends.

Johnny was the first guy I faced in batting practice in spring training. He was still the ace of the Giants staff, but he was great to me from the start. He'd picked up on my strong affinity for Latin music and bestowed the name "Cha Cha" on me, one of the two nicknames that followed me throughout my career. "Chi chi chi, cha cha cha," he'd say to me each day.

Phoenix was not in the South, but once we left the ball field it was not a comfortable feeling. In the movie theaters blacks and Latins had to sit in sections separate from whites, in designated rows.

Ruben Gomez would play golf every day with Hank Sauer. Valmy Thomas, a catcher from the Virgin Islands, used to go with Willie Mays every night to a black social club. Valmy had played winter ball with Willie in Puerto Rico. I'd hang out some with Felipe, but he wasn't a night person particularly so he didn't like going out that much.

Bobby Thomson, the hero of the 1951 pennant race, had returned to the Giants in late 1957 after three and a half seasons with the Milwaukee Braves. Before long he would be off to the Chicago Cubs, where he would have one last good season in 1958. But not before I beat him in a foot race.

When he broke camp in the spring, Rigney had Herman Franks clock every runner. A couple of days before I had run against Bobby Thomson and beat him in a 75-yard race. That last day they clocked everybody. The next morning the sports headlines read, "Orlando Cepeda, the Fastest of All the Giants' Rookies." I had the best time on the stopwatch.

We played exhibition games in two California cities: El Centro and Los Angeles. In LA, Leo Durocher came to a game that Herb Score was pitching. Herb threw me a curveball, and I hit a line drive to right field. Leo was so impressed that he told reporters that he had never seen anyone hit a curveball like "that kid at first base."

Chub Feeney, the Giants' general manager, said very little to me during the spring, even though I was hitting up a storm. Chub was Horace Stoneham's nephew. He was the one who made the trades, but those in the know said there was always tension between Horace and him.

When *The Sporting News* picked me as the prospective Rookie of the Year in mid-March, I felt I had earned the starting job. Willie McCovey, who had a good Double A season with Dallas in 1957, would be the starting first baseman for the Giants' Phoenix club.

When we broke camp in Phoenix, we barnstormed through minor league cities in Texas, Oklahoma, Iowa, and Nebraska, before flying to San Francisco on April 13. Such barnstorming tours were common practice in those days.

We traveled with the Cleveland Indians to Houston, Dallas, San Antonio, Tulsa, and Oklahoma City, playing them in a series of exhibition games. In Texas we had to stay in black houses outside of Houston. We also had some problems on the train—they didn't want to let the black players eat in the dining car. But the Latin blacks were treated even worse than the American blacks. There were three types of people on the train: whites, blacks, and them. We were the "them."

We arrived in San Francisco by plane on Sunday, April 13. I was tingling all over. This was it. This was the famous City by the Bay. Originally I had been disappointed to learn that the Giants were moving west. My sister lived in New York, I had relatives there, and there was a strong Puerto Rican community and a lot of Latin music. But Willie Mays had told me what a nice city San Francisco was and that I would really like it.

When I got off the plane some Puerto Rican people were waiting for me at the airport. Some were waving Puerto Rican flags. About 400 fans were awaiting the team at the airport. I was so touched. It was something I had never expected.

There was a huge ticker-tape parade for us the next day through downtown San Francisco and a Play-Ball Luncheon at the Sheridan Plaza Hotel. Shirley Temple Black was the parade queen. Throngs of people lined both sides of Montgomery Street and welcomed us as we drove in open convertibles. We were headline stories all over. Local newspapers and radio and TV stations feasted on us. Bill Rigney was given the key to the city.

I was confident. I knew I could play ball. I knew that one way or another I was going to make it. San Francisco was a long, long way from the ghettos and barrios of Puerto Rico. It was a dream come true.

Still, I was in limbo. I had made the team, but I had yet to sign a contract. Believe it or not, with all the excitement and hoopla they had forgotten about me. Here I was, about to open the 1958 baseball season for the San Francisco Giants as their starting first baseman, and I had no contract.

I said to Ruben Gomez, "Ruben, I haven't signed a contract yet. What's the matter?" Ruben quickly made a phone call, and Chub Feeney came scurrying down in a matter of seconds with a contract offering me $7,000. I signed my name on the dotted line ten minutes before game time.

One night around that time I was lying in bed. It was about 11:30, and I was half asleep. I looked up and saw Perucho. As clear as can be, I saw my father. He stood there, then he put his arms around me and smiled. Then he left just as quickly as he had appeared. I knew then that things would be just fine. I was a Major League Baseball player.

·5·

Rookie of the Year

$\mathbf{M}$ajor League Baseball had arrived in San Francisco at last. And just five years before, at age fifteen, I had first picked up a baseball bat with real purpose in mind. It had been only three years since I left the Puerto Rican slums to play professional baseball in the United States.

Things were far from easy. I was black and I spoke a different language. Many customs were new and strange to me. There were days of struggle and lonely moments of tears. Once I almost quit. There was sadness and loneliness, but there was also kindness and friendship along the way.

I was twenty years old and suddenly felt that the world was mine. San Francisco may have been new to me, but the city, I would soon learn, was hardly a stranger to baseball. Born and raised in Puerto Rico, I had not known that the Bay Area was home to three Pacific League teams; the San Francisco Seals, the Mission Reds, and the Oakland Oaks. Nor did I know that the term "sandlot" baseball had been coined right in San Francisco.

There was a longtime Bay Area baseball heritage that I was unaware of. For example, I never realized that so many great major league players hailed from the Bay Area. We didn't pay attention to things like that in Puerto Rico. I had no idea that in the 1930s the San Francisco Seals alone sent thirteen players to the majors, including the great Joe DiMaggio.

Originally I wanted to play in New York, but when I was in Triple A, a lot of Pacific Coast League players told me what a great city San Francisco was. Willie Mays had told me I would really like it there, and he was right. In some ways San Francisco seemed like a smaller New York. It had the same music and the same entertainment, and it was easier to get around. I fell in love with the city from the beginning.

The city went bonkers for us immediately. Bay Area fans had been expecting Major League Baseball since the end of World War II, so we were the talk of the town. Win or lose, we were big-time conversation. The five Bay Area papers made us front-page news. Everywhere the bars and restaurants were alive with Giant chatter. Each day of a home game busloads of fans were dropped off at the ballpark gates at 16th and Bryant Street.

Bill Rigney was smart enough to give fans the pleasure of creating their own frontline stars. He played his rookies immediately and had faith in us. It was an ideal setting for a newcomer like me. And I became an instant celebrity.

Our weekend games were played in the afternoon, except for Fridays. Monday was usually an off day, so Sunday and Thursday night we could stay out without breaking curfew, which we occasionally did.

What great night spots! Some, like the Copacabana and the Blackhawk, were second homes. On Tuesdays I'd go to the Copacabana for Latin music and Cal Tjader. Sunday night was the Blackhawk with Miles Davis and John Coltrane. Wes Montgomery was at the Jazz Workshop. I was "Cha Cha, the Dancing Master," and the music was made to order.

Many people tended to associate the Giants only with Candlestick Park. What they forget is that we played our first two major league seasons, 1958–1959, in Seals Stadium. I liked that park. It had a warmth and a sense of community not unlike Wrigley Field or Fenway Park. Giants announcer Russ Hodges called it a "beautiful little watch-charm ballpark, all green and cozy."

The city was in a frenzy. Writers were swarming from the rafters. Bill Rigney had two other rookies in the starting lineup: Jim Davenport at third base and leading off, and Willie Kirkland in the right field batting cleanup. Bob Schmidt was to have started behind the plate, but Rigney decided instead to go with Valmy Thomas. A native of the Virgin Islands, Valmy had caught Ruben's screwball before.

Willie Mays, starting his sixth season with the Giants, was in center field batting third. Already one of the game's anointed superstars, Willie was Rookie of the Year in 1952 and National League MVP in 1954. Our keystone combo was eight-year veteran Danny O'Connell at second and seven-year vet Daryl Spencer at shortstop. At the last minute Rigney penciled in left-handed hitting Jim King to replace Hank Sauer in left field. I'm not sure why Bill made the change, but Hank was understandably hurt. He and Rigney were good friends, but Hank did not talk to him for two weeks.

One of baseball's true power hitters with the Chicago Cubs in the late forties and early fifties, Hank was Minor League Player of the Year in 1947 and National League MVP in 1952. Hank, who was forty-one years in 1958, hit 281 of his 288 career home runs after his thirty-first birthday. He might well have shattered some records had he made it to the big leagues in his early twenties like today's players.

Felipe Alou made the club. So did Leon Wagner. Because the Giants were planning to send Felipe to the minors, he only signed for $5,800. When he got word he was being sent down, he simply refused to go. It took real guts. His wife, who was only eighteen at the time, was pregnant, and Felipe did not want her to have to go to Phoenix, where the temperature can sometimes reach 120 degrees. Felipe decided he would return to the Dominican Republic and then report to Phoenix in 1960 after the baby was born. Just before he was about to leave a spot opened up on the Giants roster, and Felipe was able to stay.

Until the Milwaukee Braves dethroned the Dodgers as National League champs in 1957, the Dodgers or the Giants had taken every National League flag since 1951, the year the two teams locked horns in that historic playoff series. Just another reason that game was so memorable.

As long as I live I'll never forget Opening Day, April 15, 1958. It was a warm, breezy day, the sun was shining, and we were making history. The first West Coast major league game was about to unfold, and it was the Giants against the Dodgers, the new Los Angeles Dodgers. The historic feud had moved west, and a standing-room crowd of 23,449 packed Seals Stadium.

Tingling with excitement, I looked across the field to see those blue Dodger uniforms. These were my boyhood heroes: Duke Snider, Gil Hodges, Don Newcombe, Pee Wee Reese, and Carl Furillo. This was the real thing.

On the mound for the Dodgers was their ace, twenty-two-year-old hard-throwing Don Drysdale. With a record of 17–9 in 1956, Don threw smoke. He was fast. And when his fastball lost some velocity later on, he learned to change speeds beautifully. Like Bob Gibson and Juan Marichal, Drysdale wouldn't give you an inch. On more than one occasion he had me hitting the dirt. Don was one of baseball's best big-game pitchers. He was the guy you wanted out there when the stakes were all or nothing.

Bill Rigney surprised the pundits by bypassing Johnny Antonelli for Ruben Gomez. Bill must have known something, because Ruben shut out the Dodgers 8–0, allowing them only six hits. Born in Arroyo, Puerto Rico, Ruben was a legend back home. His screwball was baffling. And he had given the Giants some good years. He was 17–9 in 1954, and he had outpitched Mike Garcia in Game Three of the Giants' World Series sweep of the Cleveland Indians. With the sixth-place New York Giants in 1957, he'd gone 15–13 to lead the staff.

I was hitting fifth, behind Willie Mays and Willie Kirkland. We got to Drysdale early, knocking him out of the box with 3 runs in the 2nd and 4 runs in the 3rd.

Daryl Spencer became the first player to hit a West Coast home run. I was the second. After grounding into a double play my first turn at bat, I squared off against Don Bessent with the bases empty in the third. I worked the count to 3 and 1. Bessent fed me a changeup, and I was ready. I got good wood, and the ball sailed 390 feet over the right-field fence. The crowd went crazy.

The home run did it for me. It established a love affair with the city of San Francisco. If Perucho was the "Bull," I was the "Baby Bull." I had not known anything like this before. Willie Mays was New York, part of the old guard, an established star.

I was the new kid, the rookie. In other words, I became a San Francisco original. I was theirs from the beginning.

Columnist Herb Caen took after me first, though. He called me the Copacabana Kid, and he knew every move I made. Each time I went into a slump he'd slam me with something like, "He can't hit . . . he stays up all night." Later Herb and I became good friends. I grew to like him a lot.

The next day was different. The Dodgers jumped all over Ray Monzant in the 2nd inning, and behind the excellent pitching of Johnny Podres, they downed us 13–1. We came back to take Game Three 7–4, with Curt Barclay getting the win in relief of Johnny Antonelli.

On April 19 I homered in Los Angeles, a 3rd-inning solo shot off Ron Negray. Behind Ruben Gomez, we slammed the Dodgers 11–4. On the 23rd I tripled as we came from behind with a four-run 9th-inning rally to beat the Cardinals 8–7. Daryl Spencer's two-out, two-run homer in the 9th was the margin of victory.

I connected with my third home run of the season against the Cubs on April 27. On the 30th I hit homer number four, a two-run shot off Philadelphia Phillies Hall of Famer Robin Roberts.

On May 4 I hit consecutive home runs off the Pirates' Bob Smith. The next day I homered again for number seven, and then on May 6 a solo shot made it 4 home runs in three days against the Pirates. The fans went wild. "The public loves a slugger," wrote the Chronicle's Bob Stevens, "and this boy is the Rocky Marciano of the batter's ring."

How does a twenty-year-old handle instant celebrity? All I can say is that I was having a very good time. I was having fun. We weren't paid great salaries back then. I had signed a $7,000 contract ten minutes before game time. Like many others, the money was secondary for me. I truly loved the game. Free agency and multiyear contracts were years away, and we played for our pay. If you didn't produce, you'd be sent down to the minors. Someone else was always waiting in the wings to take your job.

I was on a roll. Every day was a highlight. We'd start with the

Dodgers. Then St. Louis would come to town with Musial, Ken Boyer, Sad Sam Jones, Larry Jackson, and Lindy McDaniel; then Pittsburgh with Dick Groat, Bill Mazeroski, Bob Friend, Vern Law, and Roberto Clemente; then Cincinnati with Gus Bell, Frank Robinson, and Johnny Temple; then Philadelphia with Wally Post, Granny Hamner, and Richie Ashburn; and finally we'd go to Chicago and face Ernie Banks, Walt Moryn, and Dale Long.

The national media was paying attention "The Rookie Bull of Baseball" was featured in the June 30, 1958, issue of *Life* magazine:

> Orlando Cepeda has been playing Major League Baseball only two months but has already earned a formidable nickname: "The Bull." He runs bases like one—madly and with grotesque expressions . . . In the field . . . the twenty-year-old Puerto Rican recklessly charges in on bunt situations. At bat, following Willie Mays, he unsettles opposing pitchers almost as much as Willie does. By last week he had hit as many homers (14) and driven in as many runs (42) as Mays had. He's baseball's outstanding rookie and a prime reason why the Giants have jumped from second division into a fight for first place.

Because I was the son of a baseball legend, the name "The Bull" soon evolved, and the "Baby Bull" was officially born. I also got a pay raise. I was doing so well that on June 1 the club increased my salary from the minimum $7,000 to $9,500. I wasn't worldly or money-wise. We were in Milwaukee on payday, and there was an additional check for $1,800 waiting for me. I thought it said $18 so I took it to the bank to cash. Imagine my surprise when the bank gave me $1,800. That night I went to my room and spent all night counting my money. I had never seen so much.

Felipe and I lived in Daly City, just outside San Francisco, with Ruben Gomez and his wife. I was the only one who liked to go out at night. Felipe was very religious and rather quiet. Ruben was married and liked to play golf. But I was single, and I loved the town.

I dated a lot. Girls would find all sorts of ways to meet me. Some would call the ballpark and say they were writers. They'd say they wanted to interview Orlando Cepeda. Sometimes I'd meet a girl before the game. Then after the game, I'd find out she wasn't a writer at all. Many of these women were beautiful. It was that easy for me. I was a baseball hero.

That occasionally presented problems, mainly racial and cultural. Because I lived in Daly City with Ruben, who was a light-skinned Puerto Rican and considered white, some black players resented that I didn't live with the black people. And since I sometimes dated white girls, some teammates were not exactly kindly disposed. Poor Bill Rigney. He had to call me into his office more than once to tell me to stop dating white women. Not that Bill cared a bit, but word had it that there were others who cared a lot.

But I sure drove Bill crazy with mental lapses. I made a lot of mistakes, and it was hard making the necessary adjustments. I did a lot of dumb things, like running through coaches' signals. Sometimes Willie had a base stolen, and I'd swing and foul off a pitch. I had a lot to learn yet. Bill could be patient. But he could also be tough.

I had good speed, but I didn't harness it well. Once I overran second base and was thrown out by twenty-five feet at third base. Rigney slapped a $50 fine on me. I learned my lesson. The next game I went 4 for 4.

I always tried to please the fans. Once there was a pop fly behind first base. As I circled to my left and extended my glove into the first-base seats to snare the ball, a twelve-year-old kid hoping for a souvenir touched the ball and knocked it out of my glove. The ushers yelled at him and were about to throw him out of the ballpark. I told them to leave the kid alone. The fans gave me a rousing ovation.

At the start of the season, Ruben Gomez told the press that I was the "best player to come out of Puerto Rico since Ruben Gomez." By midseason fans and writers were going even further, calling me perhaps the best player ever to come out of Puerto Rico. Although Roberto Clemente came up with the Pirates in 1955, his big numbers didn't begin until 1961. By then

I had been named Rookie of the Year and a three-time National League All-Star.

As my popularity increased and his career began to slide, Ruben became more jealous and began taking jabs at me. Once in St. Louis Sad Sam Jones was pitching. Sam had a hell of a curveball. I always looked for a fastball, knowing I could adjust to a breaking ball. Well, Sam threw a fastball, and I pounded it 420 feet for a double. When I came to the bench, I said, "Ruben, I was looking for a breaking ball." That's all I said. Then he yelled out, "Bullshit!" He was really angry at me.

I bought my first car in 1958, a Chevrolet Impala. I really loved that car. Of course, San Francisco is not the easiest place to drive. One day I wrecked the car and was so devastated. I called Ruben, asking him to help me out. He was older and knew the ropes far better than me. "Help yourself!" he shot back at me. He couldn't have cared less.

That winter in Puerto Rico he made it a point to tell my mother that I was getting a big head. I trusted Ruben, and that really hurt. Maybe he didn't really want me to do well after all. I would be Rookie of the Year in 1958, and Ruben, after a good start, would fall to 10–12. The following year he would be traded to the Phillies. Among other things, the Giants felt he was a bad influence on me.

The real irony was that I always followed Ruben into battle. That was the biggest rap sportswriters had against me in 1958. But I was Latin, and I had a temper. And Ruben Gomez was my *compadre*, my friend, my teammate.

I had been given the heave-ho by umpires early in the season for protesting their calls, but Bill Rigney convinced me that I was far more valuable to the team in the game than out. So I curbed my temper and mended my ways. At least I thought so.

The big flare-up occurred on June 25, 1958. There was bad blood between the Pirates and the Giants that afternoon. Ruben and Pirate pitcher Vern Law had both been warned against throwing at batters. "The crowd sensed the outbreak of a fight at any time," is how one writer described the scene.

In the 4th inning Ruben plunked Bill Mazeroski on the shoulder. Home plate umpire Frank Dascoli gave Ruben a stern warning. When Ruben came up in the 5th inning, Dascoli remembered that he had beaned Vern Law the year before and warned Law against any retaliation.

Pirates manager Danny Murtaugh charged out of the dugout and chased after Dascoli. En route, Murtaugh looked at Ruben and pointed to his head, an indication that the Pirates were going to throw at Ruben's head.

All hell broke loose after that. Herman Franks, our third base coach, bore down on Murtaugh. Murtaugh broke free and rushed toward Ruben, his arms swinging wildly. There was bedlam on the ball field. Players were throwing long wild punches everywhere. All of the sudden I got clobbered in the back of the neck. The bat boy had hit me, and my hat fell off.

I was from a Puerto Rican slum, and I was used to grabbing the nearest thing to protect myself. I ran to the dugout and was about to grab a bat, but Willie Mays ran in from the outfield and dropped me to my knees with a flying tackle.

Without knowing the whole story, much of the press was all over me. Looking back, it was a dumb thing to do. It was also costly. Ruben and I were each fined $100 by National League President Ford Frick. There was a torrent of jeers and boos whenever we went to Pittsburgh to play the Pirates.

That winter in Puerto Rico there would be another incident in which Ruben would hit an opposing player. In Puerto Rico you're lucky just to get away with hoots and howls after pulling a stunt like that. Ruben and I had to be escorted by car off the playing field and out of town, away from 4,000 angry and screaming partisan fans with an assortment of sticks, stones, and blades.

I was fortunate. I kept an even pace all season. My average was never lower than .305 that year, ranging from .339 on May 1 to a low of .305 on September 1. I finished the year at .312. Willie and I formed a potent tandem in the middle of the order. Willie batted third, and I usually hit fourth.

When the month of May ended, we were 27–17 and tied for first place with the Milwaukee Braves. On June 4 the cover story in *The Sporting News* was "Can the Giants Capture Pennant? Why Not?"

On June 22, Willie Mays collected his 1,000[th] career base hit. Five days later, on the 27th, I drove in my fifteenth home run of the season. By June 30 our record stood at 37–33, 3 games behind the first-place Braves.

My best display of long-ball hitting began on July 11 against Cincinnati. In the 12th inning, with the score tied at 4–4 and with two on and two strikes, I tagged Hal Jeffcoat for my seventeenth home run of the season.

The next day against the Braves, I took two strikes before leveling a Warren Spahn pitch 420 feet into the right center-field bleachers, as Johnny Antonelli beat the Braves 5–3. The following day was more of the same. For the third day in a row I had the key hit. This time it was a two-strike home run against Don McMahon. Our upstart San Francisco Giants were looking like pennant contenders as we marched into first place once again.

In his "Hats Off" column, Bob Stevens wrote, "After Cepeda put on a terrific batting exhibition against Milwaukee in County Stadium the first time around, a Brave pitcher sneered, 'Wait for the second time around. The kid will be chopped down to size.' The second time around arrived, and Orlando did terrible things to Spahn, who is not a bad pitcher, indeed. Shortly after Orlando's loft into the bleachers, the same Brave who had taken Cepeda so lightly smiled an embarrassed little smile and said, 'Well, he's good.'"

It was hot and humid on July 28 when 28,305 fans poured into Philadelphia's Connie Mack Stadium for a doubleheader. I had 5 hits as we swept the Phillies by scores of 3–2 and 2–1. Mike McCormick, our classy nineteen-year-old southpaw, upped his record to 8–2 in the opener, while Ruben Gomez battled to victory in the second game. Philadelphia's famous boo birds hooted throughout both games, filling the field with paper airplanes, beer, and other assorted debris as we moved within .001 points of the league-leading Braves.

July 29, 1958, we were back in first place with a record of 54–43. It was our last day on top.

On July 31, I hit 2 doubles in a losing cause against the Reds, as Bob Purkey beat us 5–1. But Red's manager Jimmy Dykes touted me with the words "Rookie of the Year." Dykes told the press, "Cepeda is as strong as a span of mules. Without him the Giants would be nowhere."

Dykes wasn't the only one. Babe Pinelli, a National League umpire for twenty-two years, wrote in his *Call-Bulletin* column that I had the inside track over the Cardinals' Curt Flood and Gene Green for National League Rookie of the Year honors: "To date Orlando leads the Giants in home runs (19) and runs batted in (58). He is traveling at a faster pace than [Frank] Robinson did his rookie year."

It was an interesting baseball year. Tragically, a January car accident in New York left Dodger great and three-time MVP Roy Campanella permanently paralyzed. As a youngster I had watched Campanella play winter ball in Puerto Rico; he was one of my favorites.

Years later, in 1970, he managed one of the teams in the second annual Martin Luther King All-Star Game at Dodger Stadium. Roy made it a point to tell me and everyone else in sight what a great ballplayer my father was. It was a kind and thoughtful thing to say, and it would have made Perucho proud.

When the dust settled at the end of the season, Ted Williams won the American League batting championship at age forty. The White Sox's Nellie Fox played a major league record 98 games without striking out. Ernie Banks led the National League with 47 home runs and 129 RBIs and was named National League MVP for the fifth-place Chicago Cubs. He won again in 1959 with the Cubs still in second division. Richie Ashburn won his second batting title in four years, hitting .350, three points higher than Willie Mays. Our own right-hander Stu Miller led the league with a 2.47 ERA despite a losing record of 6–9. Willie Mays, Johnny Antonelli, and catcher Bob Schmidt were on the National League All-Star team.

The Milwaukee Braves again were the class of the league, winning their second straight National League title. They had an outstanding team with the likes of Hank Aaron, Eddie Mathews, Johnny Logan, Del Crandall, Billy Bruton, Red Schoendienst, and Wes Covington, who hit .330 and slammed 24 home runs in less than 300 at-bats.

But it was pitching more than anything else that put them over the top. Warren Spahn went 22–11, the ninth of thirteen times Spahn would top 20 wins. Lew Burdette, the World Series hero of 1957 with three wins against the Yankees, was 20–10 with a .291 ERA.

Spahn was one of the all-time greats. One time I slammed one of his pitches into the right-field seats for a three-run homer. He was angry and made it known to the press. "I tried to jam him," he told reporters, "and he hit a home run to right center off me." Del Crandall, his batterymate, joined in by saying that I hit a breaking ball better than any rookie he'd ever seen.

Some of the best advice is the advice you don't take. Lefty O'Doul was a great hitter and a San Francisco icon. In 1929 he batted .398 for the Phillies and set a National League record with 254 base hits. Lefty spotted me in Phoenix during spring training and said I was hitting too many balls to right and right center. He wanted to change my swing and make me a dead-pull hitter. I didn't listen, so he walked away and rarely spoke to me again. Lefty didn't like the way I swung inside out. But that was exactly why I hit to both fields with power. Today many young players learn to hit that way—with excellent results, I might add. I was just a bit ahead of my time.

Like most young teams, we slipped some during the last two months, going 26–30 in August and September. The Braves just had too much of everything. But for four months we turned the rest of the league into true believers and made the city of San Francisco and all its baseball fans very proud. For thirty-three days we held first place.

Though picked for no higher than sixth place, we finished third with a record of 80 wins and 74 losses, behind the Braves and the surprising Pittsburgh Pirates. We led the National League in runs scored (727) and in doubles (250). Willie Mays caught fire and finished the year at .347. Jimmy Davenport established himself as one of baseball's best third basemen. Willie Kirkland, Davenport, Leon Wagner, and I made *The Sporting News* All-Rookie Team for 1958.

My 25 home runs were second on the club to Willie's 29. For most of the year I led the team in RBIs, but Willie caught me on the final day to tie for the club lead. Our 96 RBIs were bettered only by Ernie Banks (129), Frank Thomas (109), and Harry Anderson (97).

At twenty years old I had come of age with a new major league franchise and an adoring city. I hit .312 and led the league in doubles with 38. I hit for 309 total bases and had a slugging percentage of .512. Only Banks (379), Mays (350), and Hank Aaron (328) hit for more total bases. I had more putouts than any National League first baseman.

Willie Mays and I were the only two National League players to finish in the top ten in the following six categories: hits, runs, home runs, batting average, runs batted in, and stolen bases. I was unanimously selected as National League Rookie of the Year. Only Frank Robinson in 1956 had ever won the award by a unanimous vote. I was in good company.

"Cepeda is Tops" said an editorial in a leading San Francisco paper:

> Now that the "keed from Puerto Rico" has made it, we want to be counted among the thousands of baseball fans who probably would have demanded a Congressional investigation if he hadn't been so honored.
>
> We're talking about Orlando Cepeda being named National League Rookie of the Year [for] 1958.
>
> San Francisco, in turn, can feel as proud of the coveted award bestowed upon the genial first baseman as the young athlete himself feels about being named the top rookie of the year.
>
> It is more gratifying to red hot Giants fans in view of the fact the honor was won by one of their boys in San Francisco's freshman year in the big leagues.
>
> But with Orlando performing the way he did, we can't see how those who elect the Rookie of the Year could have missed naming him—unless there were two Cepedas.

As great an honor was my being named the Most Valuable Giant by Bay Area fans in a poll conducted by the *San Francisco Examiner*. I received 18,701 votes. Willie Mays was second with 11,510 votes. In a pregame ceremony on September 28, *Examiner* sports editor Curley Grieve presented me with a $275 watch and a handsome plaque. I won on consistency, according to the thousands of letters that accompanied the vote. *The*

Sporting News responded that although Willie Mays was "terrific at the start and finish, [he] faltered badly during midseason."

With the season over, ballplayers packed their gear, exchanged good-byes, and wished each other well. We were a baseball club, a unit all season long. Now we were going our separate ways for the winter months.

The December 1958 issue of *Sport* magazine proclaimed the San Francisco Giants as the baseball success story of 1958. "The story of the Giants is partly the cornball legend of young America—a bunch of brash swaggering youngsters going forth to challenge the world."

Felipe and I were due to catch a plane for New York. Felipe would then fly to the Dominican Republic to see his family and his baseball-playing brothers who he talked so much about. I was off to see my mother and buy that new house she so richly deserved.

As we left the clubhouse, most of the guys shook my hand and thanked me for a great season. They congratulated me on being chosen the Giants' MVP and most popular player. Two teammates neglected to congratulate me. I was surprised. One was Ruben Gomez; the other was Willie Mays.

I was also hurt. Ruben had been my mentor, one of my heroes growing up as a kid in Puerto Rico. He was an icon back home. Willie was the "Say Hey Kid." He was everyone's hero, the greatest in the game.

I never understood why being named Giants MVP rattled Willie. I still don't. Sportswriter Glenn Dickey interviewed Willie for his recent book on the Giants called *The San Francisco Giants: 40 Years* (Woodford Press, 1997). Dickey concluded that Willie was "still obviously nettled by that vote nearly forty years later."

Nevertheless, being chosen National League Rookie of the Year and Most Valuable Giant by the fans as a twenty-year-old rookie in 1958 remains one of my brightest and most cherished baseball memories.

·6·

The Georgia Peach and the Say Hey Kid

I returned to Puerto Rico a hero. Perucho would have been proud. Even my staunchest critics considered me a worthy successor to my father. No Puerto Rican had ever put together a major league season like mine. Not even Vic Power or Roberto Clemente, whose greatest seasons were still in front of him.

There was something else too, something far more important. I became a pioneer for the great wave of Latin ballplayers of the future. Giants outfielder Stan Javier said recently that people like his dad (Julian), Roberto Clemente, and me were the Jackie Robinsons for the Latin kids of his generation, the role models, much like Minnie Minoso, Chico Carresquel, and Bobby Avila had been to mine.

It was a thoughtful thing for Stan to say and so nice to hear. I've know Stan since he was born, and there was never any doubt that he wanted be a ballplayer. But as a good friend of his parents, Stan thought of me more as an adopted uncle than a baseball star. A lot of people don't know that Stan Javier was named after Stan Musial. That's how much his father, Julian, admired Stan Musial when they were teammates together with the St. Louis Cardinals.

After my rookie season, scouts from many big league clubs started going to Puerto Rico searching for top prospects. Charlie Metro, who was one of the major leagues' top scouts, wrote to

Pete Zorilla asking him to look for more Orlando Cepedas. Clearly the Giants had a head start on the Latin market. On our 1958 squad alone Ruben and I were Puerto Rican, Felipe was from the Dominican Republic, Ramon Monzant was Venezuelan, and Andre Rogers a Bahaman.

Until then only a few scouts went to Puerto Rico looking for prospects. I still have copies of letters explaining how the Giants got a jump on the Latin market by signing players like the Alous, Jose Pagan, Juan Marichal, Manny Mota, and others.

The Giants' Latin connection had been well-established. Jose Pagan, who came up through the ranks with me, joined the Giants in 1959. He would become our starting shortstop in 1961, go on to play for the Pittsburgh Pirates, and complete his career with the Phillies in 1973.

The Giants also signed Felipe's two younger brothers, Matty and Jesus. In 1963 the three Alous would start a game in the same outfield. It was a major league first, and I don't believe it's ever been repeated.

The Dominican Islands were also home to Hall of Fame pitcher Juan Marichal, who ranks among the best ever. Juan came up in 1960 and pitched for the Giants through 1973, before finishing up with the Boston Red Sox in 1974 and ever so briefly in 1975. Juan racked up 238 of his 243 wins in a Giants uniform.

The best Puerto Rican pitcher I ever saw was Juan Pizarro. He was one of the fastest I ever faced. He came up in 1957 with the Milwaukee Braves, where manager Fred Haney once chewed him down for pitching too tight to Stan Musial and knocking him down. Juan's best years were with the Chicago White Sox in the early to mid-sixties, when he won 61 games from 1961 through 1964. It was White Sox manager Al Lopez, Juan insists, who kept him from winning 20 games in 1964 by refusing to pitch him more often.

Juan Pizarro was just awesome when he pitched for the Santurce Crabbers in the mid-fifties. But Santurce was in a money crunch, and in December of 1956 they sold him and Roberto Clemente to the Caguas Crilloes. At the time, Roberto was enjoying an 18-game hitting streak en route to his only Puerto Rican batting championship.

The Caguas Crilloes had a close working relationship with the Milwaukee Braves in the 1950s, much like the Santurce/Giants link back then. Personal friendships helped. That's why Hank Aaron joined Caguas in 1953 and why the Milwaukee Braves later signed Felix Mantilla, a close friend of Hank's, a short time later. Remember, Horace Stoneham sent Willie Mays to Santurce as a personal favor to Pete Zorilla.

I had a great season that winter, winning the batting title with a .362 average. We played Caguas for the championship in a best-of-nine series. I homered twice in Game Five as we beat Caguas 9–3, and again in Game Six to help Santurce to a 9–2 win. We eventually won the series five games to two.

In the era before multiyear contracts and high-powered agents, we waited to receive our contracts in the mail. Then the negotiating began. Thank God for my brother, Pedro, or else I'd really have been in the wilderness. Pedro was a college graduate with a degree in business administration. My mother had saved every nickel and dime to help him with his tuition. Now he was my unofficial agent in dealing with Giants General Manager Chub Feeney. Remember, I had signed the year before as a nonrostered player for $7,000, then received a raise to $9,500 during the season. This time their offer was $12,000. I wouldn't take it.

We felt strongly that my numbers alone warranted more than a mere $2,500 raise. I was the Giants' Most Valuable Player, Most Popular Player, and the National League Rookie of the Year. I had finished ninth in the MVP voting, behind Bill Mazeroski and ahead of Del Crandall. We were asking for $20,000, which was less than one-third of what Willie Mays was making. Since Willie and I had comparable years in 1958, we felt this request was reasonable.

Pedro did what he could, negotiating by phone with Chub. But the Giants were tough. Eventually we settled for $17,000. We could do little else realistically. It was not what we thought I was worth, but it sure beat being poor in Puerto Rico.

It was a different feeling when I reported to spring training in 1959. I was brimming with confidence, secure that I was a major league ballplayer and a good one. Lots of people were talking "sophomore jinx." That's when a player who has a good rookie season falls flat his second year. It's happened more than once. But I didn't give it much thought. Some critics said that a full season of winter ball could take a toll on my endurance. I never gave that another thought either. There was no way I could return to Puerto Rico and not play ball there. When you're twenty-one and physically fit, you think you can go on forever.

The general feeling in 1959 was that more pitching was needed. It was pitching more than anything else that fell short late in the season. Johnny Antonelli had paced the staff with a 16–13 record. At age nineteen, Mike McCormick was loaded with potential. His 11–8 record was an indication that he'd get better with age. Stu Miller sported the league's lowest ERA, but Ruben Gomez had slipped badly to 10–12.

We improved our rotation greatly by trading for Sam Jones and Jack Stanford. Sam Jones came to us from the Cardinals for Bill White and Ray Jablonski on March 25, 1959. It was one of those trades that helped both clubs. Sam won 21 games for us in 1959, leading the league in ERA, and he won 18 games more in 1960.

Bill became a standout with the Cardinals and Phillies for many years, then rose through the ranks to become president of the National League. One of the best fielding first basemen ever and winner of seven straight Gold Gloves, Bill had 22 home runs as a rookie in 1956. He returned to the Giants from military service in July 1958 but played in only twenty-nine games. He became trade bait only because the Giants were set with Jim Davenport and me at infield corners.

Sam Jones was one of those unforgettable characters. His trademark was a toothpick dangling between his lips. When he as on his game, no one could be tougher. Signed originally by the Cleveland Indians in 1951, he was picked up by the Chicago Cubs in 1955. That year he led the league in losses (20), bases on balls (188), and strikeouts (198).

Old-time Cub fans still talk about his 1955 no-hitter. After walking the bases loaded in the top of the 9th, he struck out the next three batters in high fashion to preserve his no-hit game. With the Cardinals in 1958, Sam was a superb pitcher. He was 14–13 with a .288 ERA and had a major league-high 225 strikeouts. Sam's 21 wins in 1959 would tie Warren Spahn and Lew Burdette for the National League lead.

Jack Sanford had been the National League Rookie of the Year in 1957 with the Phillies. That year he was 19–8 and led the National League in strikeouts. Sanford came to us in a trade for Ruben Gomez and Valmy Thomas. The deal was great for us. From 1959 through 1962 Jack won 64 games, including 24 in our pennant-winning season of 1962.

Ruben, on the other hand, was a big disappointment for the Phillies. His record fell to 3–8 in 1959. He'd win just two more games over the next two years. Ruben came back briefly with the Phillies in 1967 before calling it quits. Once he had been my friend and my hero. But we'd long since had a parting of ways and our friendship dissipated completely.

It was an interesting spring. Early on I noticed a gray-haired man watching our workouts. He seemed to know something about the game. I figured he was just another old-timer, one of many retirees soaking up the Arizona sunshine. But I figured wrong. He was Ty Cobb, the "Georgia Peach" himself, and he took a real shine to me and the way I handled myself as a ballplayer.

Cobb came to Arizona from 1959–1962, and he drove this huge black Chrysler Imperial. He'd made a small fortune from his Coca-Cola stock by then. Each time we played the Chicago Cubs in Mesa he'd see me and talk with me. He would point out Willie Mays and say to me, "Too bad you're playing with that guy there. You should be playing somewhere else where people can know and appreciate how well you really play ball."

I've heard a lot of things about Ty Cobb recently, that he was a bad man and a racist among other things. But that's not the Ty Cobb I knew, the man who befriended me. I didn't know too much about him at the time. When people asked me if I knew who the old-timer was, I'd say, "Yes, he used to play ball himself." Then someone said to me, "Don't you know that's Ty Cobb?" Now I look back and wish I had taken a picture with him. He was a humble man and treated me with decency and respect.

Cobb would sit and talk with me a lot in spring training, because in the spring you would only play about three or four innings a game. In fact, he gave me a ride in his big Chrysler and invited me to dinner once. On more than one occasion he said for the record that if Orlando Cepeda doesn't get hurt, he'll surpass Willie Mays one day.

He was not alone. In the July 7, 1959, issue of *Look* magazine there was a feature by Tim Cohane entitled "Orlando Cepeda: Will He Pass Willie Mays?":

> When Orlando Cepeda cocks his bat and bores his eyes into the pitcher, he suggests a mongoose truculently awaiting . . . a cobra. And it's no bluff. The twenty-one-year-old Puerto Rican first baseman of the San Francisco Giants has displayed such right-handed hitting power that it has evoked superlatives bestowed on few major league newcomers. Stan Musial of the St. Louis Cardinals . . . has predicted that Cepeda . . . could lead the National League [in hitting]. Leo Durocher, one-time manager of the Dodgers and Giants, calls Cepeda one of the best curveball hitters he has ever seen. Del Crandall, Milwaukee Braves catcher, concurs. And Giants manager Bill Rigney terms Cepeda the best young player since his spectacular teammate, center fielder Willie Mays.
>
> Some even believe Cepeda will surpass Mays. They point to his first-year performance in 1958: a .312 average, 96 runs batted in, and 25 homers, compared with Mays' .274, 68, and 20 during his first year in the majors in 1951. Each was twenty at the time. Cepeda's supporters feel he is basically a sounder hitter than Mays. They concede that he will never equal Mays defensively, but they argue that his bat may ultimately resolve the comparison in his favor. . . . The theory does not sound exaggerated.

First let me say that I doubt if anybody could surpass Willie Mays. He was the greatest ballplayer I ever saw. I never saw Joe DiMaggio play baseball, but Willie could do it all. I'm not sure anyone will ever play the game of baseball better than Willie Mays. His numbers alone speak volumes, and as an outfielder he had few peers. Many old-timers say that Willie could have been a big star at any position.

To be truthful, though, I believe that playing with Willie did hurt me. He was a great player, but because he came from New York, they built him up so much in San Francisco. When I did well a lot of people who relocated here, as well as some writers, seemed to resent that.

It's not a secret that Willie Mays and I didn't get on that well. Certainly there was never the feeling of friendship and camaraderie that existed—and still exists—between Willie McCovey and me, and I feel badly about that. Willie was a private person and a loner, so it was hard to figure out what he was thinking. I was hurt when he didn't congratulate me on being named the Giants' MVP, Most Popular Player, and National League Rookie of the Year. I was also hurt by his silence later when internal strife was tearing our team apart.

When I hit 3 home runs in three days following the 1958 All-Star Game, the headline on Jack MacDonald's column read: "Cepeda Powers Giants' Surge, Now Rivals Willie in Spotlight: Frisco Fans Cheer Rookie's Clutch Homers as Mays Struggles to Halt Slump." The article read, "The Giants have shed their label as a 'one-man' club. While he is still around and frequently gets into the thick of the plot, it's no longer just Willie Mays with a supporting cast of eight basking in his reflected limelight."

At the time I was leading the club with 19 home runs—ten hit in Seals Stadium—and 57 RBIs. But I wasn't in competition with Willie or with anyone else, for that matter. I was a baseball player doing my best for the team and for myself. I felt very lucky to be there and was literally playing for my keep. It was that very paycheck that would make things better for my mother and take her away from the slums she was living in.

But Willie began to distance himself from me almost immediately. I enjoyed my popularity and the city of San Francisco could not have been nicer, but somehow I felt that Willie resented the attention I was getting from the Bay Area. When the national press began taking notice as well, Willie distanced himself even further.

For seven years (1958–1964) Willie Mays and I gave the San Francisco Giants the most potent one-two power punch in baseball. We hit 488 home runs between the two of us, which was nine more than Hank Aaron and Eddie Mathews hit for the Braves. But off the field he all but ignored me. We put on a good front for the press and public. We said nice things and engaged in a number of photo ops, but privately he kept his distance and we had little to do with one another. We were great on the field together and put up outstanding numbers, but not once in the seven years we played together for the Giants did Willie Mays treat me like a friend.

Nineteen-fifty-nine was an interesting year. On May 26 Harvey Haddix of the Pittsburgh Pirates threw a twelve-inning perfect game against the Milwaukee Braves, then lost the game 1–0 in the 13th inning.

Pirate reliever Elroy Face put together a remarkable 18–1 record, including 17 straight wins in relief, for the best single-season pitching record in history. A record crowd of 93,103 attended a game at the LA Coliseum for a Yankee-Dodger exhibition to celebrate Roy Campanella Night.

Stan Musial, who had never hit less than .310 since coming up with the Cardinals in 1941, dipped to .255 in 1959. And a milestone was achieved when Pumpsie Green became the first black player to wear the uniform of the Boston Red Sox. The Red Sox were the last major league team to break the color line. What Jackie had started in 1947 had gone full circle.

To raise extra money for the players' fund and other causes, a second All-Star Game was scheduled for the first time in 1959. The first game was played at Forbes Field in Pittsburgh. The National League won 5–4, with Willie Mays's triple to center field as the game-winning hit. The second All-Star Game took place in Memorial Coliseum in Los Angeles. The American League evened the score by beating the National League 5–3.

I started in both All-Star Games in 1959. As a youngster you can only dream about playing alongside baseball's very best. But there I was on the same field, sharing the same locker room with the likes of Hank Aaron, Ernie Banks, Eddie Mathews, Stan Musial, Ken Boyer, and Warren Spahn. It was a thrill beyond compare.

The 1959 National League All-Star team also included starters Johnny Temple of the Cincinnati Reds (Redlegs), Wally Moon of the Dodgers, and the Braves' Del Crandall. In addition to Willie Mays and I, who were All-Star starters, manager Fred

Haney named Giants left-hander Johnny Antonelli to his All-Star squad. Bill White, whom we had traded to the Cardinals, was also named to the squad.

The Milwaukee Braves were favorites to take their third straight National League flag. They were a complete team with no real weakness. Hitting, defense, pitching, a starting rotation of Warren Spahn, Lew Burdette, and Bob Buhl—the Braves had it all.

But they were hampered by the absence of Red Schoendienst, out for the season due to tuberculosis, and by the vast improvement of both the Giants and the Dodgers. What followed was one of the most dramatic pennant races in a long time—a race that ended in a dead-heat tie between the Braves and Dodgers, forcing a playoff. We were in the race all the way, and what a time we had. With a week left to play, we seemed to have the National League flag locked up. We had a two-game lead over the Dodgers and Braves.

But the Dodgers came into town and swept us three straight. We never recovered. We dropped four of our last five games to the Cubs and the Cardinals to finish the year in third place with a record of 83–71, two games behind the Braves and Dodgers.

The surprising Dodgers swept the Braves two straight in the playoffs, then went on to defeat the Chicago White Sox 4 games to 2 in the World Series to bring a World Championship to Los Angeles in just their second year there.

Willie and I both had fine years in 1959. I led the club in hitting at .317 and in RBIs with 105. Willie finished at .313 with 34 home runs and 104 runs batted in. With Willie Kirkland chipping in 22 home runs, and Willie McCovey's tremendous season after being called up from Phoenix, our offense took a backseat to no one.

Our pitching made the big difference. We had four excellent starting pitchers in 1959: Sam Jones (21–15), Johnny Antonelli (19–10), Jack Sanford (15–12), and Mike McCormick (12–16). Stu Miller (8–7) was a spot starter and relief pitcher. Our 3.47 ERA was the best in the National League.

There was no sophomore jinx. I opened the season with a nine-game hitting streak. I had 15 hits in my first 39 times at bats, eleven for extra bases. On April 15 I hit consecutive home runs against the Chicago Cubs' Moe Drabowsky at Seals Stadium. The next day I cracked a solo shot off Don Elston. One day later I hit my fourth homer of the young season off Cardinal left-hander Vinegar Bend Mizell.

My average dipped to .274 in mid-May, but I found my stroke again soon. On June 4 in County Stadium I hit a powerful home run off the Braves' Lew Burdette, a 500-foot-plus shot that cleared the last row of the thirty-five-foot high bleachers.

It was homer number 12 for me, and never before had a baseball been hit beyond the left-field bleachers. I hit four more home runs in June, five in July. In August I belted 4 homers, including a pair again off Lew Burdette. In September I added two more for a total of 27 on the year.

I really came into my own in 1959. The big difference between 1959 and my rookie year was that I made fewer mistakes. I avoided the mental lapses of the year before, those base-running blunders that drove Bill Rigney crazy.

My .317 batting average was third best in the National League, behind Hank Aaron (.355) and Joe Cunningham (.345). Only Hank Aaron (223) and Vada Pinson (207) had more hits. My 192 base hits included 35 doubles, 4 triples, and 27 home runs. I had a career-high 23 stolen bases, which tied Tony Taylor and Junior Gilliam for second in the National League behind Willie's league-leading total of 27.

But no story of the 1959 season is complete without highlighting the appearance of Willie McCovey on the major league scene. Willie Mac, whose 521 home runs are the most by a left-hander in National League history, was hitting .372 with 92 RBIs for Phoenix when the Giants called him up on July 30.

He was a human dynamo from the start. In his first major league game he went 4 for 4—2 triples and 2 singles—against Philadelphia Phillies Hall of Famer Robin Roberts. Willie went on to hit .354 with 13 homers and 38 RBIs in just 52 games. He was named National League Rookie of the Year by a unanimous vote.

Willie Mac and I went back a long way to when we were raw, nonrostered players in 1955 seeking a tryout. Much was made later on over who should handle first base. I didn't want to vacate first. It was my position, and I felt that I had earned it. But with McCovey and I on the same squad, it was a tough choice for any manager.

To make room for Willie in 1959, I moved to third base for four games. It was a disaster for all: Bill Rigney, the team, me, and the fans. In one game I threw the ball so far over McCovey's head that it sailed into the stands where it hit a lady in the face and emptied the seats. A noble experiment that clearly didn't work. So I went to left field and played 44 games in the outfield that year.

Willie and I alternated between first and the outfield in 1960 and 1961. From 1962 through 1964 I was used almost exclusively at first base. In 1965, when I was sidelined almost the entire year, Willie Mac had a great season at first base. When I was traded to the Cardinals in 1966, Willie became a deserving fixture at the Giants' first base.

Although we were competitors, we were always in each other's corners. It never affected our friendship. Willie Mac felt the same way, and he said it in a recent issue of *Giants* magazine. "I really hated to see Orlando go," Willie told writer Richard Keller. "If anything I felt more pressure with him gone. Other people created so-called controversy [over who should start at first]—not us."

This is important because the press sure had a field day. Sure there were hard feelings, lots of them. But these feelings were directed at two people in particular, Alvin Dark and Herman Franks, the two managers who succeed Bill Rigney.

The 1959 pennant race was an exciting one. But finishing third may well have sealed the fate of Bill Rigney. The Giants brass wanted and expected a pennant, and nothing short of a Russian invasion would have saved him.

In 1960 we looked to be strong contenders once again. We took advantage of interleague trading to tighten our pitching staff further. We sent outfielder Jackie Brandt and two others to the Baltimore Orioles for pitchers Billy Loes and Billy O'Dell.

Jackie had been our regular left fielder in 1959, winning a Gold Glove and batting .270. Billy Loes immediately joined the bullpen, while Billy O'Dell, an American League All-Star in 1958 and 1959, joined the starting rotation. He would win 19 games for us in our pennant-winning year of 1962.

We got off to a good start in 1960. We were in second place on June 18 when Rigney was suddenly fired.

Losing Bill was disappointing. I have indicated repeatedly how he built our club from the ground up. He was not afraid to go big time with his younger players, hardly the rule back then. He gave San Francisco a baseball team the city could be proud of. He took a sixth-place club and almost overnight made us a force to be contended with.

Bill was (and still is) a skilled baseball man, and a fair human being. He gave me my chance and always supported me. He knew I had talent and did his best to develop it. I had the natural tools from the start, but I was raw. Bill taught me how to play the game, to avoid mental lapses, to run the bases better, and to play with more finesse.

Bill was replaced by Tom Sheehan who guided us through the final 96 games of the season. I loved Tom Sheehan. Tom had been in my corner from day one. No one in the organization had more faith in me or cared about me more. He saw me change from an awkward youngster who could hit into a well-rounded, seasoned professional baseball player.

But Tom's business was scouting, not managing. It was clear that he was interim until the Giants found the man they wanted to lead the club on the field in 1961.

The 1960 season was a disappointment. We moved to Candlestick Park in April. The cold and wind was unbearable at times. That was before they enclosed the stadium with the bleachers. One evening during a night game in July the wind chill factor dipped to 29 degrees. There's a picture of four of us in the dugout wrapped in blankets and freezing our butts off. And that was July!

Under Tom Sheehan we went 46–50 and finished in fifth place with a 79–75 record on the year. We were 16 games behind the Pittsburgh Pirates, who won their first National League flag since 1927, and 9 games behind the second-place Braves. The Cardinals, anchored by the pitching of Ernie Broglio, Larry Jackson, and Lindy McDaniel, finished third at

86–68, as Bill White hit .283 and won the first of seven consecutive Gold Gloves at first base.

The surprising Pittsburgh Pirates were led by National
League MVP and batting champion Dick Groat (.325) and
Roberto Clemente, now a budding superstar (.314, 16 HR, 94
RBIs). Cy Young winner Vern Law (20–9) and Bob Friend (18–12)
headed up the pitching staff. Badly outhit and outscored in the
World Series, they beat the Yankees to become the World
Champs on Bill Mazeroski's heroic 9th-inning home run off
Ralph Terry.

Willie Mays hit .319 for us with 29 homers and 103 RBIs.
Willie Kirkland hit 22 home runs and drove in 63 runs, but
he failed to live up to the great expectations three years earlier when he was the most highly touted rookie in the
Giant organization.

Willie McCovey hit only .238 and was shipped back to the
minors. I was glad to nail down first base yet saddened to see
Willie Mac sent down. But we all knew it wouldn't be long
before he would be back in top form again.

At age twenty-one, Mike McCormick surfaced as the ace of
the staff with a 15–12 record and a league-leading 2.70 ERA.
Sam Jones was 18–14 and struck out 190 batters. Jack Sanford's
record was 12–14, though his six shutouts were tops in the
National League.

However, Johnny Antonelli suddenly lost his stuff. A two-
time 20-game winner with the Giants, Johnny had slipped badly
to 6–7 in 1960 and lost his place in the starting rotation.
After playing with the Cleveland Indians and Milwaukee Braves
and winning only one more game, he retired from baseball the
next year.

I had a good year but not vintage. I hit .297 with 24 homers
and 96 runs batted in. It was the only time in my first seven
major league seasons I failed to hit better than .300.

In 1959 I moved from Daly City to the Sunset District of San
Francisco to be more a part of the city, and the atmosphere
there was perfect for me. After a season ended, I'd stay an extra
two or three weeks before returning to Puerto Rico. With no day
games to worry about the next day, I could really do the town.
I'd go out with Felipe occasionally, and I hung out a lot with

Willie Mac. In 1960 I moved to 19ᵗʰ and Pacheco. The next year Willie found a place he wanted to buy at 48ᵗʰ and Pacheco, just a stone's throw from the ocean. He called me in Puerto Rico during the winter and I flew out before spring training to take a look. We bought the building in 1961. I lived there until I bought a house in Diamond Heights shortly before I was traded.

The Copacabana, the Blackhawk, the Jazz Workshop—they were my second homes. And what music! There was great jazz by Cal Tjader, Mongo Santamaria, Willie Bobo, and Wes Montgomery. One Sunday night there was a jazz session at the Blackhawk, and all the greats were there: Miles Davis, Cannonball Adderley, John Coltrane. I walked in and suddenly they began playing a new song that went, "Cepeda, Cepeda, Viva Cepeda!" They were making it up as they went along. Cal Tjader recorded the song, and it became a big hit in Latin jazz. I'll never forget that night.

At the end of 1960 Johnny Antonelli and Willie Kirkland were traded to the Cleveland Indians for former American League batting champion Harvey Kuenn. Horace Stoneham also found his new manager, the skipper whom he felt could take us to the top.

Alvin Dark was an astute baseball man whose Giants' credentials were excellent. The Major League Rookie of the Year with the Boston Braves in 1948 and a fine shortstop, he'd been a member of both the 1951 National League Champion and the 1954 World Champion New York Giants.

I gave the matter little thought at the time. Like Bill Rigney before him, Alvin's baseball credentials were solid. But Alvin was no Bill Rigney. And my four years under his stewardship would become rife with pain, publicity, and controversy.

· 7 ·

A Team Divided

They should have been two of my happiest seasons. Instead, they were years of sheer frustration. By the charts alone 1961 and 1962 were years that every ballplayer dreams of: a home-run and RBI championship in one year, and a World Series the next.

Between 1961 and 1965 the San Francisco Giants had the best talent in the National League. We were the most balanced club by far. Our hitting was second to none; our defense was sound; and our pitching, although not up to the Dodgers, was certainly good enough with the likes of Juan Marichal, Jack Sanford, Gaylord Perry, Mike McCormick, Billy O'Dell, Billy Pierce, and Stu Miller.

The fact that we didn't win more pennants falls squarely on the shoulders of Alvin Dark. He was the wrong man to manage a team like the Giants. My difficulties with Alvin Dark have been well chronicled. Time and time again I am asked to talk on the issue. It was one of the most frequent questions asked me on national shows prior to the Hall of Fame voting in 1993. But my Buddhist faith does not allow bitterness or hate. It's self-defeating and only manifests the poison inside a person.

Alvin, to his credit, offered me an apology of sorts at an old-timers game a few years ago. But if my story is to have any validity, I have to tell the truth—the way things really were and not how Alvin and some members of the press corps made them out to be. To be blunt, on many occasions Alvin made my life a living hell. Things got so bad at times that there were days I didn't want to go to the ballpark.

What's ironic is that during those times of stress, my numbers were steadily improving. By age twenty-four, I was already 17 home runs ahead of Hank Aaron's pace at a similar age. During my first six years (1958–1963), I hit 191 home runs, drove in 650 runs, and hit at a .310 clip.

I believe that Alvin's racial attitudes were harmful to the best interests of the ballclub in general, and to the Latin players in particular.

Bill Rigney knew how to bridge the ethnic and cultural diversity on the team. Many were the times he chewed me out for making dumb mistakes, especially on the basepaths. But that was to help me become a better ballplayer and enable me to reach my full potential. Alvin, on the other hand, managed with a vendetta and a meanness that was detrimental to all of us.

We were never a unified team, in spite of our incredible numbers. That cost us pennants. We were a club made up of three distinct groups: whites, blacks, and Latins. And even among the black players, there was animosity between American blacks and Latin blacks. When I was traded to the Cardinals in 1966, I realized for the first time how well a team could work together both on and off the field.

By 1960 Matty Alou, Felipe's younger brother, had joined the club. Six years later he became batting champion with the Pittsburgh Pirates. In 1965 Jesus Alou joined the club. Jose Pagan came up to the club in 1959 and became the Giants' starting shortstop in 1961. Juan Marichal, the best right-handed pitcher I ever saw, first came to spring training in 1960. One day he was hit in the testicles while pitching batting practice. Since I arrived to camp late that year, I met Juan when he was in bed, still in dire pain. A couple of days later he was sent down to the minors for more seasoning.

The Giants called him up in July and he went 6–2 with a 2.66 ERA for the rest of the year. In his major league debut against the Philadelphia Phillies on July 19, 1960, Juan threw a one-hitter and struck out twelve. During his Hall of Fame career he would win 243 games and lose only 142. Without taking a thing away from the likes of Greg Maddux, Steve Carlton, or Tom

Seaver—all superb Cy Young pitchers—Juan Marichal had six 20-game seasons, winning 25 or more three times but never winning the Cy Young Award.

Alvin Dark was a sound baseball man. No one should take that away from him. I had every reason at first to feel that he would be a worthy successor to Bill Rigney. But we got off to a bad start early on.

One of the first things Alvin did in spring training was to try to stop the Latin ballplayers from speaking Spanish in the clubhouse. I'll never forget that day. He called us behind second base and said we had to stop speaking Spanish in the clubhouse because other players were complaining that they didn't know what we were talking about. I said, "Alvin, I won't do that. I'm Puerto Rican, others are Dominican, and I am proud of what I am. This is a disgrace to my race." I went on to tell him that I didn't know who it was that was doing the complaining, but if some players really had complaints, they should have the guts to tell us directly and not be sneaky about it. Whether or not there were really complaints, let's remember that no other team had as many Latin players. For many of us, our native tongue was the only way we could converse coherently.

Alvin had little respect for Latin players. I don't think he liked black players in general. He brought the attitudes of the Old South to the ballpark with him. Others who might have thought the same usually left these thoughts at home. Whenever there was a meeting in the clubhouse he'd avoid the Latin ballplayers—that is unless he had a reason to yell at us. I love music, as everyone knows. It's been a big part of my life from the beginning. I was "Cha Cha, the Dancing Master." Everyone knew that.

Alvin decided I shouldn't play Latin music in the clubhouse. He wouldn't even let me carry my record player with me. One day I was about to leave for the airport when our clubhouse man, Eddie Logan, told me point blank that I couldn't take my record player along. I made it clear that if I couldn't, I would just stay home. I took that record player with me.

On the road the blacks, whites, and Latins each dressed in a separate corner of the clubhouse. When Alvin made his rounds, he'd growl out a thing or two. Once when we were in St. Louis for a series, Harvey Kuenn and Don Larsen got drunk and made some noise. Somehow Alvin managed to blamed the noise on the Latin players instead. More than once he said that blacks and Latins were dumb. If he'd chew out the team, he'd make sure the black and Latin players got more than their proper share of the blame.

One afternoon in Chicago Willie was playing a shallow center field. That's because the wind was blowing in. As so often happens in Wrigley Field, the wind suddenly shifted. Billy Williams knocked a ball out to center field that went over Willie's head. We lost the game 9–8.

Now the only possible way Willie Mays was going to misjudge a fly ball was a shift in the velocity or direction of the wind. When we got to the clubhouse, Alvin called Mays a clown. Then he said something unpleasant to McCovey. I had done my part that day and hadn't messed up anything. I figured I was okay. As I was washing my face Alvin yelled, "And Orlando, get your fingers out of your ass!"

Mays never said anything. If I was Willie, I would have spoken out more. Willie had the stature, the leverage. He was an icon, and he carried a lot of weight with the management. I was very disappointed because I looked at him—we all looked at him—as a leader. When Dark gave the Latin players a hard time, I hoped that Willie might say something on our behalf, but he never did. When I was out almost the entire 1965 season, writers generally asked Willie how my absence would hurt the club. Most of the time he would just change the subject. I'm not sure I've ever figured out why.

Things are much different for today's Latin players. Managers like Tony LaRussa and Dusty Baker either know enough Spanish or have people who can readily communicate with the Latin players. But back then Latin ballplayers who came to the United States were susceptible to anything.

I was still just a kid myself. I probably was a little too hotheaded and sensitive for my own good. I had to grow up. Instead of just going out and playing my game, I let Alvin's remarks throw me too often. But again, ours was a different culture. Alvin never took the time to try and understand these problems and work them out for the betterment of the entire team.

Latins generally have a need to be loved. We want to like people and want people to like us. Our culture is clear on this. We are warm people, but we can't be demeaned as men. The big rap on us was that we were lazy and sulked a lot. Maybe we did sulk. But what I told one writer shortly after my trade to the St. Louis Cardinals sums up how I felt back then as well as anything. "If you do something to hurt me, I'll stay away from you, I won't talk to you," I told Bill Conlin. "But I won't smile in your face and twist a knife when your back is turned. You will know where you stand with me."

Lots of times it wasn't easy. In cities like St. Louis, Cincinnati, Chicago, and Pittsburgh, we stayed in the nice hotels but couldn't eat in the nice restaurants. We either had to eat in our rooms or in the black section of town. Felipe and I might have been authentic big league stars, but that didn't stop people from calling the police on us in Chicago.

The team stayed at the Edgewater Beach Hotel on Chicago's Lake Shore. Back then the north side of Chicago was almost totally white. So there were Felipe and I, walking down Sheridan Road. We were dressed in jackets and ties. Ballplayers were expected to dress that way then. Someone happened to see two black guys speaking Spanish and came to the conclusion that we must be up to no good. We went to a restaurant and waited nearly two hours without being served. We finally got up and left far more hungry than when we arrived.

Sometimes you had to have a sense of humor to survive. During a road trip in Pittsburgh, Felipe and I had finished working out. We were dressed well and decided to stop in a restaurant for lunch. We walked in and waited to be seated. Somebody came by and apologized warmly. We were told there were no more kitchen jobs available. If we were looking to wash dishes, we might try the place down the street. We had to laugh about that or we would have cried.

On numbers alone, 1961 was my best major league season, arguably an MVP year. I led the league in home runs (46), runs batted in (142), and home run percentage (7.9). My RBI total tied Roger Maris for the major league lead in the year Roger hit his record-breaking 61 home runs. I batted .311, was second to Frank Robinson in slugging average (609), second to Hank Aaron in total bases (356), and scored 105 runs.

Together Willie Mays and I hit 86 home runs and drove in 265 runs that year. Felipe Alou and Willie McCovey each hit 18 home runs. Stu Miller was 14–5 and led the league in saves, and Mike McCormick, Juan Marichal, and Jack Sanford each won 13 games.

We scored more runs than any team in the National League (773), led the National League in slugging average (.423), and hit 183 homers. Our staff ERA of 3.77 was the second best in the National League. We still finished the year in third place with a record of 85–69, 8 games behind the Cincinnati Reds, who won their first National League flag since 1940.

On September 18 I hit a two-run, 9th-inning home run off the Braves' Bob Hendley to give us a 3–2 win. Otherwise we might have finished fifth. The Braves ended the year 2 games behind us in fourth place, and the fifth-place Cardinals were just 2 games behind the Braves.

But at no time did Alvin Dark come up with a favorable word on my behalf. To the contrary, he said for the record that I didn't deserve to be the MVP. I finished second to Frank Robinson in 1961. As a ballplayer, Frank was right up there with everybody. Frank had a hell of a year in 1961 but not like mine. Frank Robinson could do it all, but I should have been National League MVP in 1961. I thought so then, and I think so today.

In 1961 I made $30,000. I asked for a $20,000 increase, which I did not think was unreasonable. *Baseball Digest* had named me as the major league ballplayer most likely to break Roger Maris's home-run record. *Look* magazine was set to do an article calling me one of the best right-handed hitters ever, based on my record over the first four years of my career.

The Giants would not hear of it. A $50,000 contract was too much for a fifth-year player. MVP caliber season or not, I would be making too much money too fast, they insisted. I had to really fight and hold out before finally settling for a $16,000 raise to $46,000 in 1962.

What a club we had that year. On sheer talent few if any clubs could match us. Take a look. We led the National League in runs scored (878, more than any other major league team between 1954 and 1981), home runs (204), batting average (.278), and slugging average (.441).

Willie Mays had another superb year, hitting .304 with 49 home runs to lead the league and 141 runs batted in. I hit .306 with 35 home runs and 114 runs batted in. Felipe finally came into his own, leading the team with a .316 average and a then career high 25 homers and 98 RBIs.

Our outfield of Mays, Felipe, and Harvey Kuenn was as good as any. Harvey, a former shortstop and eight-time American League All-Star, hit .304 for us in 1962 and helped us in many ways. Jim Davenport had a career year at third base, hitting .297 and winning a Gold Glove. Willie McCovey had 20 runs and 54 RBIs in just 229 at-bats. Former University of Illinois quarterback Tom Haller and veteran Ed Bailey combined for 35 home runs and 100 RBIs behind the plate.

We had our best pitching in years: Jack Sanford (24–7), with 16 straight wins; Billy O'Dell (19–14); Juan Marichal (18–11); and Billy Pierce (16–6). Pierce was the one who really put us over the top that year. The fine left-hander, one of baseball's very best in the 1950s, still holds the all-time Chicago White Sox record for career strikeouts and wins by a southpaw pitcher.

The White Sox, thinking Billy Pierce was over the hill, traded Pierce to us for pitchers Eddie Fisher and Dom Zanni. In spring training it sure looked like he was. Billy couldn't get anyone out. They just killed him. I felt sorry for Billy because he was once of the nicest guys and one of the best teammates I ever had. But once the season opened, BOOM, BOOM, BOOM, he started winning. He won all 12 starts at Candlestick Park, the most home wins without a loss in baseball history. Billy's accomplishments in 1962 included a playoff win and a World Series victory over Whitey Ford.

We were well-represented at All-Star time, too, with Felipe, Juan, Willie Mays, Jim Davenport, and myself representing the National League in the midsummer classics, which the National League and American League split.

Our main competition was going to be the Dodgers. This was the year the Dodgers moved from the Coliseum to the new Chavez Ravine Stadium. They had an excellent team and were genuine contenders.

Maury Wills broke Ty Cobb's record of 96 stolen bases in 1915, stealing 104 and being named National League MVP. Tommy Davis hit a league-leading .346, with 230 base hits and 153 runs batted in, the most in baseball since Ted Williams and Vern Stevens each drove home 159 runs for the Boston Red Sox in 1959. Big Frank Howard hit 31 home runs.

And the Dodgers had plenty of pitching. Drysdale was 25–9 and was named National League Cy Young winner by a comfortable margin over Jack Sanford. Sandy Koufax was 14–7 with 216 strikeouts and a league-leading 2.54 ERA, the first of five successive earned run titles for Sandy.

On September 1, the Dodgers held a two-and-a-half-game lead over us, with a four-game series coming up on the 3rd. We split the first two games and won the last two to pull within a game and a half of Los Angeles. After the Pirates beat the Dodgers 10–1 and we beat the Cubs 6–5, their lead was half a game.

Then the Dodgers pulled away and opened up a four-game lead on September 16. Most of us had resigned ourselves to a long winter. Bolstered by a pitching staff of Drysdale, Koufax, Johnny Podres, and Stan Williams, and with Ron Perranoski in the bullpen, it seemed unlikely that the Dodgers could fade. But Sandy Koufax was sidelined by an injury most of the second half, and we managed to work our way back to striking distance. On September 30, one game was all that separated the two teams.

Alvin Dark benched Felipe and me the final day against Houston. It made no sense. I had topped the .300/30/100 mark again. Felipe had 98 RBIs and a chance to drive in 100 runs for the first time. The pennant was on the line, and he benched us!

The drama was intense. Billy O'Dell and Houston's Dick Farrell were locked in a pitching duel when Mays tagged Farrell for an 8th-inning home run. Stu Miller pitched two innings of perfect relief for a 2–1 Giants win.

All we could do was return to the clubhouse and wait for the results of the Dodgers-Cardinals game. A Dodger win would send us packing for home. A Cardinal win meant we would tie the Dodgers with a record of 101–61 to force a three-game postseason playoff. The tension could not have been thicker. The Cardinals' Curt Simmons and the Dodgers' Johnny Podres were pitching it out. When Simmons finally beat Podres and the Dodgers 1–0, the roar from the clubhouse was deafening. There would be a playoff for the National League title.

Eleven years earlier, in 1951, the Giants and Dodgers had locked up for another National League playoff. Now their West Coast heirs were doing battle once again. Back then young Billy Pierce had won 15 games for the fourth-place Chicago White Sox.

Now Billy was on the mound for Game One of the 1962 playoff series. His opponent was Sandy Koufax. Billy pitched masterfully, allowing 3 hits and striking out six in shutting out the Dodgers and Koufax by an 8–0 margin.

Willie Mays paced our attack, going 3 for 3 including a home run. Jimmy Davenport and I each chipped in with solo homers, mine a 6th-inning shot off Larry Sherry.

The Series moved to Los Angeles for Game Two. The starting pitchers were the National League's two biggest winners: Don Drysdale (25–9) and Jack Sanford (24–7). It was hardly a pitchers' duel. We pounded out 13 hits, including three by Jose Pagan and two apiece by Davenport and Felipe. But the Dodgers scored a run with two outs in the bottom of the 9th to beat us 8–7 in a game that saw thirteen pitchers take the mound.

Game Three featured Marichal against Podres. It was the top of the 9th, and we had closed the gap to 4–3. There was 1 out, and the bases were loaded when I came to the plate. It was one of the most important at-bats in my life. A pennant was on the line.

I was facing Stan Williams, the Dodgers' hard-throwing, 6'5" right-hander. His first pitch was high. I swung. Strike one. I called time out. It's now or never, I told myself. At the least I had to get that runner in from third. I swung at the next pitch, got good wood on the ball, and hit a line drive to right field. I thought I might clear the bases, but Frank Howard made a great play. He was so tall that he reached up and caught it. But the tying run crossed the plate. We scored two more times to take a 6–4 led into the bottom of the 9th. Pierce held the Dodgers hitless, and it was on to the World Series.

The city of San Francisco had its first National League flag. With our backs up against the wall, we had brought home a pennant and a shot at the New York Yankees in the World Series. With the playoffs taking up so much time, we had to get ready for the World Series immediately. So we didn't have much time to celebrate.

In fact, when we arrived at the airport, we were so overwhelmed by throngs of excited fans that many of us bucked the crowd all together and found alternate ways to get home. I walked to the back of the airport, made my way to the freeway, and hitchhiked home.

We were as good a team as the Yankees in 1962, maybe even better. We'd won 101 regular-season games to the Yankees' 96. Make no mistake, they had a great team. They could beat you in so many ways. Bobby Richardson, Mickey Mantle, Roger Maris, Yogi Berra, Bill Skowron, Tony Kubek, and Elston Howard were all members of that squad. Ralph Terry led the American League with 23 wins. Whitey Ford went 17–8, and Bill Stafford was 14–9.

Game One opened in San Francisco. Whitey Ford defeated Billy O'Dell by a score of 6–2. It was Whitey's tenth and last World Series win. We evened the Series in Game Two when Sanford threw a three-hit shutout to beat Ralph Terry 2–0.

It was Bill Stafford over Billy Pierce as the Yankees took Game Three by a score of 3–2. In Game Four Chuck Hiller's grand-slam home run broke a 7th-inning tie as we evened the Series with a 7–3 win. Hiller's blast was just the eighth grand slam in World Series history.

Then the rains came, and it was another five days before play was resumed. When Alvin Dark had benched me the last regular-season game against Houston it hurt. But we'd tied for the pennant that day, and I was happy as anyone with the outcome.

But nothing ever hurt me as much as his benching me for two games in the World Series. My family and friends had come to see me play in New York. Some came from as far as Puerto Rico. Alvin Dark's excuse was that I was struggling at the plate. But so were Mickey Mantle and Roger Maris on the other side. That was the deepest cut of all. I was embarrassed and humiliated. I could hit; my teammates knew I could hit; and the Yankees knew I could hit. In the sixth game I had a chance to prove it.

It was back to San Francisco for Game Six. We were down three games to two. The Series was on the line. Before a hometown crowd of 43,948 at Candlestick Park, I had 3 hits and 2 RBIs as Pierce beat Ford 5–2, limiting the Yankees to just 3 hits. As he had done so many times for us in 1962, Billy Pierce was there for the big one.

Game Seven was among the most dramatic and exciting contests in World Series history. I saw that final dramatic play from the on-deck circle. I can still see it.

Matty Alou was on third and Mays was on second. It was the bottom of the 9th and two were out. The Yankees, who'd scored in the top of the third, were leading 1–0. McCovey came to bat. Ralph Terry delivered. Willie Mac sent a tremendous line shot to right. I could visualize Mays crossing the plate with the winning run from second. Then, in the blink of an eye, it was all over. Second baseman Bobby Richardson caught the ball.

Actually, I was expecting it to all come down to me. Manager Ralph Houk had gone to the mound to talk to Terry. He had some choices. He could pull Terry and bring in a left-hander to face McCovey, or he could walk McCovey, load the bases, and pitch to me from the right side.

He decided on neither. He allowed the right-handed Terry to pitch to Willie Mac. Terry had given up that 9th-inning home run to Mazeroski in the 1960 World Series. Could history repeat itself? It could have, but it didn't. This time it worked for Terry, but just barely.

I had a chance to talk to Ralph Terry and Ralph Houk at a later time. They both said they'd do it the same way again, and with no second thoughts. They'd have pitched to McCovey even with first base open. Terry told me he knew in his gut that I would have gotten him because I had come so close the time before. He took a chance with the left-handed hitting McCovey rather than pitch to me.

So in the end I watched helplessly as Bobby Richardson speared Willie Mac's screaming liner to right field. It's a moment frozen in time.

You want to win. Oh, do you want to win! But to get that far, down to the wire, we had every reason to feel proud. We got as close as you could get. We gave it everything we had. We just came about an inch short. We played the best team in baseball, a club that dominated the game for three decades. And although we didn't win, we outhit, outpitched, and outhomered the world champs through seven games.

Jose Pagan led all hitters with a .368 average; Tom Tresh was the Yankee leader at .321. I did not have a good Series, only 3 hits in 19 at-bats for a .158 average. Interestingly, Roger Maris hit only .174 and Mickey Mantle just .120 for the Yankees. So some of the biggest bats were silenced in the Series.

It was a bittersweet season, a mixed bag of memories. The pennant race was exciting. We brought home a National League flag for the people of San Francisco. We gave an excellent account of ourselves in the World Series against the Yankees, who had won 13 American League pennants and 11 World Series titles since 1947.

I had a good year, hitting .306 with 35 home runs and 114 RBIs. I had 191 base hits, scored 105 runs, and hit for 324 total bases. For the fourth straight year, I was the National League starting first baseman at the All-Star Game. But somehow, through a strange plus-and-minus theory that Alvin Dark concocted, it was determined that my value to the team was negligible.

He used a late-season slump to contend that I was the only team regular who didn't warrant a raise. Rather, he persuaded the Giants to cut my salary by $7,000 for 1963. Usually managers did not become directly involved in salary negotiations. But Alvin made me a pet project.

I have given these matters much thought over the years. Time and distance tend to yield a more balanced perspective. But in my heart of hearts, I believe that Alvin Dark tried to destroy me emotionally. During the next two years he came very close to achieving that end.

·8·

A San Francisco Farewell

My last three years with the San Francisco Giants were clouded by several things. On the surface, though, things could not have looked better.

On December 3, 1960, I was married to my girlfriend, Annie Pino, in San Juan. We had a small church wedding with my mother, my brother, and some close friends and relatives attending. A large reception of more than 200 people at the San Juan Hilton followed.

Annie joined me for spring training, then we moved to the house I had bought at 48th and Pacheco in San Francisco. We socialized with Juan Marichal, Felipe Alou, Jose Pagan, and their wives. Willie Mac lived next door and was still a bachelor so we had him over for dinner from time to time.

Before re-injuring my knee and missing most of 1965, my career was on an upswing. I was Rookie of the Year in 1958, then an All-Star first baseman each year since 1959. Based on statistics some people argue that I might well be the best right-handed hitter ever. Maybe that's true, maybe not. But just the fact that more than a few people said this meant that I was in some select company. My .308 lifetime was third best in the National League. Only Hank Aaron (.320) and Willie Mays (.313) were higher.

But there was a dark underside. My hassles with Alvin Dark became more bitter and disturbing. My salary disputes were headline news. Trade rumors were persistent. Suggestions that the Giants might let me go for a frontline pitcher were rampant. I was a big favorite with the fans, but with the exception of a few writers like Harry Jupitor, Roger Williams, Charlie McCabe, and Jack MacDonald, the press generally was not friendly. They reported the spin Alvin Dark gave them—whether that spin was true or not.

In 1962 the New York Mets and the Houston Colt .45s joined the National League as its first expansion teams. New York hadn't had a National League franchise since the Giants and Dodgers left town in 1958.

Our first game against the Mets was unbelievable. The stands were filled with every devout New York Giant fan imaginable and a number of Brooklyn Dodger faithful as well. The number-one attraction was Willie Mays, as it should have been. We were stunned by the ovation he received. He was the conquering hero returned. Felipe, Juan, and I were quite moved. Willie's reception by the New York fans was touching, and we were all happy for him.

But Alvin Dark put his own spin on the occasion. He told *Look* that I had been jealous of Willie's stature, so uncomfortable in fact that I became a less productive hitter in the second half of 1962. Nothing could have been further from the truth. My second-half slump had everything to do with my playing 152 games in 1961, a full season of winter ball in Puerto Rico, and a full 162 games in 1962. I wasn't disturbed by the well-earned acclaim Willie received in New York. I was very proud to be playing on the same team and in the same San Francisco ballpark as Willie Mays.

To compound matters, Dark revealed his complicated plus-and-minus system, which I never understood for a moment. What he deduced was that I had minus value to the team, that I didn't get the big base hit or hit in the clutch.

That year *Look* magazine published an article about me that had been in the works for a year. Photographers shot me at the beach stripped to the waist. I was told the article would tout me as the best right-handed hitter in baseball. But when the article finally appeared, the tone had changed dramatically.

Alvin Dark's plus-and-minus system was the centerpiece of the article. Willie Mays was a hefty plus, Jim Davenport was a plus, Harvey Kuenn was a plus, and I was a minus. My productive value to the club, according to Alvin, was something like a negligible 37.

I thought it was unfair. You don't have to be a rocket scientist to determine that 553 RBIs over five years is clutch hitting under any stretch. Through my first five seasons (1958–1962) I had more RBIs than Willie Mays (514), Ernie Banks (512), and Hank Aaron (494) during their first five major league seasons.

In 1963 I hit .316 with 34 home runs and 97 RBIs while in constant pain. My average jumped to .321 late in the year. Suddenly I was fighting for a batting title along with Roberto Clemente, Dick Groat, and Tommy Davis. Alvin moved me up to the third slot, making it more difficult for me to gain ground. My usual slot in the order had been fourth or fifth.

I thought it strange that he did this only when I was contending for a batting championship. At .316 I finished the year behind Tommy Davis (.326), Roberto Clemente (.320), and Dick Groat and Hank Aaron (.319 each).

But I had played hurt all season and would do so again in 1964. I damaged my knee badly in Puerto Rico in late 1962. I was working out when a weight fell on my knee. Because I knew that the team would give me flack, I didn't tell a soul other than my wife. I was determined not to let Dark get on my case any more than he already did.

Looking back, I know I should have said something. I was playing hurt and ultimately it cost me greatly. But day in and day out I struggled and played on in great pain. I managed to play 156 games in 1964. I missed the first three weeks in 1964 and still batted .304 with 31 home runs and 97 runs batted in. Yet Dark never really let up on me.

In 1962 we were playing a series in Milwaukee against the Braves. When I was nineteen years old and playing for the Minneapolis Millers, a woman named Juanita had taken care of me and treated me like a son. I was a long way from home and confused like any nineteen-year-old might be. I'd go to her house every day for lunch.

Since Milwaukee was within driving distance, she and her two daughters drove to see me in 1962. It was Sunday at eleven o'clock in the morning and we were on the bus waiting to go to the ballpark. Juanita and her daughters came by the bus to say good-bye to me. I left the bus to kiss and hug them.

When Dark saw this, he got so mad he screamed, "Let's go!" at the bus driver. All three women were light-skinned Puerto Ricans. I don't think he could accept that.

The night before I'd had a hell of a game. I went 3 for 4 with two stolen bases and beat Warren Spahn with a home run. When we got to County Stadium that afternoon, I didn't see my name in the lineup. Dark was mad because he saw me with the three light-skinned women and was taking it out on me. I was angry, really angry. Hank Sauer had to calm me down.

In the 9th inning we were behind 9–1. There were two outs when he decided to use me as a pinch hitter. I didn't want to go to the plate, but Hank reminded me that I had to. I hit a ground ball to second base and was so fed up I just walked halfway to first.

When I got back to the clubhouse, Dark told me I was fined for not running the ball out. I snapped. I was crying because I was so mad. I jumped up and ran after him. I had reached my limit. It had finally gotten so that there were days I didn't even want to go to the ballpark. He was breaking my spirit.

Earlier I mentioned that Dark had become involved in contract negotiations. I made $46,000 in 1962, and at Dark's suggestion the Giants wanted to cut my salary by $7,000. I held out while we negotiated with Chub Feeney. Finally I was able to coax a $1,000 raise for 1963 to $47,000—although according to Dark five players were ahead of me in team productivity.

The *Look* article—"Orlando Cepeda: Can He Slug His Way out of the Doghouse?" suggested that I was expendable for several reasons: (1) I didn't produce the crucial hit often enough; (2) I wasn't a team man; (3) when things went wrong, I blamed everybody but myself; (4) I didn't rebound and take it out on the opposition; (5) and I was a hearty holdout every year.

Public sympathy was in my corner, although most of the writers were not. Dark said my late-season slump did not help the team during the stretch drive when we were making a run for the flag. Everything he said publicly was negative. It was as if I had nothing to do at all with getting into the playoffs or winning the National League pennant.

Horace Stoneham backed me. "You can say no, no, no, all the way," he told writer Roger Williams. "Sure Orlando has been a holdout, but other than that there is no truth to the charges listed."

And one sympathetic writer noted the following:

> [The Giants'] attitude all along was Orlando was a minus player all season and of little help to the club in its stretch for the flag.
>
> Little mention was made of the games he helped win earlier in the race, yet, without them, the Giants would never have qualified for the playoff with the Dodgers. . . .
>
> Granted that Orlando tailed off toward the end. He helped put a lot of hay in the barn before the Giants started asking, "What has he done for us lately?"

In a piece called "How the Giants Can Lose Flag," Charlie McCabe urged Dark to leave me alone in 1963. "Dark talks about hitting. *Cepeda* can hit," he warned.

The Latin players, he went on to say, "are a marvelous lot, alienated from the rest of the club by more than the language barrier. Cepeda is the cement which keeps them functioning as part of the team. . . . And let us not forget for a minute that the fortunes of the Giants rest on the Caribbean fellas more than any other single group."

Early in his career, Matty Alou hurt his leg. He was running a ground ball and his leg completely collapsed on him. The next day Dark sent him down to Tacoma. After the Giants traded Matty to the Pirates, he immediately won a batting championship, hitting .342 in 1966. For the next three years he never hit less than .331. Dark never gave Matty the opportunity to show what he really had. Felipe had already been traded to the Braves, where he became a big-time star.

On September 17, 1964, I turned twenty-seven years old. I had hit .300 or better six of my seven major league seasons. I already had 222 home runs, an average of more than 30 per year. There probably would have been more had it not been for the winds and chill of Candlestick Park. Bob Stevens, who covered the Giants for many years, pointed this fact out during batting practice recently. Mays, McCovey, and I, all of us, could have added about sixty more career home runs playing in another ballpark.

But 1963 and 1964 had taken a huge toll on my injured knee. When I went to Puerto Rico after the 1964 season, the knee got so bad that I had to fly to New York to have it looked at. That's when the doctors decided I had to have surgery. I had the operation in the winter of 1964. In 1965 I was in such bad shape that I missed almost the entire year.

But a lot had happened. Alvin Dark was fired by the Giants after the 1964 season. The big rap against him was that he not only divided the team along racial and ethnic lines but that he had done everything possible to exacerbate the problem.

He had told a *Newsday* columnist earlier that year that he was having trouble with the club because there were too many black and Latin players on the team. He said that the Negro and Latin players did not have the same pride as the white players, that we were not able to perform with the same mental alertness as the whites.

There was also another factor. With all our talent, except for our pennant-winning year in 1962, we'd never finished above third place. On paper we were the best team in the National League.

In 1963 we finished in third with a record of 88–74. We were 11 games behind the Dodgers and just a game in front of the fourth-place Phillies. We were a powerhouse, with five players hitting twenty or more homers. McCovey hit 44 home runs, Mays hit 38, and I hit 34. Ed Bailey hit 21, and Felipe chipped in with 20. As a team, we hit 197 home runs, 58 more than the Milwaukee Braves who were next in line.

Although the Dodgers pitching staff was outstanding, we had good pitching ourselves. Juan Marichal topped the league with a 25–8 record. Jack Sanford was 16–13, Billy O'Dell 14–10, and Bob Bolin 10–6. Mike McCormick and Stu Miller had been traded to the Baltimore Orioles. Stu promptly led the American League's best relief pitchers for a number of years.

Mike, who won 51 games for us before he turned twenty-four, hurt his arm and was shipped off to Baltimore as damaged goods. After four years in the American League, he came back to the Giants in 1967, led the league with 22 wins, and was the National League's Cy Young winner. A great comeback for a great guy.

On July 2, 1963, Juan Marichal and Warren Spahn engaged in one of the greatest games ever pitched. It's certainly a game I'll never forget.

Juan was twenty-five years old. Warren Spahn, at age forty-two, would win 23 games that year. They put nothing but goose eggs on the board for nine innings. Braves manager Bobby Bragan suggested Spahn should come out of the game. Who could ask for more? Spahn refused. Dark asked Juan if he had had enough. Juan replied, "A forty-two-year-old man is still pitching. I can't come out."

And so they kept on pitching scoreless ball, tossing shutout inning after shutout inning until the 16th, when Willie Mays hit a home run to win the game 1–0.

In 1964 we were involved in one of the most exciting pennant races ever. With two weeks to go, the Philadelphia Phillies led by rookie Richie Allen and John Callison and the pitching of Jim Bunning and Chris Short were ahead of the pack by 6 games. But suddenly the Phillies lost ten straight to hand the pennant to the St. Louis Cardinals.

Going into the final weekend we still had a chance. But so did the Cardinals and the Reds. A loss to the Cubs on the last Saturday of the season finished us off. The Reds were eliminated too.

The Cardinals marched into Shea Stadium needing to win only one of three games against the Mets, losers of 109 games that year. The Cardinals lost the first two games and trailed on the final Sunday before rallying to win the ballgame and the National League flag. It was the Cardinals' first National League pennant since 1946, and they went on to beat the New York Yankees in an exciting seven-game World Series.

We made history in 1964 when left-handed pitcher Masanori Murakami became the first Japanese-born player in the major leagues. He did a good job for us too. Over two years he had a 5–1 record with 100 strikeouts in 89 innings. I had played in Japan in 1960 and was very impressed by the quality of their ballplayers. They played hard and took the game seriously. But there would not be another Japanese player in the major leagues until Hideo Nomo was named Rookie of the Year for the Los Angeles Dodgers in 1995.

There were other milestones too. On May 31, 1964, we beat the Mets in a doubleheader that lasted a record ten hours. On the 10th day of July Jesus Alou went 6 for 6 in one game. Jim Ray Hart took over third base from Jim Davenport and set a Giants franchise rookie record in 1964 with 31 home runs. And Duke Snider completed his Hall of Fame career with the Giants in 1964, hitting just .210 in 167 at-bats.

Willie Mays topped the league with 47 home runs and drove in 111 runs. Juan Marichal was 21–8 with a league-leading 22 complete games. Gaylord Perry, in his first productive season, was 12–11 with a 2.75 ERA. I hit .304 to lead the team, with a .539 slugging average. For the third year in a row we led the National League with 165 home runs. My 31 homers (tied with Jim Hart and John Callison) was third-best in the National League behind Willie (47) and Billy Williams (33).

And Herman Franks replaced Alvin Dark as the Giants manager. Herman and I went back a long way. He had managed at Santurce when I was a fifteen-year-old kid working out with the club. He served as a coach for 1949–1955 in New York and came back to coach for Bill Rigney in 1958 when the team moved to San Francisco. Dark brought him back as a coach in 1964. Herman, who spoke Spanish, had a long history with the Giants. He also had a temper.

The day after Alvin Dark was fired, Herman came to my house. He told me that the reason he was taking the job was because Willie, Juan, and I formed the nucleus of a great team that he felt should have won more pennants.

But when I showed up at spring training with my bad knee and in constant pain, Herman picked up where Dark left off. He accused me of faking it. But unlike Dark, Herman had no racial problems. He never showed signs of bigotry. Yet life with Herman was one big nightmare. In baseball lingo, he tried to take bread out of my mouth.

Foolishly, I told Juan Marichal that I would try playing with the bad knee. I would show them. And I tried, believe me. But I was in pain, real pain. Herman kept saying I was faking, that there was nothing wrong with my knee. He said it was all in my mind and that I should get my ass on the field and earn some money.

I was sitting in the clubhouse one day very depressed. I was almost crying. I had taken enough—too many—accusations, first from Alvin and now from Herman. A friend of mine, a Mexican guy, brought me a jar of alcohol with marijuana inside to rub my knee with. It was an old Mexican remedy. The clubhouse kid asked me what it was. I told him it was to rub my knee. The kid said, "Why don't you smoke it? It's better that way." I hadn't smoked marijuana in a long time, not since my boyhood in the slums of San Juan.

So he went out and got me a couple of joints. After the game I smoked a joint and felt great, relaxed. That night I went out for dinner and smoked another one. Right after that I started smoking the weed regularly. How little I knew then that my association with marijuana would one day destroy the life I knew and the very people I loved.

When the 1965 season opened, Herman was still insisting that my problem was not my knee. It was all in my head, he said to everyone within shouting distance. I was moody, I was lazy, I sulked, I was faking. He hit all the bases. His words made me determined to take the field no matter how much pain I was in.

We went to Los Angeles to play a night game. Maury Wills was shocked by what he saw. "Orlando, you look so bad. Why are you playing?" I said, "Maury, I have to play. I have to!"

I was 1 for 2, but after the 5th inning I went in the clubhouse to take a shower. I looked at my knee, and it had swelled so much that I couldn't put my pants on.

The next day I played. The doctor had to drain my knee. The following night in St. Louis I could barely walk. I was sitting in the dugout and Herman chewed my ass. I said "Herman, I just can't do it." He yelled, "Bullshit!" As usual, it was Hank Sauer who calmed me down. Later in the game, Herman put me in to hit for the pitcher. I had to walk up to the batter's box using my bat as a cane because my knee hurt so much.

I'd work out at Marine Memorial every day. Dr. Jefferson, the San Francisco specialist the team sent me to see, urged me to run. I couldn't. It just hurt too much. He, too, suggested that a good part of my problem was mental. That's when I decided to go to the Mayo Clinic. Twelve doctors saw me there. They put me through a series of tests and consultations. Their overall conclusion was that I shouldn't play ball again.

I wouldn't accept that. I couldn't. Baseball was my life. So I approached Horace Stoneham and told him I would find a new doctor, even if I had to pay for him on my own. I went back to Marine Memorial and asked my friend Bob, the trainer, if he knew a good doctor. "Orlando," he said, "I'm glad you asked me. The doctor you're seeing is too old. He doesn't know a lot of the new techniques."

He recommended a Russian doctor by the name of Gene Sollovief. He started me working with weights. The owner of the physical therapy clinic was a weightlifter and a wrestler. He started me on weights, and then he took me to a field in Golden Gate Park to start running slowly. That's just what I did, day after day, day in and day out, a little more each time. The leg was getting stronger. I knew it. I could feel it. Soon when we ran I was leaving everyone behind. It got to the point that I was in the best shape of my career.

The 1965 season was a disaster. I came to bat only 34 times. I had 6 hits for an average of .176, with 3 home runs. Pinch-hitting for Masanori Murakami on September 30, I homered off the Reds' Joe Nuxhall to break a 3–3 tie and nail a 4–3 Giants win.

But the big story of the year was the Juan Marichal/Johnny Roseboro fracas, which stole the thunder from an otherwise exciting pennant race. My good friend Juan is a fine man, a lovely person, a great guy. Juan was a tough kid. Most Latins fight back when abused. Juan and I, and others like us, had to prove ourselves. Once we did we usually had to prove ourselves again. Then, when you raised a little hell, you were considered a troublemaker.

There was bad blood between the Dodgers and us. We hated each other. And the bad blood that overflowed that August day went back a few years—in fact, way back to 1961 when we played the Dodgers in the Coliseum.

Actually, Maury Wills started the whole thing. Maury would

do anything to get on base, which is good heady baseball. Then he'd go crazy making us look bad by stealing base after base.

Juan had a great move to first base, which annoyed Maury to no end. Juan would throw to first five or six times to hold Wills tight. He wouldn't give Maury an inch. John Roseboro couldn't hit Juan with a broomstick. I could hear guys like Roseboro, Gilliam, and Wills from the bench taunting Juan with catcalls.

The feud just got worse over the years. Friday night before the big fight we were playing the Dodgers at home. Wills as usual did everything he could to get on base. One particular turn at the plate he pulled his bat back and got Ed Bailey to get his glove on the ball. The umpire called interference and Maury took first. When Matty came up to the plate in the bottom of the inning, Herman told him to do the exact same thing. Matty did and hit Roseboro in the hand. Roseboro started chewing Matty out, calling him all sorts of names. Now, Matty was a quiet guy, so Juan shouted from the bench, "Matty talk back to him! Don't let him talk to you like that!"

In the Giants' clubhouse the two teams come out the same corridor. After the game I came out as John Roseboro was coming out. He told me to tell Juan that if he didn't want him to kick his ass Juan should shut up. I said, "John, Juan is not a weak guy. Cool it."

On Sunday Juan was on the mound against the Dodgers facing Sandy Koufax. Juan was a real gamer, in the mold and tradition of a Gibson or a Drysdale. It was simply not a good idea to take too many liberties with him. I can attest to that. We may have been the best of friends, but after I was traded to the Cardinals Juan brushed me back and sent me sprawling on more than one occasion.

As we prepared for the game Juan didn't say a word. Maury Wills was the first Dodger hitter. Juan knocked him down of course. Roseboro wanted Sandy Koufax to throw at Juan, in fact to hit him in the head. But Sandy Koufax didn't throw at anybody. So he pitched high and way over Juan's head. When Roseboro threw the ball back to the pitcher he nicked Juan's ear. Juan said, "Why did you try to hit me?" That's when Roseboro hit him with his mask.

Daryl Spencer (who was with the Dodgers then), Ron Fairly,

and Roseboro went after Juan. Juan backed up and went for the bat. The whole incident was ugly.

Sunday afternoon we left right after the game. There was almost a riot. We traveled to Pittsburgh, Philadelphia, New York, and Los Angeles. Wherever we went we'd get threatening phone calls. I got one anonymous call telling me they'd find my body in the river. When we got to the LA Airport there were policemen assigned to take us to the hotel. We had to have bodyguards. I pinch hit in LA and received boos and catcalls from 53,000 people. As I said, there was really bad blood between the two teams. We wouldn't even talk to Maury Wills or Tommy Davis. Fortunately we're all good friends now.

The press didn't treat us well either. I felt sorry for Juan. The only writer who really stood up for him was Dick Young.

In Puerto Rico that winter, I worked my ass off. I would run in the water, work with weights, then run some more. I was like Rocky Balboa training for a shot at the title, working harder than I ever had before. When I arrived in Arizona in the spring, I was in the best shape of my life. Even my knee felt good, and I was running well.

But I saw the negativity in Herman's eyes from the start. He didn't seem to recognize or appreciate the shape I was in. He barely seemed to acknowledge me. Willie Mac was amazed by what he saw. We worked out together in the gym, and he was impressed. "Orlando," he said, "you're looking fit. You look terrific!" He even told Herman, "Orlando's in great shape. He's looking good and ready to play."

But Herman was determined to start Willie Mac at first base. He'd hit 39 homers in 1965 while I was injured. Herman also seemed just as determined to keep me out of the lineup period. I believe it had become personal.

I wasn't in the starting lineup for the season opener, not even in the outfield. Willie Mac was at first, and Len Gabrielson and Don Landrum played alongside Willie Mays in the outfield instead of me.

Herman kept calling me lazy. I was faking, he insisted. McCovey had played his heart out for him in 1965. I had done nothing but go to the doctors. The past winter I'd bought a beautiful house in Diamond Heights. Annie and I were expecting the birth of our first child, Orlando Jr. I certainly would not have invested in a home if I knew I'd be traded the following year.

We were in St. Louis playing the Cardinals on Mother's Day weekend. McCovey got hurt, and I played first base that series. I was lining the ball all over the place. I went something like 11 for 15, including a grand-slam home run off Art Mahaffey. Juan Marichal was all smiles. "They'll never trade you now," he said putting his arm around me. "Not with the series you just had."

In the clubhouse after the final game I was as pleased as I could be. I was in the groove. That's when I saw Herman Franks walking toward me. I thought he was going to congratulate me, tell me what a good series I'd had. Instead, he told me I was traded to the St. Louis Cardinals. Just like that. No explanation. Nothing. Just that I had been traded. It came as a total shock. During the tough times I had occasionally asked to be traded. His answer then was that nobody wanted me.

To this very day, Herman rationalizes the trade by making me the heavy. On one hand he says I was a fearless hitter, one of the best he ever saw, and that it was my refusal to play left field that prompted the trade. On the other hand he did everything he could to humiliate me. My medical problems were there for the record. Harry Jupitor, in his *Sporting Green* columns, kept abreast. "Cepeda Has Date with Doctor Today" headlined his June 7, 1965, column:

> Orlando Cepeda has an appointment with Dr. Herman McLaughlin today in New York. . . .
>
> He can go back on the active roster whenever he's ready to play. Unfortunately it doesn't appear that Cepeda will be ready for a while.
>
> He's been taking batting practice on the Giants' current trip, and his batting eye seems to be getting sharp. But Cepeda still cannot run or slide, or put sudden or severe pressure on his knee.

Charlie Einstein, no media friend, noted in his August 15, 1967, column for the *Chronicle* that Dr. Sollovief told the Giants I was not only as good as new but that I was better. I begged

Herman to give me a chance at first base again. His answer was, "McCovey breaks his back for me, but you don't try to do a damned thing. Why should I do anything for you?"

I told Hank Sauer that if need be I wanted to be the best left-fielder in the league since McCovey had taken over first. I had no chance though. Herman said I couldn't play for the club with my knee. Herman's story is that I made it impossible for him to play me because I wouldn't go to the outfield. The truth is that Herman made it impossible for me to play anywhere.

Herman Franks turned his back on me, humiliated me, and then traded me. I'll leave it at that.

So I was shipped to the St. Louis Cardinals on Mother's Day weekend 1966. Initially I was crushed. So were my wife and my mother. At times I had hoped a trade might happen. But it still hurt. There were wonderful memories of the team, the fans, and the city of San Francisco. The day I was traded I sat by my locker alone and cried. Jim Davenport was the only non-Latin player to bid me good-bye and wish me well.

·9·

"El Birdos"

How often have I heard that a trade to the St. Louis Cardinals was a blessing in disguise? Actually, it was a blessing among blessings, because I received a warm reception from the beginning. That left me little time to dwell on my departure from San Francisco.

It was awkward at first, because I was traded on a Sunday, when we were in St. Louis playing a series against the Cardinals. So I joined the Cardinals right there in St. Louis and flew with the team to Chicago for a Monday afternoon game with the Cubs.

A major leaguer only knows players on other teams from his experiences on the field. So with the exception of Julian Javier, most of my new teammates were strangers of sorts.

The person who surprised me the most was Tim McCarver. Tim is from Tennessee, and my past experience taught me to tread carefully with people from the Deep South. My first encounter in Salem, Virginia, and then my later encounters with Alvin Dark had left me a bit uneasy. Yet Jim Davenport, who was born and raised in Alabama, was as nice a teammate and as good a friend as I had on the Giants.

Tim McCarver was a special guy. He still is. His father was a policeman and instilled in Tim a strong sense of fair play and justice. Years later, during the tough times, Tim never turned his back on me. He showed a strength of character and an unwavering friendship that I have not forgotten.

That first day in Chicago he saw how sad I looked. When we got to the ballpark he broke the ice immediately. He told me, "Orlando, you're here now. Screw the Giants. Screw Herman Franks. We really want you here." That made a big difference. It doesn't matter how big a guy is, he still wants to feel wanted.

Lots of people had been wondering why Herman Franks hadn't played me more. A couple of weeks before I was traded I'd hit a home run in Chicago off Ernie Broglio. The next day I didn't play. Ernie Banks asked me, "Orlando, what's going on here?" I told him I didn't know. Herman had cast a shadow on me.

But with the Cardinals it was different from the beginning. Stan Musial, now in the Cardinals' front office, came down to see me and to tell me how happy he was to have me with the club.

Bob Bauman, the Cardinals trainer, made his position clear as well. "I'll take care of your leg," he said. "You take care of the hits." When people began talking MVP in 1967, I said many times that if I was named Most Valuable Player, Bob should be named Most Valuable Trainer.

The following morning I had breakfast with Red Schoendienst. The Cardinals presented me with a new contract reinstating the $53,000 the Giants had offered me before cutting my salary to $40,000. Red told me I was going to play first base and hit cleanup. My first time at-bat as a St. Louis Cardinal I homered in Wrigley Field off pitcher Bill Faul.

I have already mentioned Tim McCarver. The rest of my Cardinal teammates were an incredible group of guys. Many of us are still friends today, thirty years later. I had never particularly cared for Bob Gibson or Curt Flood when I played against them. How that all changed once I joined the ballclub. Both Bob and Curt became instant friends.

Bob was never too friendly to players on other teams. To Bob, you were the enemy. He was a tough adversary who wouldn't give you an inch. But once we became teammates he was a different guy. I couldn't ask for a better friend.

Bob was tough, no doubt about that. He was a competitor, and he had to be. Bob grew up in a rat-infested Omaha, Nebraska, ghetto. In fact, as a baby his ear was bitten by a rat.

He had asthma as a kid and never knew his father. A superb athlete, Bob was an excellent basketball player at Creighton University and toured with the Harlem Globetrotters before starting his baseball career.

Bob was twenty-three years old when he joined the Cardinals in 1959. At the time he was basically a thrower. I faced him at Omaha in Triple A, and he overpowered me. He could throw 98 to 100 mph. But he was wild. The scoop was that if you stayed close to him you could beat him.

By 1964 he had put everything together. He went 19–12 with two World Series wins against the Yankees, including that all-important seventh game. By 1967 he was easily one of the two or three best pitchers in the National League, if not one of the two or three best in baseball.

There's one Bob Gibson story I have to tell. As teammates with the Cardinals, he was like a brother to me. When I was traded to the Braves in 1969, the Cardinals rolled into Atlanta for a big series. I saw Bob on Friday night and made it a point to invite him to dinner on Saturday. My wife Annie was a great cook, and Bob always loved her cooking.

I didn't know that Bob was scheduled to pitch against us on Saturday. My first time at bat, Bob knocked me down. He wasn't going to let me dig in. Bob was a good hitter, too. He got on base, though I don't recall whether he had a base hit or a walk. But he was perched on first. I reminded him about dinner and said I would meet him in the clubhouse after the game. "Don't talk to me now," he growled. "You're the enemy and you're making me lose my concentration." Bob won that game.

After the game Bob came over for dinner, and it was like old times. I let the issue drop. But three-year-old Orlando Jr. did not. "Hey, Bob," my son asked, "How come you throw at my dad?"

Then there's Lou Brock. When the Cardinals traded Ernie Broglio to the Chicago Cubs for Lou in 1964, a lot of people thought the Cardinals would come out on the short end. Ernie had won 21 games for St. Louis in 1960 and 18 games in 1963. In fact, when Ernie was in the Giants organization in 1958, Bill Rigney called him the best-looking rookie pitcher in spring training.

The general feeling on the club was disbelief. Why would the Cardinals let go a 20-game winner for an unproven ballplayer?

But to those really in the know, Lou had great potential. He had played in St. Cloud in 1961 and had actually lived in the same house where I stayed in 1956. People I knew in St. Cloud spoke highly of Lou back then. Today we laugh a lot because of how much more he had to pay for rent than I did.

Lou, who was hitting in the .250 range for the Chicago Cubs at the time of the trade, hit .348 for the Cardinals the rest of the year and .315 on the season. Not only did Lou help bring a World Championship to St. Louis, but he is also one of the nicest human beings you can meet.

I had a lot of fun with him after I joined the Cardinals. Lou happened to be in a slump and struck out about fifteen times in the first four or five games after my arrival. "Is this the way you hit?" I'd ask him. I'd call him "The Whiff."

Mike Shannon was another super guy. Mike, an outstanding high school quarterback, turned down a football scholarship to the University of Missouri to sign with the Cardinals. We called him "Moon" or "Moon Man" because he was such a character.

Mike really loved Chicago. You could walk down Rush Street at any time, twelve midnight or six in the morning, and Mike would be there. Then he would go to the ballpark and go something like 3 for 4 that same day.

Dal Maxvill, a great guy and a defensive wizard, replaced Groat at shortstop, and Julian Javier was a fixture at second base. They were an excellent double-play combination. I've played with a lot of great ballplayers, but I can tell you that "Hoolie" was the best second baseman of the lot, a very underrated player. It's too bad that players like him don't get the recognition they deserve.

I also helped Hoolie a lot; I was good for him. When I first got to St. Louis he was the only Latin on the club. He had difficulty expressing himself and wasn't particularly happy in St. Louis. Hoolie and his son Stanley, who plays for the Giants today, are both beautiful people. They are real gentlemen.

Because Hoolie wore glasses and was dealing with a language problem, people made it rough on him at times. When I got there Hoolie changed. He just needed someone to talk to and share things with. We went back a ways too. Like Felipe Alou, Julian and I first met as teenagers playing for our Amateur Caribbean All-Star teams years earlier.

The Cardinals' regular second baseman since 1960, Hoolie was always a good clutch hitter despite somewhat low averages. He hit .281 with 14 home runs in 1967, both career highs. He holds the Cardinals' all-time record for career games at second base.

There was a burning intensity in Curt Flood. His mind was always working overtime. I'm reminded of Curt when I look at Michael Jordan or Mark McGwire, that look of intense concentration. You saw it in the clubhouse and you saw it on the ball field. But when you met him personally there was nothing but sincerity and warmth. It made no difference to him if you were famous or not, if he was a major league ballplayer and you were just an ordinary guy.

The unfortunate thing is that, if you did not know Curt, it was possible to misjudge him. Because he was sensitive, he carried a lot of pain with him. It was harder for him to shake off the injustices of the past than it was for some other fellows.

Curt challenged the baseball establishment when he refused to be traded to the Philadelphia Phillies. At first I didn't understand what he was doing. I was confused. But Curt was very upset with Bing Devine for trading him. He had established roots in St. Louis.

It was a mission with him. That's how Curt was. Trading ballplayers is part of the game., How well I understood that. But what the public at large never fully recognized is that being traded, especially midseason or during the spring, changed everything.

Curt couldn't accept the premise that he belonged to one particular owner or one particular club in perpetuity. He challenged this in court and he lost. In 1971 he tried a comeback with the Washington Senators but was unsuccessful. That spring we played an exhibition game in Virginia. He told me, "Charlie" (he always called me Charlie), "if I had to do it, I'd do the same thing all over again. Maybe someday it will help other ballplayers."

We lost a wonderful man and a loving friend when Curt

Flood died in 1997. In addition to being an outstanding baseball
player, Curt was an excellent artist. He painted a beautiful portrait of my son that still hangs proudly in my front hall.

Before he died, Curt wrote a note to his wife in which he told
her to make sure I was one of his pallbearers. I did so with
honor. The funeral was held in Los Angeles. Bill White, Bob
Gibson, Lou Brock, Maury Wills, and Steve Garvey were among
those who attended.

When I joined the Cardinals in May 1966 the team's big concern was scoring runs. That's why Cardinal GM Bob Howsam
wanted me so badly. He was a student and protégé of Branch
Rickey, and his mentor always stressed the necessity of balance
for a winning ballclub.

The Cardinals needed a cleanup hitter to balance the team,
and Bob Howsam felt I was the man for the job. In St. Louis all
they asked of me was to swing the bat. The pitching staff,
anchored by Bob Gibson, Al Jackson, Ray Washburn, and Larry
Jaster, was a good one. In fact, it had the second-lowest ERA in
the National League in 1966.

But the Cardinals gave me more than the opportunity for
base hits and RBIs and a career comeback. They allowed me
the latitude to be myself and to be appreciated for that. That
was very important to me. The last few years in San Francisco,
no one seemed to realize that all I wanted to really do was play
baseball. It got so that I was afraid to make an error at first
base. I never felt up against a wall in St. Louis.

Playing for a club that wants you makes an enormous difference. I became a big favorite with the St. Louis fans. The city
took to me from the beginning. "Cepeda for President" signs
were carried into Busch Stadium and motorists pasted "Cha
Cha" bumper stickers on their cars.

My stereo system, which had been taboo with the Giants,
was a welcome addition to the Cardinal clubhouse. I played it
regularly, and the sweet Latin beat helped loosen up the guys.
If I'd done that with the Giants, they'd have given me a funny
look and decided it was wrong.

We were certainly the most relaxed team I ever played for.
We'd play around in the clubhouse until five minutes before
game time. But make no mistake—once we were on the field it

was all business. We were professional ballplayers to a tee. We thought of ourselves as a team, and we played smart baseball. We rarely if ever made glaring mistakes.

The city of St. Louis had changed quite a bit since the late fifties. Until expansion broadened the demographic limits of Major League Baseball, St. Louis was its western frontier. The civil rights legislation of the sixties opened the door to many changes. Back then the black ballplayers had to eat in their rooms. I recall once when Tony Bennett was in town. He had a black trumpet player who couldn't stay in the Park Plaza Hotel. He had to stay with blacks on the black side of town.

Annie and Orlando Jr. would join me soon. I didn't want them to live in a hotel suite. Bob Gibson and Julian Javier stayed at the Washington Hotel during the season. Bob would return to Omaha for the winter. I told Bob that living in a hotel on the road was bad enough, but with my wife and son on the way I needed a house. I asked the black players about renting a house in a nice neighborhood. But that was still pretty hard to do in St. Louis.

So I talked with Harry Caray, who was announcing the Cardinals games. Harry agreed to mention on the air that I was looking for a house in a nice neighborhood no matter what I had to pay. Over one hundred people responded and were eager to help. Finally I settled on a house in Olivette, Missouri.

It was a great neighborhood, almost entirely Jewish. My neighbors couldn't have been nicer, and the community as a whole couldn't have been warmer. Whenever I was on the road two motorcycle policeman watched the house for me. Lou Brock bought a house there too a short time later.

I think the best way to understand my two and a half years with the Cardinals would be to look at the period immediately following the championship year of 1964.

When the Cardinals beat the New York Yankees in the 1964 World Series, a strange thing happened. The Yankees fired Yogi Berra after just one year at the helm. They replaced him with Johnny Keane, who had just resigned as the Cardinals' manager a few days earlier.

In a great public relations coup, Mr. Busch signed Red Schoendienst to be the team's manager. Red was one of the most popular players ever during his playing days in St. Louis and had been a coach with the Cardinals since 1961. Red was quiet, but he was a sound baseball man who let you do your job as long as you were doing it right.

But 1965 turned out to be a disaster for the World Champs. The Cards tumbled badly, from 93 wins and a World Championship in 1964 to 80 wins and seventh place in 1965.

The pitching faltered. Bob Gibson was on target with a 20–12 record and another great season. But Ray Sadecki and Curt Simmons—two mainstays from the 1964 staff—slipped badly. Sadecki, a 20-game winner in 1964, fell to 6–15 in 1965, and Simmons, 18–9 in 1964, dropped to 9–15.

Bill White, Curt Flood, Tim McCarver, and Lou Brock had decent years. But Ken Boyer and Dick Groat had disappointing seasons. Boyer, the National League MVP in 1964, fell from .293, 24 home runs, and a league-leading 119 RBIs to .260, 13, and 75 in 1965. Groat, who hit .319 and .292 in 1963 and 1964, hit only .254.

Someone had to pay the price for the big flop. The two fall guys were Kenny Boyer and Bill White, both huge favorites with Cardinal fans. Boyer, who had played eleven years with the team, was traded to the New York Mets for third baseman Charlie Smith and left-handed pitcher Al Jackson.

Barely a week after the Boyer trade, the Cardinals dealt Bill White, Dick Groat, and catcher Bob Uecker to the Philadelphia Phillies for catcher Pat Corrales, pitcher Art Mahaffey, and outfielder Alex Johnson, who had loads of potential. Trading Bill White opened first base for me. There's a touch of irony. Remember, Bill had been the Giants first baseman in 1956 who lost his position to me after spending two years in the service.

I played in just nineteen games and was hitting .286 when the Giants traded me to St. Louis. Even then we had the nucleus of a fine club. The outfield of Lou Brock, Mike Shannon, and Curt Flood was as good as any in the league. Curt hit .310 and drove in 83 runs to lead the club in both departments in 1965.

Lou Brock hit .288 with 63 stolen bases. Tim McCarver joined the Cardinals as a seventeen-year-old rookie in 1959. By 1964 he had gained a lot of strength; he led all hitters with a

.478 average in the World Series. He was recognized as one of baseball's best catchers.

My trade coincided with the opening of the new Busch Stadium on May 16 against the Atlanta Braves. The Braves had moved from Milwaukee to Atlanta, and on April 12 they played the first-ever regular-season game in a southern state.

The old Sportsman's Park in St. Louis—renamed Busch Stadium—had been home to the Cardinals since 1920. The St. Louis Browns had played there too. More major league games were played in that park than any big league ballpark, or so I've been told.

I played in 123 games for the St. Louis Cardinals in 1966, hitting 17 home runs and leading the team with a .303 average. I was very happy when I was named National League Comeback Player of the Year. Whoever said that the best revenge is living well sure knew what he meant.

One of the most emotionally taxing times was when we played the Giants in Candlestick Park. After being a San Francisco Giant for more than seven years, I was returning in a different uniform. What followed was touching. The Giants fans gave me a warm ovation.

Horace Stoneham called me at home to talk to me personally. He told me how sad he felt when I was traded, that he liked me and would miss me. Horace and Tom Sheehan had been in my corner for years.

Tom and I went back a long way. He knew me when I was an awkward, untamed fifteen-year-old who could slug the stuffings out of a baseball. He was a wonderful man, a real gem. But an interesting thing happened when Tom Sheehan paid me a visit in the Cardinals locker room. We talked about old times and many different things. Then he said something that disturbed me. He told me that Herman Franks had been one of the people who wanted me traded.

Before the 1966 season began, Sandy Koufax and Don Drysdale became the first teammates in major league history to stage a dual holdout over their contracts. Then, after leading the league in wins (27), complete games (27), strikeouts (317), and earned run average (1.73), Sandy retired after the season because of an arthritic elbow.

On June 1 the Cardinals' record stood at 20–21. It moved steadily upward to 54–48 on August 1, then dropped a bit to 67–66 on September 1. We finished the year with a sixth-place record of 83–79. We were 12 games behind the pennant-winning Dodgers, but just 4 behind the third-place Pittsburgh Pirates.

We were building, and building well. There was still a hole or two to be filled. We were just a player or two away from becoming true contenders. We were lucky to find just the man we needed to help bring a championship to St. Louis. His name was Roger Maris.

"The Babe Ruth of Puerto Rico"—
My father, Perucho (in the hat),
celebrating with friends in 1946
after Caguas won the Puerto Rican
Championship.

When this photo was taken I was
fifteen years old and had just
graduated from junior high school.

A Baby Bull in the making. Here I am as a sixteen-year-old with my City Taxi team (*back row, second from left*). One scout called me a "young Josh Gibson."

Here I am (*front row, left*), eighteen and hopeful, in 1956. What a year! My second season of professional ball I won the Northern League Triple Crown at St. Cloud in Class C (.393, 26 home runs, 112 RBIs). Despite these lofty numbers, the Giants wanted to move me up just one notch to Class B for the 1957 season.

Hoping for the Big Show. Here I am (*front row, third from left*) at spring training rookie camp with the San Francisco Giants in 1958. What a talented group! In the back row are Alex Pompez (*far left*) and my mentor Pete Zorilla (*third from left*).

As a twenty-year-old rookie with the great Willie Mays during spring training, 1958.

Me and my family, 1958. I am hugging my grandmother upon returning to Puerto Rico as my mother and brother look on.

My mother, Carmen, and me in October 1958. I had just received word that I was unanimously selected National League Rookie of the Year.

Excited friends and relatives greet me after I was named National League Rookie of the Year in 1958.

Those were the days. Felipe Alou (*left*) and I hitting the town. Felipe and I first met as teenage All-Stars in the Caribbean.

A favorite shot—connecting against the Chicago Cubs in 1959. There's nothing like the feel of good wood on the ball. (Lee Balterman Photography)

A trio of hitters: (*from left*) Felipe Alou, Willie Mays, and me in 1959.

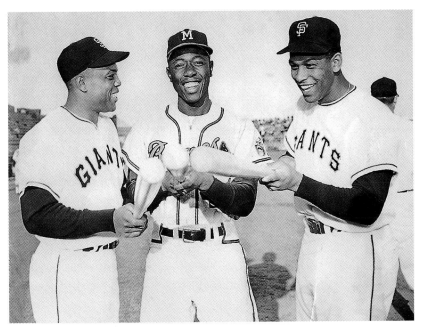

Here I am at age twenty-one in the presence of two of the all-time greats—Willie Mays (*left*) and Hank Aaron (*center*)—in 1959.

Roger Maris and me at the 1961 All-Star Game. Roger broke Babe Ruth's home run record that year by hitting 61 home runs in one season. Roger and I tied for the major league lead for RBIs with 142 apiece. A wonderful guy, Roger and I would be teammates with the 1967 World Champion St. Louis Cardinals and the 1968 National League Champion Cardinals.

Two hometown boys who made good. Here I am with the great Roberto Clemente in a 1961 parade down the streets of San Juan. Together, Roberto and I captured the National League Triple Crown in 1961. Roberto hit .351, and I topped the National League with 46 home runs. My 142 RBIs in one season is still a San Francisco Giants' record.

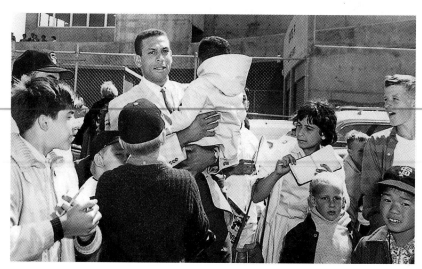

Me holding Felipe Alou's son in 1961. (Eddie Murphy)

Winter ball 1961, Santurce vs. Caguas. Here I am with slugger and future home run king Frank Howard.

Dressed to the hilt. Here I am clowning with the great Juan Marichel (*center*) at the 1963 All-Star Game in Cleveland. Kneeling is my good friend and retired Philadelphia writer Alan Lewis.
(Lee Balterman Photography)

Music has always been a major part of my life. Here I am with Pepo Talavera, my music teacher and former high school PE teacher, in 1967.

Here I am with Orlando Jr. and my first wife, Annie, at a Father and Son Game in 1967. (Alfred Fleishman)

I was drenched in champagne by my teammates after the Cardinals clinched the 1967 National League pennant. Behind me are (*left to right*) Tim McCarver (behind champagne bottle), Ed Spiezio, and Jack Lamabe. I was also named MVP that year.

At bat with the 1967 World Champion St. Louis Cardinals. The 1967 and 1968 St. Louis Cardinals were the most perfect baseball units I ever played for—a great bunch of guys.

What a pitcher! Tim McCarver and I congratulate Bob Gibson (*center*) after Bob's record-setting 17 strike-outs against the Detroit Tigers in Game One of the 1968 World Series. In the Year of the Pitcher, Bob was the National League Pitcher of the Year and captured both the MVP and Cy Young Awards in 1968 (22-10, 268 strike-outs, 13 shutouts, 1.12 ERA).

I helped bring a division title to Atlanta in 1969—but 1969 was to be the year of the Mets. I had my last great National League season with the Atlanta Braves in 1970. (Gary Williams)

With the Boston Red Sox in 1973 I was named the American League's first Designated Hitter of the Year—a very proud moment. Here I am with Hall of Famer Luis Aparicio.

Sad times. This was the last picture taken of me in my home before my prison sentence. A few days later I was off to the minimum security facility at Eglin Air Force Base. (Gary Williams)

Here I am with youngsters Sammy Sosa (*left*) and Candy Maldonado (*right*) in 1993. Who could have guessed that five years later Sammy would shatter Roger Maris' all-time single season home run record?

(*From left*) My pal Juan Marichal, Barry Bonds, and me in the San Francisco Giants dugout in 1993. The Giants finished at 103-59, but the Atlanta Braves were one game better and took the National League West with a record of 104-58. (Martha Jane Stanton)

Two sons: Ali (*left*) and
Orlando Jr. (*right*) at our
home in 1993. There I am
in the background.

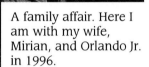

A family affair. Here I
am with my wife,
Mirian, and Orlando Jr.
in 1996.

A night on the town. My
wife, Mirian (*standing,
left*), my idol Tito Puente
(*seated, left*), and actor Al
Pacino (*seated, center*).

Two guys and a gal. Here I am with Mirian
and actor Danny Glover.

• 10 •

A Very Good Year

I was pushing thirty and still going strong. Things were changing very quickly all around the country. There was political and social unrest. Sideburns were longer, miniskirts were shorter, and love was freer. To the flower children flooding the streets of San Francisco, and the counterculture in general, the summer of 1967 was known as the "Summer of Love."

It was a summer of love for me as well. It was the year everything came together. The Cardinals became the baseball champions of the world, and I was chosen unanimously as the National League's Most Valuable Player. I was at the top of my game. And when the fall came a decade later, it sure was a long way down from the top.

But in 1967 the Cardinals had a date with destiny. The odds-makers had pegged us at 12 to 1. Yet one Chicago writer was smart enough to note that we just might be the best 12-to-1 bet in baseball. Tim McCarver was confident from the start. "We're going to win because we have Orlando Cepeda from the beginning," he insisted.

But we had a hell of a team. We were a perfect unit on and off the ballfield. It was a team that rarely made a mental mistake. We were solid offensively and defensively. We had a group of guys who were complete ballplayers, smart, talented, and unselfish. And no two exemplified this more than Roger Maris and Mike Shannon.

Roger Maris was one of the best ballplayers I have ever seen. He had no weakness, and each part of his game was totally developed. He was a real student of the game, as adept as anyone I had seen in fielding, base running, and moving guys from first to third. He could do it all. He may not have been the power hitter he once was, but National League pitchers didn't seem to know this. Many times they walked him to get to me.

It seemed a bit ironic that Roger and I, who in 1961 had led our respective leagues in home runs and tied for the major league lead in RBIs, were now teammates. Roger had long played in the shadow of Mickey Mantle, just as I had played in the shadow of Willie Mays. In 1962 I was generally considered the best prospect among active players to top Roger's record-setting 61 home runs in 1961.

Breaking Babe Ruth's home run record was no picnic for Roger, believe me. Roger talked to me a lot about the ordeal of playing in New York. Members of the press had tried to destroy him because he was doing better than Mickey, who was a Yankee farm product and a New York favorite. It was a double-edged sword for Roger. He'd get hate mail from people who didn't want him to break Babe's record. Then he took shots in New York because, if the record was to be broken, Yankee fans wanted Mickey Mantle to be the one to break it.

Every time Roger said something for public consumption, the press would twist it. Roger Maris was a quiet guy who wouldn't harm anyone. So his only recourse was to retreat and keep the press at a distance. Of course they didn't like that; it led to a media war that, in the end, took a heavy toll on Roger.

When Roger first joined our club for spring training in 1967, he had a reputation for being a loner and being distant. We were National Leaguers, and Roger had played his entire career in the American League. Because we were just beginning spring training, Roger didn't know most of the fellows. But there was a real closeness on our club. We'd barbecue and drive back to the ballpark together. We'd socialize after hours. Black or white, it didn't matter a bit.

One day we were leaving the motel for the ball field when we saw Roger by himself waiting to catch the bus. We stopped the car and invited him to ride to the ballpark with us. This broke the ice. It did not take long to find out what a decent guy Roger was.

After a couple of days everyone was impressed by Roger—especially his work ethic. He had reported to camp overweight, maybe even fat. By the time spring training was over, he'd worked that weight down and was muscular and fit. Roger was a professional, a complete ballplayer who I never saw make a mistake. He won the respect of the entire team and became one of us. He was instrumental in the great success of our 1967 and 1968 championship teams in St. Louis.

When Roger died in 1985 at age fifty-one, I was deeply saddened. I had been going through my own personal hell, and I hadn't stayed in touch. I wish I had. He was not a selfish man. Late in the season I blew a play running the bases. It was a dumb mistake, and I was really down in the dumps. He came over and put his hand on my shoulder and said, "Don't worry about it, man. You got us here. We're here because of you. Because of all the guys." That was Roger.

A few years ago there was an Old-Timers Game in St. Louis. Roger's wife was to throw out the first ball. She asked me if I would take her throw from behind the plate. She told me how highly Roger always spoke of me. She said that I had been a good friend. I was touched. Just recently I was invited by Roger's widow to fly to North Dakota and participate in the Roger Maris Golf Tournament. I was honored to attend.

Bob Howsam had known for a long time that what we needed was a left-handed power hitter. Charlie Smith had not lived up to our expectations at third base. But there weren't any power-hitting third basemen from the left side of the plate except Eddie Mathews, and he wasn't available.

With that option closed, a left-handed hitting outfielder might do. Roger had withered under the pressure of the New York media and really wanted out of New York. He would not play another season there under any circumstances. So Roger was traded to the Cardinals in a deal that sent Charlie Smith to the Yankees.

Roger was a right fielder. So Mike Shannon agreed to make the transition to third base. I've never seen anyone work harder than Shannon that spring. He took ground ball after ground ball, sometimes for more than two hours at a time. Other days Red would bunt more than 200 balls to Mike. Mike had a tough time. He was discouraged. But he wouldn't give up. He stuck with it, fielding thousands and thousands of ground balls all spring. By Opening Day he was ready.

Most of us felt the Giants were the team to beat in 1967. With Koufax gone, the Dodgers didn't seem as ominous. I was at my best against the Giants. In 1966 we eliminated them from the pennant race. They came into town locked in a tight race with the Dodgers and Pirates.

I had been in a big slump. I think I was 0 for 20. But once the Giants arrived I went crazy. I won one ballgame. I tied another. I stole a couple of bases. Herman Franks went bonkers. He was really angry. "Look at that guy," he'd scream. "He wasn't doing anything. We come to town and he starts hitting the ball." The Giants finished the year 1 1/2 games behind the Dodgers.

I picked up where I left off in 1967. I never got so many big hits in my life. I drove in 7 runs in one game against the Cubs. We had a little game among us. Each Cardinal batter who left a runner on third was fined a dollar. The money went into a kitty to pay for a postseason, maybe even a World Series, party. After the first 83 games, I had contributed a grand total of five dollars.

We had a three-game lead, so I asked Red if I could have the night off. Three hours later, in the bottom of the 7th against the Pirates, we were losing by a score of 1–0.

There was one out. The tying run stood on second base, the lead run on first. Eddie Bressoud was scheduled to bat, but Red decided I should pinch hit for him. The clubhouse boy found me in the dressing room talking on the phone to a friend in Chicago. I hung up, ran to the dugout, grabbed a bat, stretched, and stepped to the plate.

Fans were screaming with excitement. There was pandemonium. Pirates pitcher Tommie Sisk had allowed only two hits all night. I leaned into a 3–2 pitch and hit a shot between short and third. It sent Alex Johnson home with the tying run and moved Julian Javier to third. A minute later Hoolie, with some dazzling base running, scored on an error. We hung on to win the game 2–1.

Our main rival over the season's first two months was not the Giants. It was Leo Durocher's Chicago Cubs. After losing 103 games in 1966, Leo put together a surprisingly good team, a club with three future Hall of Famers—Ernie Banks, Bill Williams, and Fergie Jenkins—and potential Hall of Famer Ron Santo.

But timely hitting was the biggest difference between this year's Cardinals team and last year's. On June 18, after a tough ten-game road swing, we found ourselves in first place.

We'd won eight out of ten on the road. We took the Pirates and the Giants two out of three, and both the Astros and Dodgers two of two. By June 23 our spurt reached 13 victories in 15 games. After we shut out the Dodgers and Don Drysdale 2–0, Don proclaimed us the team to beat in the National League.

We were a fun team too. Before we began the streak, Red Schoendienst didn't like the way we were playing. That was especially true after a tough thirteen-inning loss to the Atlanta Braves. The next day our trainer decided to try something that might change our luck. So he made a heaping pot of tomato rice soup. You guessed it. We took a doubleheader from the Braves, and the soup became an everyday lucky charm.

But soon we got tired of eating the same soup over and over. We needed something red and white to replace the soup as our lucky charm. So we took a baseball and painted it half red. That became the only baseball we used in infield practice before each game.

At the end of our infield warm-ups, I'd throw the ball to coach Dick Sisler—only to Dick Sisler. No one else was allowed to catch it. Protocol demanded a new red-and-white ball for each series. Each time we lost a game the ball was discarded and a new one was painted and put into use. I really messed things up once and almost became a big goat. I accidentally threw a winning ball into the stands after one game. Two balls had to be given to the fan who'd caught the elusive red-and-white ball before we got it back.

I was hitting the ball better than I ever had and so was Tim McCarver. During our June surge Tim hit at a .441 clip. Both our averages stayed over the .350 mark.

Line drives were flying off my bat as never before. By June 25 I had 20 doubles, tops in the league, and just six short of my 1966 total. On the 20th of June I clinched a 6–2 victory over the Astros with a three-run homer in the Astrodome, my first ballgame under glass. But I actually hit the ball harder when I doubled to right center that same game.

Defensively, around first base I had never been better. I'd become an expert in scooping up throws in the dirt. Bob Gibson told the press that only Bill White was a better first baseman. Coming from Bill, that meant a lot.

We played the All-Star Game in Anaheim. It was my sixth All-Star Game as a National League starter, and my seventh overall. Bob Gibson, Tim McCarver, and Lou Brock were also on the National League squad. We won the game 2–1 when Tony Perez homered off Catfish Hunter in the top of the 15th. Thirty batters went down on strikes that night, shattering the previous All-Star Game record of twenty set in 1955.

In those days we didn't have a union. Today there's a three- or four-day rest regardless, but we had to immediately go to Pittsburgh to make up an earlier game against the Pirates. Then we flew to St. Louis, and from July 11 through the month of August we played 53 games in 48 days. We also blew things wide open.

We were tied for first place in July when we made a shambles of the pennant race by winning 21 of our next 25 games. We even survived the loss of Bob Gibson, who suffered a broken leg when he was hit by a line drive off the bat of Roberto Clemente.

I'll never forget that night. Clemente rocketed a shot back at the mound and Bob went down in a heap. His face was contorted in pain, but he was able to hobble to the dugout on his own.

What other team could survive losing a pitcher like Gibby? He was our meal ticket. He had averaged more than 20 wins over the past three years—twice with second-division clubs. But like real champions, we took up the slack. Nelson Briles, a relief pitcher the year before, went 14–5. Dick Hughes, a twenty-nine-year-old rookie who spent ten years in the minors, led the staff with a 16–6 record. Steve Carlton, just twenty-three years old, went 14–9 for us.

Bill White said that we were a better club than the 1964 Cardinals, a team for which he hit .303 with 21 homers and 103 runs batted in. Phillies manager Gene Mauch saluted Red Schoendienst and told Bob Broeg, the sports editor of the *St. Louis Post Dispatch*, that the reason for the unexpected Cardinal runaway could be summed up in two words: Orlando Cepeda.

"He has been inspirational," said Mauch. "He never was the big man in San Francisco. At least he was never made to feel he was, but now the man doesn't think anyone can get him out. Brock hit with him early. Then McCarver hit with him. Then Flood, after he came off the disabled list, hit with him, but always there was Orlando. He'll probably be the first unanimous choice as Most Valuable Player in our league."

My teammates were great to me. Roger Maris, who'd played on some very good teams with the Yankees, said, "We have speed and power, and we have guys who know what they are doing. One of the few things that sometimes bothers us is that people are in such a hurry to compare us with the Gashouse Gang. We are *El Birdos* because Cha Cha named us that, and that is what we want to be called and remembered as."

Once when we were going strong, a writer in Chicago asked me the Cardinals' secret. "Here we have no superstars," I said. We were a team, a unit. No superstars. The next day the sports headline read, "Orlando Slapped Willie Mays in the Face." I hadn't meant that at all. Willie never entered my mind when I said that. There are writers and there are writers. Ballplayers have to be careful. I learned that. Roger Maris learned that. We all learned it sooner or later.

A case in point was Charlie Einstein. After my big season in 1961 he came to my house and gave me $500 up front to write a book with me. I signed the contract and never spoke much to him again. I visited some hospitals with him in San Francisco, but he never really talked to me.

I never saw the book either. Six years later when I was with the Cardinals I got a call in Pittsburgh, where we were playing the Pirates. It was the book's publisher telling me the book would come out that year. I reminded them that six years had passed, I was having my best year, and I wanted more money. Of course, the publisher would not hear of such a thing. In 1968 the book came out. It was entitled *My Ups and Downs in Baseball* by Orlando Cepeda with Charlie Einstein.

Charlie never even interviewed me. He spoke to people like Ruben Gomez, who gave him less than reliable information. Ruben and I had long since ended our friendship. To date I haven't read that book.

We were running away with the National League. Writer Bill Conlin called it "the worst runaway since Goldwater vs. Johnson." We were getting pitching, defense, offense, and speed. We could win so many different ways. We could get the other team in the 1st inning or the 9th. We could beat you 16–1 with power, or 2–1 with pitching and defense.

What's more, we were having lots of fun. I was playing for a manager I liked and respected. Herman Franks was 2,140 miles away and Alvin Dark was at the other end of Missouri managing the Kansas City Athletics.

My soapbox routine of "Down with Herman Franks, Down with the Giants" became a favorite clubhouse routine. I had everyone in stitches. And why not? Herman didn't trade me, he kicked me out. We all knew that. I was having a ball and becoming, among other things, the team's favorite funny man and clubhouse jockey.

Before the trade, Ray Sadecki was part of a favorite clubhouse routine with Tim McCarver. Ray played Joe the Bartender and Tim played Crazy Gugenheim, two characters on Jackie Gleason's TV Show. It became part of the daily repartee. But at a certain point it got old, and all too predictable. We needed a new voice.

There was a clubhouse meeting before a game in Philadelphia to discuss Phillies pitcher Chris Short, whom we were facing that night. Chris was a left-hander who threw a screwball that tailed away from a right-handed batter. "You've got to stay with Short all night," Red instructed. From the back of the room I yelled, "You mean I got to go out with Short after the game?" Everyone started laughing. We went out and won the game. I hit a two-run homer off Chris Short.

Then there was the time in Atlanta when we boarded the team bus after the game to return to our hotel. There was one problem. The driver was missing. So a few guys fiddled with the controls until Joe Hoerner got the bus started. We took off with Hoerner at the wheel. While driving the bus through downtown Atlanta, it dawned on him that he was driving a stolen bus in the middle of the night.

The bus passed four police cars, but nobody stopped us. But a squad car pulled over another bus. One of the guys yelled to Hoerner, "Look, Joe, some nut must have stolen a bus." We made it back to the hotel, where Joe managed to smash a street sign parking the bus. The bus company later apologized to the Cardinals for the missing driver. Pranks like that kept us loose and close, and in the right frame of mind for winning baseball. I truly believe they made a positive difference.

I saved some of my best hitting exploits for the Giants. In June we hit San Francisco with a four-game lead over them. I had been suspended for the first game for arguing with umpire Stan Landis, and the Giants beat us, cutting our lead to 3 games. The next day I was back in the lineup and hit a two-run, 8th-inning homer to beat Gaylord Perry 2–1.

On August 22 we destroyed the Giants 9–0 in Candlestick. I drove in 4 runs off Ray Sadecki with a single in the 1st and a three-run homer in the 5th. It was the fifth time that year that I had accounted for the winning run against the Giants. Not bad for a fellow they once said did not hit in the clutch.

I'll never forget flying back to St. Louis after that series. Roger Maris was sitting next to me. He said without qualification or reservation that he had never seen any one player so single-handedly beat another team like I beat the Giants that year. I didn't key myself up just for the Giants. If you make it too personal, you tighten up too much. You never want to put that kind of pressure on yourself. The real trick is to stay calm, swing the bat, and just let your skill take over.

By September 18 we had opened a thirteen-game lead over the Giants. We finished the year with a record of 101 wins and

61 losses, 10 1/2 games ahead of the second-place Giants. Leo Durocher's surprising Cubs vaulted to third place with an 87–74 record. It was the Cub's highest finish since 1946.

I finished the year with a career-high .325 average and added 25 home runs and a league-leading 111 RBIs. Most important, I had 21 game-winning hits.

But I hardly did it alone. McCarver was superb behind the plate and as a team leader. Tim hit .295 and was runner-up in the MVP voting. Curt Flood led the team with a .335 average and was brilliant defensively. Lou Brock had 206 hits, 21 home runs, and a league-leading 52 stolen bases. Mike Shannon made the transition from right field to third base beautifully and was second to me on the team with 77 runs batted in.

Anyone who watched the World Series saw our double-play combination of Julian Javier and Dal Maxvill at work. They were outstanding, maybe the best-kept secret in baseball. Roger Maris was superb. Numbers do not always tell the whole story. Roger won so many ballgames by just doing the right thing at the right time, those timely things when the game is on the line that make a difference but don't show up in the box score.

And I can't say enough about our pitching. A lesser club may have faltered with Bob Gibson out for six weeks. But our guys picked up the slack superbly and pitched us to a runaway pennant. Gibby was ready to return for the World Series and make the Red Sox wish they had never heard of him.

Although we had no 20-game winners, five of our starters won 10 games or more: Dick Hughes (16–6), Nelson Briles (14–5), Steve Carlton (14–9), Bob Gibson (13–7), and Ray Washburn (10–7). Our bullpen, anchored by Ron Willis and Joe Hoerner, led the league in saves.

Nelson and Steve, both with earned run averages under 3.00, developed into fine starting pitchers. Dick Hughes threw a hard slider that was almost unhittable. He gave up just 164 hits in 222 1/3 innings in 1967, and his 16–6 record gave him the best winning percentage in the National League.

Dick was named *The Sporting News* Rookie of the Year in 1967—the Baseball Writers of America gave it to Tom Seaver—but that was pretty much it for him. He hurt his arm the following spring and was never an effective pitcher again. Of his 20 major league wins, 16 came in our 1967 championship year.

Because we clinched the pennant so early, we had no idea who we would play in the World Series. The Tigers, Twins, White Sox, and Red Sox were battling down to the wire. It was a four-team race and the winner would be anybody's guess. It was the most exciting American League pennant race ever, with all four teams heading into the last weekend with the chance to take it all.

When the dust cleared, the Boston Red Sox, led by Triple Crown winner Carl Yastrzemski and 22-game winner Jim Lonborg, came out on top. At the beginning of the year Boston's chances of taking the American League flag were listed at 100 to 1.

But they were worthy adversaries in the World Series, battling us all the way. It was a hard-fought Series with bad blood on both sides. But it is baseball, and it is the World Series. Should things really be any other way?

The Series opened up in Boston on October 4. We were 3-to-1 favorites. In Game One it was Gibson vs. right-hander Jose Santiago. Bob, the World Series MVP in 1964, was in complete control and on top of his game. He struck out 10 and allowed the Red Sox just 6 hits as we took the opener by a score of 2–1.

Gibby and Santiago were locked in a tight pitching duel until the 7th. With the score tied 1–1, Lou Brock got his fourth straight hit, stole second, moved to third on a ground ball, and scored on a ground out by Roger Maris. Roger also drove in the game's first run in the 3rd inning. What a clutch hitter.

Gibson's one mistake was hanging a 3rd-inning curveball to Santiago, who hit it out of the stands for the only Boston run. But Lou stole the show with 4 hits, 1 walk, and 2 stolen bases.

The second game pitted Dick Hughes against American League Cy Young winner Jim Lonborg. We could see why. Lonborg was superb, throwing a one-hit 5–0 shutout. He was just four outs away from pitching the second no-hitter in World Series history when Julian Javier doubled with two outs in the 8th inning. But that was all we could do.

The World Series shifted to St. Louis for Game Three. A

hometown crowd of 54,575 were on hand to see Nelson Briles go the distance and Mike Shannon homer as we beat the Red Sox by a score of 5–2. Then it was Gibby again in Game Four. This time he threw a five-hitter in shutting out Boston 6–0.

With a 3–1 Series lead, we could put it away in Game Five at home. It was Lonborg vs. Steve Carlton. Steve pitched beautiful baseball, allowing only 3 hits in 6 innings. But Jim Lonborg turned in another gem. This time he held us to 3 hits for a 3–1 Red Sox win, which moved the Series to Boston for Game Six. Our only run came on Roger Maris's home run in the bottom of 9th—the only extra-base hit Lonborg gave up all day.

Gary Waslewski and Dick Hughes were the pitching opponents for Game Six. The Red Sox went homer happy as Yastrzemski, Reggie Smith, and Rico Petrocelli each hit solo shots in the 4th inning. We tied the game in the 7th when Lou hit a two–run homer off John Wyatt. But the Red Sox got four more runs in the bottom of the inning for an 8–4 Boston win. We depleted our bullpen, using eight pitchers in a losing effort. It now boiled down to Game Seven and Bob Gibson.

Nobody, but nobody, was better than Bob when the money was on the line. He'd allowed one run in Game One, then pitched a five-hit shutout in Game Four. It was the classic matchup for a final game: Lonborg vs. Gibson, the two aces.

Like Bob Gibson, Jim Lonborg had been magnificent. He'd thrown a one-hit shutout at us in Game Two and a three-hitter in Game Five.

But he was working with only two days' rest. Lonborg was tired, and we sensed that early on. We scored twice in the 3rd inning. Dal Maxvill led off with a triple off the center-field fence. After Lonborg retired the next two batters, Curt Flood singled to center, scoring Maxvill. Then Roger singled past first base, sending Curt to third. Curt crossed home on a wild pitch for the second score of the inning.

Bob again was brilliant. He walked Joe Foy to start the game, then retired thirteen in a row until George Scott reached him for a triple in the 5th with a long home run into the center-field bleachers. We scored again when Lou Brock singled, stole second and third, and scored on Maris's sacrifice fly to right. We were ahead 4–0.

In the 6th inning we had two men on base when up came Julian Javier. Red Sox manager Dick Williams wanted to take Lonborg out of the game. But Lonborg convinced him to let him pitch to Javier. Big mistake. Hoolie drove a hanging pitch into the screen for a three-run homer and we were up 7–1. The Red Sox scored one in the 8th, and that was it.

When Gibson fanned George Scott to end the Series, we all mobbed him. The only incident came when someone ran onto the field, hit me in the neck, and took my hat. I chased the guy, but he had too big a head start.

Bob Gibson had won his third World Series game of 1967. He limited the Red Sox to 3 hits, striking out ten en route to a 7–2 win.

It had not been the most gentle Series, full of brushback pitches and incessant jockeying from the benches. But in the top of the 9th, when Bob came to the plate, he was given a rousing ovation by the 35,000-plus fans at Fenway Park. When Lou Brock came up he got the same treatment. We may have ended Boston's impossible dream, but they played us tough right to the end. And their fans showed us nothing but class.

Bob's third Series win put him in select company: Only the Cardinals' Harry Brecheen (1946) and the Braves' Lew Burdette (1958) had achieved that hat trick. Bob had pitched 27 innings of World Series baseball, allowing just 14 hits and striking out 26. His earned run average for the Series was a stunning 1.00.

Lou Brock was just as remarkable. Lou hit a Series-high .414 and drove the Red Sox crazy by stealing 7 bases. His 12 base hits included 2 doubles, a triple, and a home run.

There was bedlam in our clubhouse. Before the game the Boston papers had boasted "Lonborg and Champagne." Now our players chanted, "We're drinking Lonborg and champagne!"

The Red Sox played us hard, but they ripped us hard in the press. They had belittled us in the papers. Now it was pay-back time. For Tim McCarver especially, this was far more satisfying than the victory over the Yankees in 1964 because the Red Sox had showed such a lack of respect. August Busch, as thrilled as he could be, paid a visit to the clubhouse and drank champagne with us. Tom Yawkey, the Red Sox owner, came in to congratulate Gussie Busch, Red Schoendienst, the players, and the coaches of the World Champion St. Louis Cardinals.

Someone asked Lou what the turning point of the game was. Lou thought a few seconds and answered, "Bob Gibson."

Curt Flood tore off his uniform. He was holding a bottle of champagne in his hand. He said it like it was. "All this jazz in the newspapers," he said, "I've never seen anything like it in my life. Everybody had something to pop off about." Then he added something I'll never forget. "They could have finished fourth on the last day of the season. They forgot about that!"

By then we were all chanting in unison, "Lonborg and champagne, hey! Lonborg and champagne, hey!" The St. Louis Cardinals were the best team in baseball. We'd known it before. But now everyone else was certain of it too.

I was elated. But I was also a little down. Lou, Bob, and the entire pitching staff had a great Series. Roger hit .385 and led both teams with 7 runs batted in. Hoolie had 9 hits, 4 for extra bases, and hit .360.

I came to bat 29 times and had just 3 hits, even worse than my outing in the 1962 World Series. Maybe I was pushing myself too hard to atone for my meager performance in the 1962 Series when Dark had been on my back. I don't know. Joe DiMaggio later mentioned to me that he had a dismal World Series or two. So have other top players. Gil Hodges, for one, went 0 for 21 in the 1952 Series.

At the postseason party at Stan Musial's restaurant, Tim McCarver raised his glass and looked straight at me. "Here's to you," he said.

"I didn't do anything in the Series," I shrugged. He answered, "You got us there."

It was my best big-league season. Roberto Clemente hit 32 points higher and drove in 110 runs. Hank Aaron hit 14 more home runs and outslugged me .573 to .524. Still, the Baseball Writers of America saw fit to make me the first major leaguer to be selected Most Valuable Player by unanimous choice. You can't get any better than that.

But I'll never forget something Mike Shannon said about me, because it went past my numbers alone and dealt with what I meant to the team: "It's not just his statistics. It's intangible. I really can't describe it. It's like walking down the street and two tough guys come the other way, looking for a fight. This friend comes along—a big guy—and when the two guys see him they disappear. That's Cepeda. He's a prestige player. We have him, and the other clubs don't."

· 11 ·

The Year of the Pitcher

The St. Louis Cardinals were not only the World Champions of baseball but also the highest-paid team in baseball history. I was browsing through some old *Sports Illustrated*s recently. The cover of one of the October 1968 issues is a classic. In fact, an enlarged framed photograph of that cover hangs on the wall of my den. It shows the eight regular starters and Bob Gibson sitting in front of our respective lockers in street clothes, our numbered jerseys hanging in full view. Inside that issue we see the salary listings of baseball's highest-paid club:

Maris	$75,000
McCarver	$60,000
Gibson	$85,000
Shannon	$40,000
Brock	$70,000
Cepeda	$80,000
Flood	$72,500
Javier	$45,000
Maxvill	$37,500
Schoendienst	$42,000
	$607,000

For that type of money (yes, it was good money back then), the Cardinal brass expected more of the same from us. In other words, another World Championship. Not since 1921–1922, when John McGraw's New York Giants captured back-to-back World Series titles, had a National League team accomplished that feat.

Our starting infield of Cepeda, Javier, Maxvill, and Shannon was intact. So was our outfield of Brock, Flood, and Maris. The starting rotation of Gibson, Carlton, Ray Washburn, and Nelson Briles was the best quartet of starters in the National League. Larry Jaster and rookie Mike Torrez added pitching depth, while Joe Hoerner was dependable and steady out of the bullpen. Tim McCarver was a rock behind the plate.

Among the reserves, Bobby Tolan could play first or the outfield, and he was on the edge of stardom. Utility man Phil Gagliano could play all infield positions. We had also added catcher John Edwards, infielder Dick Schofield, and outfielder Dick Simpson to the roster.

Sports Illustrated noted in its 1968 Baseball Preview issue that the Cardinals were the only team around capable of winning games consistently in any one of five ways: (1) with speed, (2) with defense, (3) with pitching, (4) with power, or (5) with overall hitting.

In 1967 we'd been a 12–1 shot. In 1968 we were odds-on favorites. One of the most telling aspects of the 1967 team had been our road record of 53–28. But such factors as injuries and complacency cannot be measured. We would not be starting the 1968 season with a ten-and-a-half game lead over the rest of the pack. But we were a team with enormous pride, lots of talent, and loads of spirit.

I was receiving more than my fair share of press. The editors of *Sports Review* put me on its special All-Star team for 1967, calling the Orlando Cepeda/Ray Sadecki trade the "greatest steal since the Brinks robbery." Tim McCarver, Lou Brock, and Bob Gibson were also selected to the first team, along with Bill Mazeroski, Richie Allen, Carl Yastrzemski, Jim Fregosi, Hank Aaron, and Mike McCormick.

I was glad to see Mike McCormick, my old pal from the Giants, named to the All-Star team. It had been a great comeback year for Mike, who, after spending four years in the American League, returned to the Giants to become the National League Cy Young winner. Mike was 22–10 for the Giants in 1967. His 22 wins tied him with Jim Lonborg for the major league lead. Fergie Jenkins of the Cubs was the only other National League pitcher to win 20 that year.

Curt Flood, whom the editors of *Sports Review* called "unquestionably the finest defensive outfielder in the game," was named to the Second-Team All-Stars. When it came to talent, there was no question that we had it big time.

Sport magazine featured a story in the October 1967 issue entitled "Orlando Cepeda: Why He Had to Come Back." In *Sports Review*'s baseball edition, Harmon Peterson wrote a piece entitled "The Revenge That Drives Orlando Cepeda."

In a *Sport World* piece, "The Inside Story of How Cepeda Makes the Cardinals Go," Clair Young assessed my value to the Cardinals. "The Baby Bull's true value goes deeper than just home runs and game-winning hits," he wrote. He quoted a number of my teammates, who gave testimony to what I meant to the club. "Cha Cha has a lot of spirit. It rubs off on the others on the field, on the bench, and in the clubhouse," said Bob Gibson.

Former teammate Eddie Bressoud, who'd been with the Cardinals in 1967, said that "Orlando always had great desire. With the Giants he was always under the shadow of Willie Mays."

Stan Fischler wrote a nice piece for the spring issue of *Baseball Sports Stars of 1968*—"Cepeda Is a Big Boy Now." He quoted Gary Schumaker, Horace Stoneham's right-hand man, after the 1961 season: "In my estimation, Cepeda is the greatest right-handed hitter since the days of Harry Heilmann and Rogers Hornsby. Cepeda reminds me of Jimmy Foxx. He has the big swing, a good eye, brute strength." He goes on to say, "Now having Heilmann, Rogers Hornsby and Jimmy Foxx all rolled into one should make a manager extremely happy. But it did not have that effect on the man who was then managing the Giants, Alvin Dark."

There was every indication that we were as good a team as last year, maybe even better. But what no one seemed to know was that 1968 would be the year of the pitcher, a season quite unlike any in recent memory.

The number that pitchers put up were astounding. Luis Tiant of the Cleveland Indians led the American League with 9 shutouts and a 1.60 earned run average. Detroit's Denny McLain went 31–6 in 1968 with a 1.96 earned run average. In fact, the top five ERAs in the American League that year were under .200.

To show how this impacted the game, consider that through the entire 1950s Billy Pierce was the only major league starting pitcher who recorded an ERA under 2.00—1.97, for the Chicago White Sox in 1955 .

Jim "Catfish" Hunter pitched a perfect game for the Oakland A's. In fact, five pitchers threw no-hitters in 1968, including our own Ray Washburn. His no-hitter against the Giants in Candlestick on September 18 was one for the books. The previous day Gaylord Perry had no hit us in Candlestick Park. The two pitchers threw back-to-back no-hitters in the same ballpark.

Don Drysdale pitched a record 58²/₃ scoreless innings in 1968. Even the All-Star Game at Houston's Astrodome was dominated by pitchers. The National League won the game 1–0, with the only run scoring on a 1st-inning double play.

As you might expect, in a pitcher's year such as this the hitting tailed off. Carl Yastrzemski won his second straight American League batting championship with an average of .301, the lowest winning average ever. The A's moved from Kansas City to Oakland and topped the American League in hitting with just a .240 average. The New York Yankees set a post-deadball era record for lowest team batting average, hitting a paltry .214 as a team.

We scored 112 runs less in 1968 than we did in 1967, yet still won 97 games and finished 9 games in front of the second-place Giants. Our home-run total dipped from 115 to 73. Busch Memorial Stadium had never been a hitter's paradise. I had 16 home runs to lead the club and Mike Shannon had 15. No other Cardinal player had more than 7.

Of the ten National League teams, only the Cubs (130), the Giants (108), the Reds (106), and the Phillies (100) hit as many as 100 home runs in 1968. Try comparing that with today's big numbers.

The collective American League ERA was 2.98, and the

National League's was 2.99. Our pitching staff led all twenty major league teams with an ERA of 2.49.

An even better illustration of the high caliber of pitching is this: Juan Marichal went 26–9 for the Giants, threw 30 complete games, struck out 218 batters, and did not capture the Cy Young Award. And Bob Gibson was the reason.

I'm not sure any pitcher ever had a year like Gibby in 1968. His 1.12 earned run average set a post-1920 National League mark. He won 22 games and struck out a league-leading 268 batters. The only thing I couldn't figure out was how he managed to lose 9 games in the process.

Bob pitched 28 complete games in his 34 starts. He allowed only 198 hits in 304 2/3 innings and walked only 62. Bob's 13 shutouts were the most since Grover Cleveland Alexander threw 16 shutouts for the Philadelphia Phillies in 1919.

In a remarkable streak between May 28 and August 24, Bob won 15 straight games, ten of which were shutouts. He missed breaking Don Drysdale's record of 58 2/3 consecutive scoreless innings because of a wild pitch that scored a run. He had pitched 47 2/3 innings before that wild pitch, and he pitched 23 more before allowing another run. He was to win both the Cy Young Award and the National League MVP Award for 1968.

And the rest of our mound corps pitched great baseball as well. Nelson Briles improved on his 1967 season with a 19–11 record and a 2.80 ERA. Ray Washburn was 14–8 (2.26), including that no-hitter against the Giants. Steve Carlton was 13–11 (2.99), and in relief Joe Hoerner was 8–2 with a 1.47 ERA.

We had a great team. No one could deny that. Yet few predicted another runaway season because the Reds, Giants, Cubs, and Pirates looked to be improved teams.

Street and Smith's Official 1968 Baseball Yearbook actually had us finishing third behind the Cincinnati Reds, although they acknowledged that very few pennant-guessing pundits gave anyone else much of a chance to overtake us. Their one concern was that we had remained rather pat during the winter meetings in Mexico City, while other teams were bettering themselves through interleague trading.

Red Schoendienst put it simply. "Championship clubs rarely

♦

make great changes, and we hadn't done much to ours." Although few expected another runaway, that's exactly what happened. By August 1, we had opened up a fifteen-game lead and were preparing to meet the Detroit Tigers in the World Series.

Sure it was the year of the pitcher. But we still had the same understanding and approach to the game we always had. We remained successful on the field and close friends off the field.

It was not unusual to see a lot of the players together in the same place after a game. We'd sit around the clubhouse for hours talking about baseball. Our attitude was always that winning mattered the most, not what your individual batting average might be.

Because winning was so important, we knew and understood that we must help one another. We could say things to each other that only true friends would dare to say. In baseball that was rather unusual.

We still had time for some fun. Our favorite activity was a postgame quiz in the locker room after each game. We patterned it after the new scoreboards. A scoreboard would put up a question, then a few innings later the answer would flash across.

Our version was a little different. We would watch each other's mistakes carefully on the field. Then when we'd get back to the clubhouse, someone would say, "I've got a baseball quiz." The guys would holler, "Yeah!" then the guy who said he had a quiz would act out a mistake someone on the team had made, and we would guess who did it.

Of course, the guy who made the mistake was embarrassed. We'd come up with silly answers: Was it Ty Cobb? Was it Babe Ruth? When we'd gone as far as we could, someone would give the guy's name. Sometimes we'd boo him, sometimes we'd cheer him for looking so foolish. The important thing was the guy would probably never make the same mistake again, and that was what our little game was really for. If the guy couldn't take it and own up to his flub, he was not the kind of guy we wanted around anyway.

The Detroit Tigers were the class act of the American League in 1968. They sailed through their season with little opposition.

Like us, they benefited from an outstanding pitching performance. Denny McLain became the first American League pitcher to win 30 games since Lefty Grove won 31 for the Philadelphia Athletics in 1931 and the first major leaguer since Dizzy Dean won 30 games for the St. Louis Cardinals in 1934.

The Tigers were a hell of a team. They won 103 games in 1968 and finished 12 games in front of the second-place Orioles. While the Red Sox had been carried by Yaz and Lonborg in 1967, the Tigers were a solid team from top to bottom. They had hitting, pitching, and defense.

The Tigers also had great power. They led the American League in runs scored, slugging percentage, and fielding. Their 183 home runs were by far the most by any major league team. On paper, at least, they were a more formidable foe than the Boston Red Sox the year before.

We weren't intimidated. We were convinced that we'd become the first National League team since McGraw's Giants to win back-to-back World Series. And we came close, very close.

Although it may have been Denny McLain's year, it was left-hander Mickey Lolich who was our nemesis, who shut us down by nailing three World Series wins. But what baseball fan or historian can ever forget Bob Gibson in Game One of the 1968 World Series?

The Series opened in St. Louis on October 2. Nearly 55,000 fans packed Busch Memorial Stadium to see the battle of the aces, Bob Gibson vs. Denny McLain, baseball's two best pitchers that year.

Denny gave up just 3 hits in his 5 innings of work. The game was scoreless until we put together 2 hits and a pair of walks, coupled with a Detroit error to go ahead 3–0 in the bottom of the 4th. Lou Brock homered in the 7th to put another run on the board.

I've never seen Gibson any tougher. He held the Tigers to 5 hits, shutting them out 4–0. But most impressively, Bob set a World Series record by striking out 17 batters. When he fanned Al Kaline leading off the 9th inning for strikeout number 15, he tied Sandy Koufax's record. Every one of the 55,000 fans were on their feet. Next came Norm Cash. Earlier in the game,

Cash had been on first, and he told me that he didn't see how anyone was going to hit Bob that day. He struck out for the third time.

The crowd was still on its feet, taking in every pitch as Willie Horton came to bat. The powerful Horton had slammed 36 home runs for the Tigers in the regular season. Only big Frank Howard had hit more. But Bob dispatched Willie Horton in high fashion by throwing a called third strike past him for strikeout 17. It was one of the greatest pitching performances I have ever seen, but Bob took it all in stride. He always did.

In Game Two it was Mickey Lolich and Nelson Briles. Of all National League pitchers in 1968, only Gibson, Marichal, and Jenkins won more games than Briles. Mickey had gone 17–9 for the Tigers and had great control, especially for a left-hander. In 1971, when he won 25 games for the Tigers, Mickey pitched 379 innings, struck out 308, and walked only 92 batters. In this particular World Series, Mickey showed he could pitch with anybody. He was quick, with great breaking stuff to go with that excellent control.

Backed by home runs from Norm Cash, Willie Horton, and a 3rd-inning solo shot of his own, Mickey threw a six-hitter and struck out 9. The final score was 8–1.

With the Series tied at one game apiece, we moved on to Detroit for Game Three. It was Ray Washburn (14–9) against the Tigers' Earl Wilson (13–12). Homers prevailed in this one.

Al Kaline, one of the very best I've ever seen, had a great Series. His two-run shot in the 3rd inning opened the scoring. Then in the 5th inning, after Tim McCarver's three-run blast, Dick McAuliffe hit a solo shot in the bottom of the inning to pull the Tigers within a run.

Plagued by two miserable World Series, I came out of my October slump with a three-run home run in the 7th inning off Don McMahon to put the game out of reach. The final score was Cardinals 7, Tigers 3.

In Game Four it was the aces again: Gibson vs. McLain. Once again it was all Bob. Lou Brock homered in the 1st inning and by the end of the 3rd McLaine was in the showers. Gibby was his usual superb self. He struck out ten and hit a home run of his own to beat the Tigers 10–1.

We were up 3 games to 1. One more win and we'd repeat as World Champions. We were confident. Maybe too confident.

But then we ran into Lolich. It was Mickey vs. Nelson Briles in Game Five. We tagged him early—my second homer of the Series was part of a three-run 1st inning—but then he slammed the door shut. The Tigers came back with 2 runs in the 4th and 3 more in the 7th for a 5–3 Tiger win.

The Series moved back to St. Louis for Game Six. We sent Ray Washburn to the mound against Denny McLain. It was all Detroit. Jim Northrup's grand-slam homer ignited a ten-run Tiger 3rd. McLain went the distance. We used seven pitchers, and the Tigers beat us 13–1. The Series was tied.

Maybe we had become a bit complacent. I can't say for sure. But we always felt that if it came to a seventh game, we had something the Tigers did not. His name was Bob Gibson. Somehow it seemed impossible that we could lose a big game with Bob pitching. We were going against Mickey Lolich, but he was pitching with just two days' rest.

It was a tight pitching duel, a scoreless game into the 7th inning. The key plays had come in the 6th inning when Lolich picked both Lou Brock and Curt Flood off at first.

With two outs in the top of the 7th, Norm Cash and Willie Horton each singled. Jim Northrup came to bat. He lined a shot to center, a ball Curt Flood would normally catch without a problem. Curt's fielding average had been a perfect 1.000 in 1966, and he was considered the best defensive center fielder in the game. This time, however, Curt broke the wrong way and didn't recover in time. The ball bounced over his head, Cash and Horton crossed the plate, and Northrup pulled into third with a triple. He later scored, and the Tigers took a 3–0 lead into the 8th inning.

The Tigers scored again in the top of the 9th to make it 4–0. We finally scored when Mike Shannon homered in the bottom of the 9th. But Tim McCarver fouled out to catcher Bill Freehan to end the game. Our back-to-back World Championship dream had been thwarted. Mickey Lolich had thrown a five-hitter to beat us 4–1. The Detroit Tigers had won the World Series.

I finally had a good Series, hitting .250 with 2 home runs and leading the club with 6 RBIs. But I have never been so disappointed. Looking back I think we were overconfident. We could smell victory. We were up 3–1. There was no way we could lose. But somehow we didn't go for the kill. We let it all fall on the shoulders of Bob Gibson. But in the long run it was a case of too much Mickey Lolich.

Nevertheless, Bob had another great World Series. He won 2 games, threw 27 innings, walked 4, and struck out 35. His Series ERA was a sparkling 1.67. His 35 strikeouts set a World Series record.

Sandy Koufax and Juan Marichal dominated hitters year after year. But I feel that in 1968 Bob Gibson was the most dominating pitcher I have ever seen. He put us in the World Series. He was also a tremendous help to Steve Carlton and Nelson Briles. In the Year of the Pitcher, Bob won both the Cy Young Award (by a unanimous vote) and National League Most Valuable Player.

I can't say enough about Lou Brock. One of the reasons we were such an outstanding team was that no one could figure out how to keep Lou off the bases. He had become the premier base stealer in baseball, stealing a combined 114 bases in 1967–1968. Lou was also a hitter, as his .293 lifetime average and his 3,023 career base hits clearly show.

As he did in the 1967 World Series, Lou led the club. He hit .464 against the Tigers in 1968. He had 25 hits in the two Series combined. You'd have to go back a long way to find a better performance in back-to-back World Series.

The year 1968 had not been a good one for me. In fact, it was the only really poor year I would have as a regular. My average fell to an all-time low .248, poor for me even in a year when pitching dominated. I'm not sure what happened. My 16 home runs and 73 RBIs were also career lows. Sometimes hitters get out of the groove and their timing is a flicker off. That's all it takes. Maybe that's what happened to me in 1968.

There were personal problems, too, which I will talk about later. But all ballplayers go through these kinds of things at one time or another. We're no different than other people operating under duress. So 1968 was just an off year for me. But it would have been so much sweeter had we taken the World Series.

Disappointment, sure, but panic? No! That was the mood in the clubhouse after the Series. Over a two-year period, we had won 198 games and finished a collective 19 games better than the Giants who finished second both years. Roger Maris had played his last major league game. He was retiring. But we had picked up Vada Pinson from the Reds to take his place. So there was no reason to believe that we wouldn't be in the thick of things again in 1969.

A new alignment of teams was scheduled for 1969. The National League was expanding to twelve teams with the addition of Montreal and San Diego. Consequently, the league was splitting into two divisions for the first time. Although the Cardinals and the Cubs were geographically Western Division teams, both were placed in the Eastern Division for the purpose of balance. I had no particular feeling one way or the other about divisional play. I never concerned myself too much about those changes. In the long run it still comes down to the same things: pitching, hitting, and defense.

The ball was still the same, the bat was the same, the bases were still ninety feet apart, and the pitching mound was sixty feet, six inches from home plate. Baseball was still baseball. Like it or not, the game must change with the times. New markets and larger revenue take care of that. But the essence of baseball and the tools and the skills required to play it were the same—and always will be.

Besides, I was confident that we would capture our division since we now had to beat just five other teams. The chances were good that I'd be playing for a division winner in 1969.

I was right. But it wouldn't be the St. Louis Cardinals, who fell to fourth place in 1969. It would be with the Atlanta Braves. In March 1969, during spring training, the Cardinals traded me to the Braves for Joe Torre.

· 12 ·

The Final Years

The year 1969 ushered in divisional play. For the first time in the history of baseball, division leaders would play each other in a five-game postseason playoff, with the winner advancing to the World Series. The Atlanta Braves were a National League West club along with the Los Angeles Dodgers, San Francisco Giants, Cincinnati Reds, Houston Colt .45s, and the San Diego Padres.

Being traded is always an adjustment. But when you're traded during the winter months, you have a longer period to adjust and to think. When you're traded during the spring or the regular season it's not so easy. You're uprooted and planted in a new location that you and your family must become familiar with quickly.

The signs are usually there if you choose to see them. You know something isn't right, something's going on. People don't treat you quite the same. You can read it in their faces. It's those little things you can't put your finger on.

Still, when Bing Devine told me I had been traded to the Atlanta Braves, it came as a shock. The Cardinals were a close unit. My teammates were also my close friends. I had learned to love St. Louis. I had a nice home for my family, and I was blessed with good neighbors.

Moreover, I had never liked Atlanta. It was one of the two major league franchises I never wanted to play for. Momentarily I even thought of giving up baseball, packing up, and going back to Puerto Rico. but my wife, Annie, put things in perspective quickly. Hurt feelings and stubbornness aside, baseball was my livelihood. It was what I knew. It was my passport to income and respectability.

Bob Howsam was no longer the Cardinals' general manager. Bing Devine was now GM. It was Bing who had made us baseball's highest-paid club. He had also taken his share of heat for it. Within two years he would break up the team. As Tim McCarver always said, we were a team of independent thinkers and unique personalities, outspoken, rebels in our own way. Bing did not like this.

I'd only really met Bing once. That was when he came to Puerto Rico to negotiate my contract for 1968. I never really got to know him as I had gotten to know Stan Musial. Bing was not terribly friendly, and he was all business. I signed my 1968 contract for $80,000. That was it until he called me at St. Petersburg in late March 1969 to tell me I'd been traded to the Braves.

With Bob Howsam and Stan Musial gone from the front office, I lost my two big benefactors in the Cardinal organization. And I knew that Bing Devine was high on Joe Torre and wanted him in St. Louis.

Later, when the Cardinals finished in fourth place in 1969 13 games behind the Mets, Devine was able to get rid of more of the old guard. Roger Maris had retired after the 1968 World Series, and I had been traded to the Braves in 1969. After the season Curt Flood, Tim McCarver, and Joe Hoerner were traded to the Philadelphia Phillies in a deal that took Richie Allen and Cookie Rojas to St. Louis. So four starters and our top relief pitcher from the championship teams of 1967–1968 were playing elsewhere in 1970.

I mentioned that Atlanta was one National League team I had no desire to play for. The other was Houston. That was because they struck me as still adhering to the Southern culture and mentality in dealing with blacks and Latins.

When Houston entered the National League as an expansion club in 1962, I was there with the Giants for a series. Because of its great music and Puerto Rican theme, I wanted to see the movie *West Side Story*, which had just come out. I asked Juan Marichal to join me, but he had something else planned. So I went alone. When I got to the theater and tried to buy a ticket, they wouldn't let me in.

On another occasion I was talking with a white girl outside our hotel. The next time I saw her there were tears in her eyes. She told me that she'd been told in no uncertain terms that she'd find herself in a lot of trouble if she talked to me again.

Atlanta had been part of the Old South, and I was worried about lingering attitudes. But I soon found out that a lot had changed, and my two years with the Braves were very happy ones. There were also two more good things about Atlanta: Felipe Alou and Hank Aaron.

Since being traded from the Giants to the Braves in 1964, Felipe had emerged as a frontline star, leading the National League in base hits in 1966 and again in 1968. He'd moved with the team from Milwaukee to Atlanta in 1966. We had been through much together and had been real friends in our younger days, so I was delighted to be reunited as a teammate with Felipe.

Hank Aaron, of course, was the Braves' reigning superstar. He'd been with the franchise since 1954. I had always admired Hank on the ball field. We had been teammates in a number of All-Star Games, and I envied his extraordinary skills. But now I would learn what a wonderful guy, decent man, and good friend Hank could be.

Hank could do it all, and do it as well as anyone. He often does not get the full credit he deserves for being such a superb all-around player. He could do all the things Willie Mays could do, he just wasn't as flashy. Just ask the people who played baseball with Hank day in and day out. They'll tell you what a complete baseball player Hank really was.

When I arrived at the Braves' spring training site in West Palm Beach, Hank welcomed me to the club immediately. He told me I'd like playing in Atlanta, and that I would help the Braves win a division title.

Braves General Manager Paul Richards was keen on me. He had been for a long time. Paul was the one who brought Minnie Minoso to the Chicago White Sox in 1951. He was a fine man, I think the best all-around baseball man I have ever known. He knew every aspect of the game and was a superb teacher. He made winners of the Chicago White Sox in the early 1950s after years in the baseball wilderness. Then, when the St. Louis Browns moved to Baltimore, he did the same for the Orioles.

Paul had always been good and fair to the Latin players. He had played against my father in Puerto Rico when he was a catcher with the Detroit Tigers. In addition to Felipe Alou and me, the Braves roster included such Latins as second baseman Felix Millan, infielder Gil Garrido, and outfielders Tony Gonzalez and Rico Carty.

Paul was one of those people who could look mean yet still be a beautiful person. When he signed on to manage the Chicago White Sox, it was Paul Richards and Frank Lane who created those exciting Go Go White Sox teams that dominated Chicago baseball in the fifties and early sixties.

He said for the record once, "If Orlando plays for a first-place club, he's the best first-place ballplayer you'll ever see. If he plays with a fifth-place club, then he's the best fifth-place ballplayer around. If you put him on a good team, he will make it better. He's a winner." Paul always was good to me.

The Braves had a good team. They were managed by Luman Harris. Luman was from the South, but unlike Alvin Dark, he had no tolerance for racism. We had a good rapport, and when I hurt my leg in 1971, Luman stuck by me.

It always makes me feel good to think that I went to the Cardinals when they were a second-division team and helped to lead them to two successive National League flags and a World Championship. Then after being traded to the Braves, I helped them jump from second division in 1968 to a division title in 1969.

I've seen a lot of great third basemen in my life, but I have yet to see a finer defensive third baseman than Clete Boyer— certainly on a par with Brooks Robinson. Hank Aaron hit 44 homers and led the league with 332 total bases. Hank and Clete Boyer were great teammates. So was Phil Niekro, who led the staff with 23 victories. And Rico Carty led the club in hitting with a .342 average.

I hit a disappointing .257 with the Braves in 1969 but helped out with 22 home runs and 88 runs batted in. The Atlanta

Braves became the third team for which I hit 20 or more home runs. More importantly, we won the National League West with a 93–69 record. It was a tight race all the way, with only 8 games separating us and the fourth-place Los Angeles Dodgers.

But when all was said and done, 1969 was simply the year of the New York Mets. They came from ninth place and 73 wins in 1968 to win 100 games and the Eastern Division title in 1969. They were a true team of destiny, as we were soon to find out.

Most experts picked us to win the playoffs. They had pitching, but on paper we probably had a better team overall. But they made believers of us by sweeping the playoffs. Then they did the impossible, beating the Baltimore Orioles, one of the best teams ever, in the World Series. And they did it in five games.

The New York Mets couldn't do anything wrong in the playoffs. Each time we went ahead, they came back to beat us. In Game One we came from behind twice to take a one-run lead. We were ahead 5–4 at the end of seven when the Mets hit us with 5 runs in the 8th as Tom Seaver (25–7) beat Phil Niekro 9–5.

In Game Two the Mets piled up a quick 8–0 lead, then held on to beat us 11–6 and go two up. We thought we'd come back in Game Three, especially after Hank Aaron hit a two-run, 1st-inning homer off Gary Gentry. The lead changed hands three different times, with home runs always paving the way.

Tommie Agee homered for the Mets in the bottom of the 3rd, and Ken Boswell hit a two-run homer in the bottom of the 4th to put the Mets ahead 3–2. In the top of the 5th, I tagged a two-run homer off twenty-two-year-old Nolan Ryan to give us a 4–3 lead.

But that was it. That's all the scoring we did. Mets rookie Wayne Garrett homered in the bottom of the 5th to put them ahead 6–4. Nolan Ryan shut us down the last four innings, and the Mets beat us 7–4 to sweep the playoffs. It was on to the World Series for them.

It was my best postseason to date. I led all Atlanta hitters with a .455 average (5 hits in 11 at-bats, including 2 doubles and a home run). But things would have been far better had we advanced to the World Series. That would have made it three in a row for me.

I really learned to like the city of Atlanta. People were far more open and tolerant than I expected. We were the first black family to live in Arrowhead County, and the people couldn't have been nicer.

Because of the warm weather and hot sunshine, Orlando Jr.'s skin got even darker. His best friend was a little white girl who was as blond as she could be. The kids played beautifully together. Nobody made an issue of their color.

I was learning a powerful lesson. Being black, Latin, or whatever really makes little difference if you are a decent human being and respect others. And I learned these lessons in two of the southernmost big-league cities: St. Louis and Atlanta.

There are haters wherever you go. Bigotry can be found in all places and with all people. In Mexico they don't like Puerto Ricans. Puerto Ricans might not like Venezuelans. There are racists of every color and ethnic group.

Yet I've learned over the years that if you conduct yourself with dignity and respect, you will usually receive the same. I remind kids about this when I visit schools and community centers around the country. Respect is always a two-way street.

While I was with Atlanta, I got to know a couple of young players who are making an impact today as two of baseball's best managers.

In 1970 I met Tony LaRussa during the Braves' spring training. He had been one of the first $100,000 bonus babies when he signed with Charlie Finley's Kansas City A's in 1963. After his playing career, Tony replaced Minnie Minoso as first-base coach with the Chicago White Sox in 1978. A college graduate and a lawyer, Tony became manager of the White Sox in 1979. He led them to a division title in 1983 before taking over the Oakland A's in 1986. In Oakland he won three American League titles and one World Championship in the late 1980s and early 1990s.

Dusty Baker was a nineteen-year-old rookie from Riverdale,

California, when I first met him in 1969. We were teammates with the Braves from 1969 to 1971. Dusty took a liking to me. He was a nice young man, and I more or less took him under my wing and showed him the ropes. Dusty went on to have a productive nineteen-year career in the majors. He hit .278 with 242 home runs and over 1,000 runs batted in.

Like Tony LaRussa, Dusty became and remains an outstanding major league manager, leading the San Francisco Giants to 103 wins his first year as skipper in 1993 and a division title in 1997. He's twice been named National League Manager of the Year.

In 1970 I had my last truly big season. At age thirty-three I hit .305 with 34 homers and 111 RBIs. We had hitting to spare. Rico Carty led the league in hitting with a .366 average, and Rico, Hank, and I each drove in more than 100 runs. But our pitching fell flat and we finished the year in fourth place, 26 games behind the Cincinnati Reds.

In 1971 I got off to a great start, one of my best ever. Then disaster struck. I hurt my knee, but this time it was the other knee. I had first hurt it in 1969, but after two weeks it seemed to have healed itself. After my big year in 1970, I had forgotten it all together.

By May 14, I had already hit 10 home runs. I was in a groove and might well have been headed for 50 home runs on the year. I was on a slightly better pace than when I hit 46 home runs in 1961 to lead the National League.

I was sitting in my house taping music one night when the telephone rang. When I got up to answer it, my knee collapsed. It just gave on me.

The next day catcher Paul Casanova took me to the team physician, Dr. Rogers. He was not an orthopedic specialist. He gave me a shot of something, which just made the knee worse. Paul, who lived close by, literally had to carry me to my car and up to my house.

Later I went to see a specialist named Dr. Funk. He was the Atlanta Falcons' orthopedic man. He took X-rays and ran some tests. His conclusion was that my knee was finished.

I hobbled around in pain and managed to play for a while,

but the injury limited my playing time and my batting fell off more than a few points. Playing part time, I managed to hit 5 more home runs. On June 8, 1971, I hit my fourteenth and final home run of the season, a three-run shot against Steve Carlton. That was it. My season was finished.

In September I had surgery in New York and returned to Puerto Rico for the winter. When I joined the Braves for the 1972 season, I was in great pain. I was discouraged, but I could play. And I wanted to play.

I got off to a good start, too. We flew to Houston on a commercial airliner (with the Cardinals we had our own airplane and would always travel the day before). After sitting for three hours, when I got up my knee was stiff. That night Luman Harris didn't play me. When I asked him why, he told me that my leg didn't look good. I said he should have asked me before he penciled me out of the lineup. I told him I'd be ready the next day.

And I was. It was May 16, 1972, and we were playing Houston. I hit consecutive home runs off Jerry Reuss. The first was a solo shot in the 2nd inning. I followed that with a three-run blast in the 4th. The next day, when we returned to Atlanta, Luman benched me. I was so disgusted that, instead of staying at the ballpark, I went home.

That was a big mistake. Eddie Robinson, who had replaced Paul Richards as the Braves' GM, called me into his office and fined me $500. We talked about it. I told him I was sorry, that I was wrong. It was a dumb thing to do, and I had acted like a spoiled kid. He said that I had to pay the fine, but he'd see to it that I'd get the money back later. But Eddie Robinson was no Paul Richards. I never saw that money again. And he never saw to it that my leg was treated. Instead, he traded me.

In July 1972 I was traded to the Oakland A's for Denny McLain. My leg was shot. Eddie Robinson knew it when he sent me to Oakland. We were in San Diego for a series with the Padres when he told me I was going to Oakland. It was the third time I had been traded, and the third time I got the news in mid-season or in spring training.

I don't know who was kidding who. But I was through. When I joined the A's in Anaheim, Mike Epstein, the A's first baseman, was complaining to the heavens and yelling that I was going to take his job. I told him to relax, that I couldn't play now if I wanted to. I told the same thing to the papers.

I was back in the Bay Area, where it had all begun years earlier. But this was Oakland, not San Francisco. I was no longer a big star; I was an injured veteran in decline. Moreover, I could no longer play. I played one week, went to bat three times, then entered the hospital, where I had my second surgery within a year.

I was completely discouraged. I wanted out of baseball. I remained in Oakland for three months before returning to Puerto Rico. When I arrived, there was a telegram from A's owner Charles Finley. The message was clear. If I didn't call him within three days, he would release me. I never called.

I was finished as a Major League Baseball player. My legs were shot. I distanced myself during the winter months in Puerto Rico. The Major League Baseball scene and the winter meetings were far away, and that was fine with me.

But I wasn't aware at all of a rule change that the American League owners were implementing for the 1973 season, something called the designated hitter. The American League had suffered through declining attendance recently and felt that the DH rule might spur fan interest.

I didn't know a thing about the new DH policy when I received a phone call from the Boston Red Sox. They knew my knees were bad but felt that I could still swing a healthy bat. I came highly recommended by Felix Maldonado, the Red Sox Latin American scout. So I became the first major league player to be specifically signed to fill the DH role.

It would be my last hurrah as a major leaguer and a season that I am especially proud of. The Boston Red Sox were managed by Eddie Kasko, a sound baseball man and a great guy to boot. Aside from Bill Rigney, he was the best major league manager I played for.

It was a new league, but not all of my teammates were strangers. As a member of the 1967 Cardinals, I had played against Carl Yastrzemski, Rico Petrocelli, and Reggie Smith in the World Series. Carl and I had been MVPs that year. I had known him then mainly as an outstanding ballplayer, but

Carl also proved to be a great teammate and a good friend in Boston.

Pitchers Bob Bolin and Luis Tiant were familiar faces. Bob had been a teammate with the Giants, and Luis Tiant's father, like mine, had been a great Latin ballplayer. Luis Aparicio was now the Red Sox shortstop, and even at age thirty-nine he was one of the best in the game.

There was a great cast of DH hitters around the American League in 1973. Tony Oliva, his legs as ravaged as mine, became the designated hitter for the Minnesota Twins. Two years earlier Tony had won his third American League batting championship. Two-time National League batting champion Tommy Davis signed on as the Orioles' DH. Frank Robinson, one of baseball's all-time greats, signed with the California Angels.

Other designated hitters around the American League included Carlos May (White Sox), Deron Johnson (A's), Frank Howard and Gates Brown (Tigers), and Jim Hart, my old teammate with the Giants (Yankees).

It was a hell of a season for me. I almost literally played on one leg. In 142 games, I went to bat 550 times as the Red Sox DH, hitting .289 with 20 home runs and 86 RBIs. After going hitless my first six turns at bat, I homered off the Yankee's Sparky Lyle on April 8.

My 20 home runs on the year established a major league record. The Red Sox became the fourth team for which I hit 20 or more home runs. And what a great honor it was to have been named Designated Hitter of the Year. Considering where my career was and the high level of competition, the Designated Hitter Award in 1973 remains among my most meaningful baseball achievements.

It might have been as a designated hitter, but I was back on top. At least, that's what I thought. I reported to Red Sox camp in great shape in 1974. I worked hard in Puerto Rico during the winter and arrived at spring training hard and fit. I was running well, too. Everyone was impressed: Yaz, Luis Tiant, Luis Aparicio. Then came the surprise. During spring training, when I was doing well again, the Red Sox decided to let Luis Aparicio and me go.

Darrell Johnson had taken over as manager from Eddie Kasko, despite the fact that Eddie had put together four straight winning seasons since he'd taken over in 1970. I was having a great spring, hitting over .400. But I sensed something. I said to Luis a few days before we were released, "Luis, I don't like what's going on with you and me here. They're not playing us enough."

Luis said not to worry. He too had had a good solid year in 1973 and was playing well in spring training. So I talked to Darrell Johnson. "Skipper, what's going on?" I asked. "I'd like to play to stay in shape even though I'm doing well."

He told me not to worry about it. He just wanted to give some of the kids more playing time to see how they were doing. Luis and I would be playing every day the last couple of weeks, he assured me.

That day we traveled to Orlando to play the Twins, and I went 3 for 4. I remember that Phil Roof, the Twins' catcher, watched me pull a Tom Burgmeier slider from the inside corner. He asked me how I could be so quick with the bat. He was amazed.

I went to the ballpark the next day and heard the news. I was finished. Peter Gammons of *The Boston Globe* told me I was going to be released. It seems that all along Darrell was telling the Red Sox owner that, instead of paying the bigger salaries to Luis, Bob Bolin, and me, he could get three younger players who could do a better job for less pay.

It came as an enormous blow. I took it hard, really hard. I went to Mexico, and a short time later the Kansas City Royals picked me up. But my heart was no longer in the game and my body had weakened. I went to bat 107 times for the Royals and had 23 hits for an average of .215. On the afternoon of August 14, 1974, I homered off the Tigers' Luke Walker. It was the 379th of my major league career, and it was my last.

After seventeen years and 2,124 big-league games, I was through, washed up as a major league ballplayer. One part of my life was over. What lay ahead would be a story in itself, a story without baseball or home runs or applause.

· 13 ·

Busted and Tarnished

Baseball had been my life. To this point I have not revealed many details of my private life, other than how it related to my youth and baseball career. There's a reason for that.

As a kid growing up in the slum sand ghettos of Puerto Rico, it was baseball that saved my life. Of that I am sure. Without baseball, the dark side of my upbringing began to surface. That same shadow my mother had warned me about, the shadow I thought I had left behind, began playing catch-up.

Even as a baseball star, some of my boyhood pals were never far away. They liked the good times. They were bums and hangers-on, I suppose, but they were friends, or at least I thought they were. They liked the limelight they could touch when they associated with me. It gave them a phony sense of respectability and importance.

Sometimes they came to San Francisco to hang around with me. People were surprised to see me with them. Once my baseball career ended, however, the tables turned. I began following them, and following them down the wrong path.

There were problems with my marriage too. Honestly, I was often unfaithful to Annie and to my second wife, Nydia (whom I married in 1975). I could use the excuse that I was famous. I was a young baseball star whom women liked. I had more opportunities than the average guy on the street, and I took advantage big time.

I still recall as a boy how shocked and hurt I was by my father playing around. Seeing my mother so sad bothered me greatly. I couldn't understand why my father could have another "wife," and children with other women—especially since my mother was so pretty and so kind, and I knew that my father loved her a lot.

This type of behavior, I'm afraid, is ingrained in our culture. Perucho, I would find out, was no different than many Puerto Rican and Latin men. Our "macho" culture tells us that women are a birthright of sorts. So as I grew older and women became more plentiful, I became what my father had been.

Even before the birth of Orlando Jr. in 1966 I had a child with another woman. I found this out only a few years ago. I shall relate the details later. For now I will say only that my son Carl has added a new and beautiful dimension to my life.

I have deep regrets about the pain I caused Annie, now even more so because she's gone. She passed away in 1982. She was such a sweet girl when I met her, just fifteen years old. She was a good kid, a pretty girl, and very much in love with me. I loved her deeply. But other women were simply there, and I didn't hold back. People can talk themselves into almost anything if they try hard enough. It's not difficult to fool yourself.

Annie deserved better from a husband, certainly better from me. Abuse is not only a physical thing. I never abused her physically. But abuse can also be mental, spiritual, and emotional. Married men who constantly feed on the love of other women are abusing their wives, whether they think so or not. Marriages cannot survive that way, at least not good marriages.

One night soon after Annie and I were married, I was in Arizona during spring training. It was 11:00 P.M. and I was leaving my room with a suit and tie on. Tommy Davis asked me where I was going. I said I was going out. "But you just got married," he said. "What about your wife?"

My reply was typical, "Hey, man," I answered, "I'm the boss in my house." Then I took off for a night on the town.

Years later, during the winter months in Puerto Rico, I was playing conga drums with a band called Apollo Sounds. There were beautiful dancers and adoring women all over the place. There were open invitations all the time. Annie found out that

I was carrying on with one of the dancers. That was the last straw. I had played around and hurt her too many times. We fought. Finally I split.

Annie and I separated in 1970. I moved out of the house, and our divorce became final in 1973. The year after we separated, I met Nydia Fernandez, my second wife and the mother of my sons Malcolm and Ali. Nydia was from a well-to-do family. Her father was the mayor of Carolina, the town in Puerto Rico where Roberto Clemente was born. She was working for the Foundation for Retarded Children when we met at a charity function.

But even after we married in 1975, my old habits continued. Late nights, other women, the works. She went through a lot with me. She stayed with me through some tough times—my marijuana conviction, my jail sentence. But when my life went from bad to worse, so did my behavior. I was Perucho reborn.

This taxed our marriage to the limit. When my life fell further apart in the early 1980s, she took our sons and returned to Puerto Rico. It was the final blow to my dignity and self-worth.

I can't say for sure when the bad times started. My release from the Red Sox in 1974 is as good a guess as any. I became bitter and angry. Worse than that, I used my anger as an excuse to do things I would have been better off not doing.

Many ballplayers find it tough when they leave the game. You may not court the limelight, and maybe you don't even want it. You play baseball because you love it. But fame and celebrity can be seductive. They get their hooks in you whether you like it or not.

For years we are cheered, and booed. The media courts us. The crowds roar. Then one day it's gone, over. Part of your identity remains planted firmly on the baseball diamonds to play on, no roar from the crowd to hear anymore. A part of you remains empty.

For years after my career was over, when I'd watch a ballgame, I'd want to cry. When you're playing you take it for granted. Every day is a new day. When you stop, everything stands still.

Financially I was doing well. I was well-known in Puerto Rico and had made $40,000 for playing two months in Mexico before signing with Kansas City. I was a driving a Mercedes, which really caused heads to turn in Puerto Rico. My brother Pedro and I were going to establish a health spa. I played one year of winter ball back home, but it was clear I didn't have it anymore. My skills had diminished and my legs were shot.

I was thirty-six years old. I had money in my pocket, and my old friends were always there and ready for a good time. I went to discos, dated lots of good-looking girls. I was having fun. I wasn't a drinker, and the only drug I did was marijuana. I had smoked the weed as a kid, then started again in 1965.

Rock bottom began when I flew to Colombia to put on a baseball clinic. I met some people and smoked some weed. Colombia was the best for that. The clinic was on a weekend. I was shipping two big boxes full of rugs and handmade dresses back to Puerto Rico for Nydia. A friend asked if he could enclose a five-pound bag of marijuana in the box. That way they could get it through without any hassle. I saw nothing wrong with it at the time, so I agreed.

Back in San Juan, I got off the plane and went home. Ten days later I called the airport and said I was expecting some boxes from Colombia and hadn't heard anything. The freight station told me the boxes hadn't come in yet. They would let me know when they did. They had been there all the time, and they were addressed to me.

Ruben Gomez was supposed to tell me not to go near the airport or retrieve the packages. But he must have forgotten.

Finally I got a call from the airport telling me that my things were there. I never received an invoice slip saying the packages had arrived, just that one phone call from the airport.

It was late Friday and too late to go to the bank. So I called a friend named Herman and asked him to drive to the airport the next day to pick up the package. The next day I called Herman's wife, who said he'd left early that morning. When I called the airport to see if the package had been picked up, I was told that nobody had claimed it.

So I drove to the airport myself, angry as hell at Herman for letting me down. The air freight station was located in the back of the airport. The boxes should have been prepaid in

Colombia. I had given my friend there the money to ship every-thing to me before boarding my flight.

When I arrived there they said I had to pay the shipping cost. I argued that I had prepaid in Colombia. But they said that since there was no record of the transaction, I would have to pay for the shipping before they'd turn the boxes over to me.

But something strange was going on. There were two guys at the air freight counter and they started arguing back and forth. One was insisting that I had to pay the shipping cost and pay it right then. But the other guy said no. "Take it," he urged. "Let him take it and pay later." What I didn't know was that there was a policeman back there who had instructed the second guy to make sure I'd take the box with or without the money.

I argued with these guys for about two hours. Finally I agreed to pay. But they didn't take checks, and Herman hadn't arrived with the money. Since it was already close to three in the afternoon, I said I'd go home, get the money from the bank, and return Monday for the boxes.

Just as I was driving out, I saw Herman driving in. He had finally come to get the boxes. When I saw him I yelled, "Herman, keep on going!" I was mad at him for not being there when he was supposed to be.

But Herman drove in, and I followed him back to air freight. I stopped the car and got out to talk to him. I told him to forget it, to go home, that I'd go back Monday with the cash myself. I was about to walk back to my car when suddenly the boxes appeared. My back was turned, and I didn't even see the air freight guy bring them over. The next thing I knew, the police had their guns pointed at me. They were nervous, their hands were shaking. I was arrested on the spot.

It was front-page news. The media had a field day. Over-night I had become a fallen hero, a bad apple. I suppose I was set up. I believe I was. To this day, however, I'm not sure how or why. I imagine the authorities were tipped off about two boxes addressed to me. Otherwise Ruben Gomez would not have been alerted to tell me not to go to the airport. Why Ruben neglected to tell me I don't know. But I don't think that he was involved in this or knew what the stakes really were.

How quickly we fall from grace, especially in Puerto Rico. If it had happened in Los Angeles or New York, I would have been put on probation and received no jail time. The probation people in Florida assured me of that.

But with Roberto Clemente's tragic death, I had become Puerto Rico's reigning baseball hero. I had been arrested for importing marijuana with the intent to distribute it. In the eyes of many Puerto Ricans, I had disgraced my people and the memory of the great Perucho.

The incident may have been blown out of proportion. But in Puerto Rico it was serious business. And there were people determined to see that I paid the price. It was the start of a nightmare.

When I was a boy my mother told me that there is no such thing as a small enemy. All enemies are big enemies. She was right. If you want to know how mean people can be, just get yourself in trouble.

From 1975 until I went to jail in 1978, my life was a living hell I wouldn't wish on anyone. It affected all of us. My mother would get nasty phone calls. "What are you going to do now that your son is no longer a big shot?" they'd sneer. They called me all kinds of names, names she never should have to hear.

Even through the hardest of times we had always been a loving family. I still recall my father sitting in his rocker, cradling me in his arms, caressing me as he told stories about his life as a baseball player. When things really got tough for him in later years and he left the house following a huge argument with my mother, I would go see him regularly. I might have been confused, but I loved him very much and always wanted him to know that.

When I was first arrested in Puerto Rico, the authorities confiscated my Mercedes. Later when I contacted the lawyer who was working on my acquittal, he wanted to charge me $3,500 to get my car back. Because I didn't have the money to give him, I lost my car. Soon I'd lose much more in the way of dignity and self-respect.

It was a nightmare every single day for three years. People would insult and challenge me on the streets. Twice a day I'd have to sign in at court. Once I was driving to court with my mother. A guy in the next car opened his window and shouted something. My mother heard him and motioned to me just as I was reaching down for a cassette.

When we got to the courthouse, a policeman arrested me. I asked why. He said a man in a car told him that I had pulled a gun on him. I never touched a gun in my life. It took all the restraint and courage I had to walk away.

I was accused of complicity in the transporting of 170 pounds of marijuana in Puerto Rico. My lawyer really threw me to the dogs. Nobody ever showed me what they found in those boxes. No evidence was ever produced except for a few small plastic bags. My friends kept insisting that my lawyer demand that the prosecution show the full evidence being used against me, but he never did.

Some experts testified that there were traces of marijuana. They never produced five pounds, much less 170 pounds. The best they could come up with was maybe one-fourth of an ounce. The newspapers got their information from the district attorney, who gave them his own spin. One of the writers who did his best to destroy me had been close to my father. He felt I had betrayed Perucho. I was the one who felt betrayed.

Meanwhile my ex-wife Annie was after me. She wanted more money for herself and the kids. I had used all my money for legal fees, but that didn't stop her lawyer, who came after me with a vengeance. To top it off, someone else was suing me because I was unable to pay him for merchandise I'd purchased from him earlier.

So I was involved in three different trials at the same time: one for importing marijuana; another for child support and alimony; and third for not paying a bill. Some days I would go from one trial to another with hardly a break. The pressure was enormous and the stress unbearable. Things went from bad to worse.

The press had a field day. If there was something bad to say, they said it. If there was something bad to write, they wrote it.

I found out who my real friends were. Tim McCarver and Cookie Rojas worked on getting a petition on my behalf from the players. Minnie Minoso said good things about me when he was in Puerto Rico. He gave a couple of interviews, but the press never quoted him. Minnie supported me all the way, but his words were not what the press was interested in reporting.

Vic Power was different. Vic was a great defensive first baseman, maybe the best of his era. But he turned on me and made his feelings known. Vic made it a point to tell the kids in his baseball clinic not to be like Orlando Cepeda. He continued this when I was out of prison as well. Once he said these things at an Old-Timers Game in front of Orlando Jr.

I was able to draw 10,000 people to a baseball clinic near my hometown in Puerto Rico before my arrest. Now I was an outcast. All TV commercials featuring me were taken off the air. In time my name was removed from the ball fields where my three sons played ball. Even merchants turned down my business.

For three years I was an outcast at home. I was also going broke. When I retired from baseball I had some deferred money, but I never got all the money I earned playing baseball.

Finally in 1978 my case came to trial. The trial took only three days. The prosecution tried to prove that I was a dope dealer. There was never a presumption of innocence. I was found guilty and sentenced to a five-year jail term and a $10,000 fine. I would become eligible for parole in twenty months.

We appealed the case, but eventually lost. In the meantime a close friend hired me to coach a team. Because I had no money, he paid me $200 every Sunday. I had gone through all my money paying my legal fees.

The daughter of the district attorney went to the same school as Orlando Jr. They were classmates. I was told the DA was sending federal marshals to take me to *El Presidio* for the weekend. It was a tough place, but he wanted me there under lock and key until I left for Eglin Air Force Base in Ft. Walton, Florida, on Monday to begin my prison sentence.

My mother begged me to come to her house and stay there for the weekend. I told Nydia to go to her mother's home with the kids because the marshals might show up. If they didn't find me by Monday I would already be on my way to the States and the minimum security prison at Eglin.

So I went to my mother's house on Friday to wait out the weekend. It was hell. I couldn't talk to my wife or kids. Each time the phone rang, we were afraid to pick it up. My mother was in a panic. She was worried for me. The next day, Saturday, I said, "Mother, I'm going home. If they find me, then they find me. I can take it."

I went home but they never came for me. Monday I went to court to see the judge for my final instructions before going to Eglin. The district attorney detained me in a room above the courthouse during my last five hours of freedom in Puerto Rico.

I didn't even have enough money for the plane ticket. A friend had to lend me the money to buy my ticket to prison.

· 14 ·

Eglin and Beyond

O ver the years I had seen movies about prison life. One that stands out in my mind is *Cool Hand Luke*, which was released during my years with the St. Louis Cardinals. There was a prison guard who hid behind a pair of mirrored sunglasses. I don't think he said more than a few words the entire movie. He said little, saw everything, and was as mean as could be.

People often think that because Eglin was a minimum security institution and considered a "country club" among prisons, that it wasn't like being in jail. Some people in Puerto Rico were expressing resentment that I was living the good life in jail.

It wasn't the good life. It was barely life at all. Prison is prison by any name. And bullies come in all shapes and sizes, and in any type of institution. It's sad but true. There were a number of people in Puerto Rico who were disturbed that I wasn't sent to a place like *El Presidio*, where they could have their full pound of flesh.

Eglin Air Force Base is located in Ft. Walton, Florida, near the city of Pensacola. I arrived there on June 28, 1978. At the base, the press photographers started in right away. "Go ahead and take it. I'm here," I told them, their cameras flashing every other second.

I went inside. They gave me my prison garb. "You're in jail," the guard yelled. They let me know right away. The Puerto

Rican inmates were cheering me. They were proud to have me there. "Hey, Orlando, I knew your father! I watched you play."

I wasn't the first fallen celebrity to serve my time at Eglin. Because Eglin was a prison for white-collar inmates, I met some prominent people: bankers, politicians, etc. All those guys from Watergate had been there, men like Charles Colson and E. Howard Hunt.

What I found most amusing about my fellow inmates was that they all shared the same story. None of them were guilty. It was all a big mistake. Once their lawyer got things straightened out, they would be out in no time.

The more "respectable" the guy was, the less guilty he was. There was a pilot from a major airline who couldn't understand why he was there. After an overnight stop, the next day authorities found cocaine stashed on his plane.

But the longer they stayed and the more you got to know them, the stories started changing. They were really very clever, they'd tell you. In fact, they had "outwitted" everyone and could have pulled off the crime of the century except . . . They were proud of their work.

Jail is jail. They let you know everyday. Because of my name, they wanted to make sure I knew where I was. They had a choice: to treat me normally or be tough with me.

The first ten days were orientation. They had me cleaning toilets. When I wasn't doing that, I was mopping floors or throwing out garbage. They put me in a room with bunk beds. I lay down in my bunk, looking at the ceiling, thinking of my wife, my kids, my life.

This guy in the next bunk started talking. He told me he was from Philadelphia. He remembered how I killed the Phillies with my hitting and fielding. I thought, "Oh, my God, I don't want to hear about baseball." But I didn't say anything.

The more he talked, the more he sounded like he knew what he was talking about. He knew baseball. His name was Joe Trout. Joe was Italian, tall, thin, with gray hair. He knew the streets so well because he had been a detective, one of the best in Philadelphia.

He'd been sent to investigate a cigarette scam. Because they didn't pay taxes on cigarettes in Virginia, some people were making lots of money taking cigarettes into Philadelphia illegally. Joe was sent to investigate the ring and the scam. The problem was, it was such a great scam he started doing it himself. He made so much money that he flew to Las Vegas with $200,000. But he was caught and received ten months in jail.

When you're in jail, you mingle with everybody. When you're out, you remember nobody. But Joe and I have remained great friends. Later, when I was in a halfway house in Philadelphia, Joe and his wife, Pat, were like family. I will never forget him. He's one of my best friends, and I love him dearly.

Shortly after I arrived at Eglin, the warden wanted to see me. I walked into his office to find him wearing a cowboy hat with his cowboy boots up on the desk. He had a cigar in his mouth. He said, "I don't care who you are. You came here. You won't get any special treatment because you're Orlando Cepeda. Do you think I care who you are? You're a number. Remember that. You're an inmate."

I replied, "Sir, I came here to do my time and stay out of trouble."

My doctor had prescribed some vitamins for me. One day the guards found them. That same afternoon a policeman grabbed me and took me to control. They searched me—all over. They said someone told them I was dealing drugs.

You had to have a prescription for any medication. Dr. Edwards, the prison physician, was one of the most hateful men I ever met. I showed him the prescription from my doctor in Puerto Rico for my vitamins. He okayed it. One day a "hack" found them and chewed my ass. Edwards said he didn't know anything about them or where they came from.

I worked in the laundry at Eglin. We'd get there at six in the morning. I handled the towels and passed them out. The hack was a nineteen-year-old kid. He was in charge of the laundry room and thought he was pretty important.

His father was also a policeman there. When I called the kid by his first name, he shot back at me, "Call me 'Sir!' If you call me by my first name again, you'll spend three days in the hole." From then on he was "Sir." Forty years old, and I'm calling this kid in a uniform "Sir." That was punishment.

My caseworker's last name was Clark. When I first met him

he was like a saint, the nicest human being. The next day, however, he changed completely. He was a mean, nasty man. I was getting too much attention, he felt. He was fed up because I was receiving baseball cards through the mail that people wanted autographed. He insisted that I send them back, but he couldn't enforce this because it was against the law.

There were plenty of softball tournaments at Eglin. One Saturday a policeman came in and said, "Orlando, some people want to see you." Saturday was my day to relax, and that's what I usually did. But I agreed to go.

There were two lines. The inmates were not to talk to anybody, not to say as much as "hello." But players started asking me for autographs. I signed a few. Then a guy came up and yelled in my face. "What the hell do you think you're doing here? Don't you know you're a number? Don't you know you have no rights?" He was in my face, yelling at me in front of everyone.

That did it. I yelled back at him that one of the policemen had asked me to be there as a favor. That's what was so rough, the constant humiliation. It was everyday. When a high-ranking Air Force officer came to the base, they'd usually want to see me. One in particular was a huge Cardinals fan. The hacks had a hard time dealing with that.

So that's how it was. I wore prison clothes. I barely slept at all except on weekends. Except for my wife, I hated to have people visit me. Dusty Baker offered me money to help out. He even sent Orlando Jr. a Dodgers jacket. Dusty's father had been a big Giants' fan, and when Dusty joined the Braves as a nineteen-year-old rookie, we'd become close friends.

It was Brian David, a Chicago attorney, who saved my skin. In many ways he saved my life. He was able to reduce my parole time and get me released from Eglin in ten months. Brian was introduced to my case by Cookie Rojas and a friend named Fred Sosa.

Brian came to my parole hearing in Florida. I was told not to bring an attorney, but that seemed silly to me. At the hearing two of the parole board members were big Cardinals fans. When they opened up my Presenting Investigation Report and saw there had been no real evidence presented against me at trial, they told me I could go home. The sentence reduction and the process that led to my early release is somewhat complicated. Here's how Brian David explains it:

> When I went to Puerto Rico on Orlando's behalf, there were people who supported him, but many people were against him. He'd gone from being a hero to an outcast.
>
> Here in the United States, it was a small matter. But down there it was huge. I'm not talking sports headlines. It was front-page stuff. People felt so let down. When we filed motions, I saw that attitude in the district attorney.
>
> The judge did agree to sentence him under another statute that did not allow a mandatory term before you were eligible for parole. Under the original section he was sentenced on, he was sentenced to five years, and it was mandatory that he serve twenty months to be eligible for parole.
>
> But when the judge agreed to the other statute, there was no minimum time served for parole eligibility. Theoretically, the parole board could grant parole anytime. It was a big victory for us to get him sentenced under the other statute.
>
> So when we went to the parole board, we felt we had a good chance. Also, the parole hearing was in Florida, not Puerto Rico. After the board heard his case, Orlando was released. He had served ten months.

That was not the only time Brian David came to my rescue. Since Eglin was a minimum security prison, inmates were granted furloughs for good behavior. Once I went on furlough to meet my wife in New York. Angel Cordero, the jockey, bought me the ticket. A friend was taking me to the airport to get back to Eglin, but he was late, and I missed my plane. I was in big trouble. They throw you in the hole for things like that. So I called Brian and asked him to meet my plane. He made a few phone calls, and a friend of mine picked me up. It was four o'clock in the morning.

Anyway, the day came when I was to be released. I had called my wife earlier to tell her the good news. "Listen, we're going to have Christmas together," I told her. But the district attorney in Puerto Rico had a personal vendetta against me.

He told the warden in Florida that as soon as I stepped on Puerto Rican soil, the Mafia was going to kill me. Since I still had to put in some time at a halfway house, the DA made it clear that they didn't want me in Puerto Rico. He put me in the same category as two other guys who were considered too undesirable to return home. The other two were murderers. The upshot was that I had to stay at Eglin for a while more, until I could show a way of making money.

Joe Trout had recently been released from Eglin and was back in Philadelphia. He wrote a statement saying that I was going to work for him. This ensured my release. So after serving ten months, I left the minimum security facility. I went to live in a halfway house in Philadelphia and work for Joe.

From April 19, 1979, until early June, I lived in the halfway house. It was part of the program. My wife and kids came from Puerto Rico and stayed with Joe. I would go to work for Joe each morning, then return at night. Joe paid me $125 a week to do public relations and sales work. He was like a brother to me.

It was quite an experience. There was a lady at the halfway house who woke us up at five in the morning. "Hi, love," she'd say. "It's five o'clock!" If you didn't get up and wanted a few more winks, she'd change her tone. She'd yell, "Goddamnit, it's five o'clock!" Then five minutes later, it was, "You son of a bitch, get up!" She was really very nice. She just had to do her job.

After returning from Joe's at ten in the evening, I'd kick my shoes off and go to sleep. I was so exhausted, I'd usually sleep in my clothes.

The day I was scheduled to leave the halfway house and go into the real world, I was so excited. I got up at five in the morning ready to leave just as soon as I could. But then I was told not to leave yet.

Mr. Kirkland, the head of the unit, wanted to see me. So I went upstairs. I was told I had to wait. I sure waited. It was six, seven, eight o'clock, and I had yet to see him.

Four more hours passed. Finally around noon I asked when Mr. Kirkland was due to arrive. "Oh, he's not coming," I was told. When I asked why, a woman who worked for him said he was out of town.

I said, "What do you mean? He's supposed to talk to me." About three o'clock that afternoon, a girl came in and said they were sending me back to Eglin because I was working with a felon—Joe Trout. I told them that they had known this all along, and the fact that I was working for Joe was far from a secret. Now they wanted to send me back to jail for three months.

Of course, I called Brian David immediately. He came out the next day. We went to court once again. The district attorney brought a piece of paper and was asking me some questions. They were questions the DA in Puerto Rico had sent to him, but the presiding judge saw no merit to these questions. He dismissed the case. I was officially released on April 15, 1979, and was free to go back to Puerto Rico.

When I got out some baseball people wanted me to coach in Puerto Rico. I coached Bayamon in the winter league. I worked with some good players: Dickie Thon, who went on to star with the Astros and the Phillies; Dave Bergman, also with the Astros; pitcher Ed Solomon; and former major leaguer Luis Arroyo.

Emotionally and mentally I was far from healed. There were lots of lingering scars. The ordeal of being arrested, convicted, and imprisoned for almost a year had taken a big toll on me. Moreover, Puerto Rico was far from friendly to me. In fact, my life was still a nightmare.

Looking back today, I don't know how I managed to get through everything. I was in the newspaper every single day. One day Orlando Jr., who was ten at the time, was playing ball with his team. "Dad," he asked me, "Could you work out with my team?" So one day I did. The coach said he didn't want me on the same field with him. People continued to call my mother, laughing and taunting her that I was no longer a big star.

Brian David arranged a meeting for me in Chicago with Roland Hemond of the White Sox. Roland offered me $17,000 to be a scout and batting coach for the Chicago White Sox in 1981. I am very grateful to Roland. One of the reasons he hired me was to help make me more visible to the baseball world at large. He wanted to give me a chance to redeem myself in the world of baseball.

But I was still in bad shape and getting worse. I had become my own worst enemy, and I blew the assignment. I blasted

Roland Hemond when he let me go, and I am very sorry for doing that. It was uncalled for, and I said things I shouldn't have. The White Sox organization, Bill Veeck, Tony LaRussa, and Roland were all good to me. I just wasn't ready mentally.

I was still working for the White Sox when I got the news that my mother was very ill. I flew to Puerto Rico and was at her side when she died. She had waited for me to arrive.

My mother's death was a terrible blow. She was a wonderful human being who gave so much of herself. She didn't have a selfish bone in her body, and she provided a stability in my life that was often otherwise lacking. She was sixty-nine when she passed away in 1981. I'm sure the years of stress and worry that followed my arrest robbed her of many more valuable years.

As a roving instructor with the White Sox I was sent to Lynn, Massachusetts, to work with one of their minor league teams. I was staying at a lousy hotel, a typical minor league place. My mother was on my mind all the time. I cried for three days.

One day I took a bus to Boston. I walked around the city where a decade earlier I'd played my last big season. The streets looked lonely now, especially around Fenway Park. Ten years before I had been a hero here. I was the American League's first Designated Hitter of the Year. My eyes swelled with tears. How far I had fallen.

And I was to fall further still. I went back to Puerto Rico to coach at Santurce and was fired again. The owner of the ballclub felt my conviction and sentence had disgraced my homeland and the memory of Perucho. I was going in the wrong direction. I started hanging around a lot with my old boyhood pals. My marriage was in big trouble. I didn't have much money, and I was going broke quick. To make ends meet for the family, I started to sell off some of my valuable trophies and awards, including one from *The Sporting News*.

In 1982 I attended the All-Star Game in Montreal, the first All-Star Game played outside the United States. It was quite a thrill because of the Game's international flavor. Former major leaguers like myself, born outside the continental United States, were asked to represent our respective countries.

I was there to represent Puerto Rico. Minnie Minoso

represented Cuba; Luis Aparicio represented Venezuela; Juan Marichal, the Dominican Republic; and Bobby Avila, Mexico.

The next year I attended the All-Star Game in Chicago at Comiskey Park. Then I flew to Los Angeles for an Old-Timers Game and stayed with Dusty Baker. After I returned to Puerto Rico, I got a call to play in an Old-Timers Game in Denver. My wife was having a hard time with my constant coming and going. It put an added strain on the marriage. I realized then that my mother was dead, and there was nothing to keep me in Puerto Rico. The baseball community in Puerto Rico was far more hostile than in the US. There was no longer a way for me to make a living in my homeland. It was then that I decided to move the family to the United States for good.

Because I was still on probation, I was told to check in with the probation office in Los Angeles. The woman there was named Sara Moore. Her husband was a big baseball fan. She went to bat for me, writing letters to Philadelphia and Washington to see if I could finish my probation in Los Angeles because baseball was my business and the available opportunities were there and not in Puerto Rico.

I returned to Puerto Rico and told the authorities I would be moving to the US. I had called the probation office in Puerto Rico a month before. Eventually they let me go, but they didn't let me go without a hassle.

First they told me I couldn't go. Brian David flew in and explained that I had a right to leave Puerto Rico because baseball was my livelihood. Just then another bombshell hit. One of my ex-girlfriends came out of the woodwork and slapped me with a paternity suit and child support.

Her name was Nilda. While I was in jail she'd started writing me. She kept saying how much she admired me, and that she wanted to have a baby with me. Lots of things like that. The red light should have gone on in my head instantly. But she was enticing, and when I got out of jail, I foolishly went out with her. What a big mistake.

The DA in San Juan wanted to send me back to jail because I couldn't pay her child support. My heart would sink further into my stomach every time I'd see a policeman near the house.

My wife had second thoughts about moving to Los Angeles. She was afraid of the freeways and the crime. I told her again that there was nothing left for me in Puerto Rico, and I was going to move to LA one way or another. She agreed to come with the boys once I got settled. I was still on probation, but Brian David, my attorney, flew to Puerto Rico and interceded in the paternity suit. He convinced the authorities that baseball was my livelihood and that the only way I could continue to make a living was in the US.

I arrived in Los Angeles in June 1984. The apartment I rented in Burbank wasn't particularly nice, lower middle class at best. It was quite a step down for Nydia, who came from a prominent family. It was a step down for me too. A month later she arrived with Malcolm and Ali. But by this time our marriage was reduced to fights and shouting matches. Finally she'd had enough. She left me. She took our sons and returned to Puerto Rico. It was a sad day. As with so many things in life, I never realized what I had in Nydia until it was too late.

Orlando Jr. stayed with me. He gave me support and understanding. I would cook for us and let him use the car when he needed it. He was in college and quite a baseball player. As a high school athlete at Burbank High, he had been All-City in both baseball and basketball.

I tried to open a baseball camp in Los Angeles, but no one signed up. I had no real source of income anymore, and nowhere else to go. Puerto Rico was clearly out of the question. Here at least people were still nice to me.

My mother was gone. My wife and children had left. I was bitter and angry, and my self-respect had vanished. I'd occasionally go to a baseball game when some of my old friends, like Tony Perez, were playing against the Dodgers. One afternoon in 1984 I was on the field at Dodger Stadium talking to some of the players. Someone upstairs took notice and sent a security guard down to ask for my field credentials. They knew who I was. When I said I'd never needed field credentials before, I was told I had to leave the ballpark immediately. The Dodgers even sent a memo to all their ballplayers forbidding them to have any contact with me.

I returned to my apartment as close to a broken man as I have ever been. Many things passed through my mind. The possibility of ending my life seemed quite real, at least for a minute or two.

I needed something bigger, stronger than myself. This I knew. I had been introduced to the practice of Buddhism a year earlier. Buddhism had helped me over some tough times, but I hadn't embraced it with the necessary zeal. Suddenly I knew I had to pursue it with totality and dedication. It would take work, real work—maybe even more work than becoming a major league ballplayer.

As a youngster headed for trouble in Puerto Rico, it was baseball that saved my life. Now, as an adult, it was Buddhism that would give me the tools to change my life's direction. I am fortunate that it was there. And with practice and patience, things started turning around.

• 15 •

The Miracle of Buddhism

The story of my life cannot be written without paying deference to Buddhism. More than baseball, more than the home runs and runs batted in, more than the Rookie of the Year Award and the National League MVP, Buddhism helped make me what I am today. I say this because all the records and cheers and the celebrity do not, and did not, create inner peace. Buddhism saved me spiritually and gave me the tools to turn my pain into medicine. It has helped me make myself a far better human being. And in doing so, it has made me a better husband, father, and friend.

It is not an easy practice, make no mistake. Nor does it work overnight. It takes a long time, because the necessary changes must come from inside. Through practice and guidance you feel the happiness from within. Anyone can feel happy when life is going well. But there is also real happiness in learning how to deal with problems as they unfold.

Today my practice is very serious to me. It's number one. The first five years of serious Buddhism are usually very rough. You're cleaning your own life, purging yourself of negativity and weakness. Today I chant every morning for an hour and a half, then maybe half an hour in the evening. It's become a ritual. It gives me a joy that is difficult to explain and a contentment I never experienced before.

That's a long way from where I was in 1982. I had gone to Los Angeles to do a baseball camp. A friend named Rudy Regalado, an outstanding musician who plays drums with

Herbie Hancock, saw me and was shocked. "Orlando," he said, "You don't look the same. What's happened to you?" He gave me a magazine and recommended I read it. Herbie Hancock, he told me, followed these teachings, and so do Tina Turner and Patrick Duffy. Their lives have changed tremendously for the better.

This was my introduction to Buddhism and the teachings of Nichiren Daishonin. What Rudy saw was a beaten man, maybe worse than even I was aware of at the time. Sure, the cheers were there when I appeared at Old-Timers Games. Bob Hunter wrote a beautiful article about me. So did the *Los Angeles Times* a couple of years later. I might have been putting on a good face for others, but inside I was drowning.

There was no inner peace. I was struggling financially, and except for a few appearances at Old-Timers Games and baseball camps, there was little left to hold on to. Then when I was thrown out of Dodger Stadium, it fell apart completely. I wanted nothing to do with baseball anymore.

I had been attending Buddhist meetings for more than a year. I was skeptical at first. Although I was a Catholic, I had dabbled in other faiths, ideas, and religious philosophies for a number of years. Yet none had ever changed my life. It was hard to convince myself that Buddhism would work, especially since other religions had not. The chanting was new to me, but it was a growing process. The more I did it, the more I began seeing results. I received my *Gohonzon* (scroll) on April 17, 1983. When I returned to Puerto Rico, Nydia was puzzled. "What the hell is that?" she wanted to know. Since I had dabbled in a number of faiths over the years, Nydia thought Buddhism and the *Gohonzon* was just another passing fad.

By now, a year later, she was gone. As luck would have it, Nydia was living in Puerto Rico when Nilda, the woman who wrote me in jail and bore my child, decided to pay her a visit. She brought the five-year-old boy with her. She told my wife that I was his father and that I had been in love with her. That finished our marriage. My reckless ways had caught up to me once again.

I told Nydia that I was grateful she found out, even if it had to be like this. It was like a weight that had been lifted from my shoulders. I would not have to hide it from my wife anymore. I wanted to stay together and really try to work things out, but Nydia was determined not to return to Los Angeles.

That was the lowest point in my life, even lower than prison. I was empty. I had no money, no full-time job. I called the Giants and asked Al Rosen if there was any work I could do for the club. They said they'd let me know. They never did. I didn't understand what was happening to my life. I had nowhere to go.

Then one night I was introduced to a man named Al Albergate. He did media relations as a press secretary for the Los Angeles County district attorney and really knew the ropes. The more I listened to him, the more confidence I began to have.

After Nydia took off to Puerto Rico, Al Albergate and another fellow named Bob Butts really guided me. They never let me stew in my own misery. They introduced me to a guy named Bruce who had gone through a similar ordeal. He helped me quite a bit. These people befriended me not as Orlando Cepeda the baseball player but as a man who was in trouble. That winter I went to a large gathering in Long Beach. Herbie Hancock was there. So was Tina Turner. It was an exhilarating experience and another turning point in my life.

I told Al I was through with baseball. Baseball had rejected me, and I wanted to return the favor. He helped me see that I could never be through with baseball. Baseball was what I loved. Baseball was how I'd always made my living. It was what I did best.

He assured me that with the proper work and practice, I could turn my pain to medicine. Once that happened, I'd be back in baseball, back where I belonged. I'd feel the love and hear the cheers once again. Only this time I would appreciate them even more. It would require hard work on my part and a firm belief that this day would come. When that day came, he assured me, I would be ready.

Al Albergate recalls meeting me that first fateful night:

> I met Orlando shortly before he became a practicing Buddhist. At the time, a mutual friend who was also practicing Buddhism

brought him to my house in West Los Angeles. I began practicing in 1973. I was, and still am, a lay leader in the Soka Gakkai
International (SGI). That's why he was introduced to me.

Because I was a baseball fan, I knew who he was and had
some recollections of him having some difficulty with the
law. One thing I remember is that he didn't smile very much at
that time. We were able to talk, and we met together a number
of times after that, either at my house or at Buddhist discus-
sion meetings.

We hit it off well. Once he decided he was going to practice
Buddhism, he took it very seriously and really devoted himself.
Buddhism is a religion of great hope, a hope of happiness in
this lifetime.

The change in Orlando didn't occur overnight. Orlando
tended to have a very serious demeanor. Gradually, he began
to lighten up, to get more excited about his life, and to turn
things around.

When he was campaigning for the Hall of Fame a few years
ago, it was obvious that he had regained hope and confidence
in himself. He truly has turned his life around. He's worked
through so many things himself and shares this spirit with
others. He uses his celebrity status to help people. He has a
real gift.

Because my practice is so important and such an integral
part of my life, I want to say a few words about Buddhism as
taught by Nichiren Daishonin.

Daishonin's wisdom is that we each possess the potential
for a winning life. It's within each of us to live with courage,
find fulfilling relationships, enjoy good health and prosperity,
to feel real compassion for others, and find the power to face
and surmount our deepest problems. This enables us to bring
out our highest human qualities and allows us to best change
our circumstances.

Buddhism is a way of life, a complete and dedicated way of
life. To a Buddhist, self-improvement and enhancement of our
circumstances go hand in hand. It's of no advantage to blame
others for our own failings. It was my own bitterness, anger,

and hate that hurt me the most. Before I practiced Buddhism, I used to blame everybody for what happened to me: the district attorney in Puerto Rico, baseball people, etc. I even felt guilty about my mother's death.

Through my practice I've learned that winning in life is not the absence or avoidance of problems. They will always be there. To be human by its very nature means we will encounter problems and obstacles regularly. Once I was able to channel this poison into medicine, I acquired the tools to take on whatever life presents me, each and every hurdle, and become stronger and wiser in the process.

It helped me to be philosophical rather than bitter in being denied Hall of Fame honors in 1994. I had learned to take the good with the bad and to put the past behind me. By then I was able to say, "I was a baseball player. People tell me how many thrills I gave them." This is what makes me feel wonderful. I now feel blessed that I was able to play ball and that I'm still in baseball. I'm a lucky man regardless of what happened.

Chanting enables me to experience the energy and wisdom that best fulfills my life. Unlike most western religions, when we chant, we are not praying to an external deity possessing human qualities. Our prayers are realized because we bring forth from within ourselves the wisdom to correct our actions. Yet there are some people who hold this against me because they confuse my practice with atheism. Nothing could be further from the truth.

I was happy when TV programs like *Up Close* with Roy Firestone, *Good Morning America*, and the *Today Show* asked some telling questions about my practice. There was a segment with Joe Garagiola on the *Today Show* that gave me the chance to talk candidly about Buddhism and how it changed my life.

Having had two failed marriages and enough domestic turmoil to last three lifetimes, the last thing I was looking for was a full-time girlfriend. But that's exactly when Mirian Ortiz entered my life.

She had come to Los Angeles from New York and was supervising a tour to Universal Studios. A friend of hers knew me and was planning to introduce us. When she heard she was going to meet Orlando Cepeda, she was thrilled. After all, she was Puerto Rican. She knew I was a former Latin baseball star and assumed I was living comfortably and was well off.

Of course, I wasn't. The neighborhood I lived in wasn't great. My couch was a hand-me-down from one friend, my desk and dining room table were from another. Financially, things were far from good. Nevertheless, none of these things seemed to matter to her. She too had a tough life. Sixteen years younger than me, she'd made it through much of her life on her own with a child.

We had a great time together. She returned to New York, but a short time later I asked her to come back to Los Angeles for a couple of weeks so we could get to know each other better.

She came all right—with about fifteen suitcases. We have not been apart since, and today we are happily married. Mirian was good to me—and for me—from the beginning. She put my house in order. She bought groceries and literally saved pennies with us. She was wonderful to Orlando Jr. and my other children. She gave warmth and love to a heart that was hurt and empty. My life was finally starting to change.

I had worked hard to make things better, and better things were starting to happen. In Buddhism, our faith is based on experience. Faith almost always begins as hope or an expectation that something will happen. At the start of my journey, I was willing to try the practice and anticipate some result. Because these changes develop brick by brick, I have seen actual proof of what my practice has given me.

Today many religions lack the ability to truly empower people to change. That's why people like me have benefited so much from Buddhism. And we are far from alone. Today there are some twelve million practitioners of Nichiren Daishonin's Buddhism in 128 countries.

For sixty-eight years now, this Buddhism has been widely accessible through the efforts of the Soka Gakkai, a lay Buddhist Society based on Daishonin's teachings. Through the Soka Gakkai International (SGI), President Daisaku Ikeda lectures at some of the world's most prestigious centers of higher learning, such as Harvard, Moscow State University, and Beijing University.

Mr. Ikeda has also founded the Soka schools, an educational system from kindergarten to postgraduate studies. Its purpose is based on respect for human dignity, and its aim is to nurture people of wisdom and humanity who will contribute positively to the realization of a peaceful world. In 1996, for example, Daisaku Ikeda gave a commemorative lecture at the Simon Wiesenthal Center in a solemn ceremony to remember the victims of the Holocaust. Standing in front of a majestic eighteen-foot white marble menorah in the Memorial Plaza, Mr. Ikeda lit the Flame of Remembrance. No wonder I'm so proud to be a part of this organization.

My practice was bringing me inner peace, and it helped to make me receptive to a woman like Mirian. Now it would finally help lead me back to baseball. I was on my way. Not just back to baseball but back to the San Francisco Giants, to the team where it had all started nearly thirty years ago.

· 16 ·

Return to San Francisco

Three people were largely responsible for my return to the baseball scene in San Francisco. The first was Max Shapiro, who invited me to participate in his fantasy baseball camps, where fans have a chance to train and play with former major league stars. The second was Laurence Hyman, publisher and creative director of Woodford Publishing. The third was Pat Gallagher, Giants vice president. Of course, none of this would have been possible had Bob Lurie, the owner of the San Francisco Giants at the time, not given me the opportunity to return to baseball.

When I was living in Puerto Rico, Shapiro approached me to come to Arizona for a baseball camp. It was 1981 and I didn't want to deal with baseball then. Max offered me $1,000, but I told him that wasn't enough and if he wanted me he'd have to pay me $2,500. That was it. I didn't hear from him again until 1987.

That's when I received another call from Max. Willie McCovey was ill and couldn't attend Max's fantasy camp. He needed a replacement for Willie Mac and asked me if I would attend in his place. At first I said no, but I changed my mind. I was in the process of moving from Los Angeles to Roseville in Northern California. The same day I arrived in Roseville, I took a flight to Arizona to attend Max's camp. Max was great. He introduced me to many people, one of whom was Pat Gallagher, who was participating as a player.

In the meantime, Laurence Hyman was setting out to do a series of interviews of former baseball greats. He had managed to locate me in Los Angeles when I was totally out of baseball and generally friendless in the baseball world. We met for the first time at a charity game between the 1962 Los Angeles Dodgers and the 1962 San Francisco Giants.

Laurence and I became fast friends. We talked off and on throughout the game and discovered we had a lot of common interests, especially a passion for jazz. Laurence played trumpet and I played conga drums. Later we played gigs together, once even jamming with a bunch of guys in the band Santana. He tells people that I can really play those congas well, which I must admit I can.

But we also talked about baseball, lots of baseball. In fact, the interview extended to the next day. He did a beautiful story, but more importantly than that our friendship continued. Laurence kept urging me to move back to the Bay Area. I didn't think it was a good idea at first. I was concerned about how I might be received. I'd been hurt enough, and I felt pretty much forgotten by the world of baseball. San Francisco was special, and I was afraid that I had long since worn out my welcome.

But I had occasion to visit the Bay Area. On one visit Laurence insisted on taking me to a Giants game. My knees were knocking. I had never been so nervous, although Laurence says that I kept up a good front. I had never experienced a Giants game as a fan.

We did this a number of times, and gradually I was introduced to the people Laurence knew within the Giants organization. Soon I was reunited with some of the people I had known but lost contact with over the years.

Meanwhile, Laurence continued to encourage me to try to find my way back with the club. He felt I had a lot to say and a lot to do that would be beneficial to the club. The team could utilize me in a number of ways, he insisted. He saw how people came up to me in the stands, not just to ask for an autograph but also to tell me how important I was to them. Laurence truly felt that the organization and I had been estranged for too long. It was time to get back together, he kept telling me.

Laurence brought me back into circulation. He encouraged me to contact the Giants, to write directly to Al Rosen. I had written him a couple of times before with no luck. But this time I received a reply. Pat Gallagher called to tell me that Al would like me to do some work for the club. A short time later my employment began.

I cannot say enough about Pat. Like Bill Rigney in the 1950s, Pat was in my corner from the very beginning when we first met at Max's fantasy camp. Pat, who had been with the Giants for more than twenty years now, helped persuade Al Rosen and Bob Lurie to give me a second chance.

Over the years, Pat has supported me all the way, both professionally and personally. I opened a baseball camp for kids in the late 1980s. Laurence Hyman printed my promotional material, and Pat Gallagher made sure we always had enough equipment. I also had help from Vida Blue, Juan Marichal, Dusty Baker, Jose Pagan, and others. A kid can have all the talent in the world, but you have to learn to play the game when you are young if you want to go on to college and the pros.

My first year back with the Giants I was not on the payroll per se. I was paid by individual assignment. The Giants kept me busy, sending me to Mexico, the Dominican Republic, and other parts of Latin America to scout and help develop young players.

The following year I asked Pat how I was doing. He said, "Great!" Then he told me the good news. The Giants were very pleased with my work, and they wanted me on payroll full time. I would be doing community relations for the team in the Bay Area and reach-out work across the country as a goodwill ambassador. In all cases, I would be working with and talking with kids. That made me very happy.

Like Pat Gallagher, few people have been as kind to me as Peter Magowan. Here is an owner and club president quite unique among the people that run baseball today. He's more concerned about the fans and the state of the game itself than he is about the big buck. Sure, he wants to produce a winner, and he's an astute businessman, but as an enormous fan himself, he cares deeply about the people who buy the tickets and go to the games. He's also a hands-on team president who knows the names of everyone in the organization.

Peter Magowan, Pat Gallagher, and Bob Rose, the Giants' vice president of communications, have been in my corner for years now. We are all great friends. It's so rare in a world of big bucks, business, and backstabbers to find gentlemen as fine as these three.

I was in the stands at Candlestick Park in 1987 for the National League playoff series when the Giants came within one game of the National League title, losing the National League Championship Series to the St. Louis Cardinals 4 games to 3. Two years later I watched as the Giants took the National League title, then were swept in the World Series by Tony LaRussa's outstanding Oakland A's.

One of the nicest things that's ever happened to me was being asked to throw out the first ball in the third game of the 1989 National League Championship Series against the Chicago Cubs. It was just as Al Albergate had said it would be a few years earlier. One day I'd hear those cheers again. One day baseball would welcome me back with respect and with honor. That day was October 8, 1989, and the cheers were from over 60,000 fans at Candlestick Park. There were tears in my eyes.

I was fifty-two years old, and I was back on my own field of dreams. The game would open shortly, and the Giants' Jeff Brantley would take to the mound against the Chicago Cubs' Rick Sutcliffe. But this one moment was mine. So many things crossed my mind. I thought of Perucho, "The Babe Ruth of Puerto Rico," one of the best ballplayers ever. He would have been so proud. I had come back. But even more important, I had beaten that ominous shadow that he hadn't been fortunate enough to escape. Then there was my mother, Carmen. How happy she would have been to see me back on track. Her tears might stop. I had finally outrun my environment. And this time it was for good.

The Giants kept me busy. There were countless visits to schools, community centers, and hospitals. There were so many kids to talk to, so many people to tell that life does offer a second chance, not to give up.

My sons were growing up. Orlando Jr., Malcolm, and Ali were good-looking boys and superb athletes. Orlando Jr. was twenty and had been drafted as a pitcher by the Montreal Expos. He chose to stay in college instead and attend College of the Canyon in Valencia, California. Malcolm was fifteen and already being tagged with a can't-miss label. Each time I'd look at him, I'd see my father. And Ali was growing up to be a strapping lad right before my eyes.

All these good things were a by-product of Buddhism and

my practice. So is my son Carl. I mentioned him briefly earlier. Now I can tell you the whole story.

In 1962 we were playing the Dodgers in Los Angeles. A very pretty girl from the San Fernando Valley was with a group of girls. After the game she approached me for an autograph. She was tall and looked far older than sixteen.

We talked for a while and met a couple of times after that. Following the 1962 World Series I went to Los Angeles to see Sammy Davis Jr. for a little vacation with my wife Annie. While I was there I went out. A friend of mine had pre-arranged a meeting with this girl.

When Annie and I returned to Puerto Rico I called the girl. She told me she was pregnant. Her father, of course, was furious. His attorney came after me with a vengeance and asked for $50,000 cash or he would call the newspapers.

That night I was doing *The Steve Allen Show* on television. I was on with Maury Wills. Maury was playing the banjo, and I was playing the drums. The attorney knew I was there; he came to the show and waited for me. He told me it was a shame that a black guy was dating a white girl, that I should be ashamed of myself, and that he would break me by calling the press and the Giants' front office.

Her parents wanted to hurt me, but the attorney wanted to destroy me. But the girl intervened. She told her parents that if they continued to try to punish me, she was going to disappear.

I talked to her after she had the baby. She told me it was a boy. Carl was born on July 4, 1963. Orlando Jr.'s godfather in San Francisco offered to take care of the baby. So did my mother. She wanted to raise him. But the girl's father said no. The baby was put up for adoption immediately.

Carl was adopted by a black family in Los Angeles. While he was growing up, people told him he looked far more Latin than he did black. Although he knew he had been adopted, he was sure both his biological parents were black. As time went on, he wanted to know who his biological parents were. In 1993 he started his search.

He spent a lot of money and time poring over documents in the courthouse. Somebody who worked for a judge and knew of the case saw how serious and determined he was and decided to help.

Eventually he found out that his father was a black Latin baseball player and that his mother was American and Jewish. Exactly who that ballplayer was, he didn't know. But there weren't that many around the National League in 1962. They also determined that the father most likely played for the Los Angeles Dodgers or the San Francisco Giants. So that limited the choices even further.

Finally, in 1995, Carl was able to find the identity of his mother and learned that she was still living in LA. He called her, and they agreed to meet. Not at her home, but at a neighborhood park. That's when she told him who his biological father was.

They met one more time. This time she told Carl that she couldn't have anything to do with him. She was married and had other children. Her husband's racial attitudes would never understand. She couldn't see Carl anymore.

About three years ago, he sent me a registered letter. I had been chanting to find my son for some time. I knew I had a son, and I knew his age. When I opened the letter and saw his mother's name I started crying. "Orlando," he wrote, "I don't want anything from you. I'm just happy that I found my father. You don't have to give me anything. You don't have to call me if you don't want to."

As soon as I got the letter I gave him a call. His wife, Charmaine, was the one who pushed him to find me. So when I called that afternoon she was screaming. That's how happy she was. A couple of days later they came to see me.

I was nervous. But from the start I could see what a gem he was. I'm so fortunate and so happy. He's a wonderful kid. He's a professional with a great job, and his wife is almost a doctor now.

Carl told me that when he met his mother in the park she kissed and hugged him. She was crying. But she wouldn't see him again. Anyone would be proud to have him as a son. He looks like me too. We're very close today.

My life had become so much richer. My personal life was full of joy. And the baseball world had rediscovered Orlando Cepeda. Some writers were even using the words I hadn't heard in years: Hall of Fame.

• 17 •

The Latin Legacy

The story of my life both in and out of baseball cannot be told apart from my culture and heritage. Unfortunately, the full, true story of the Latin ballplayer in the United States has not been written. Far too often the media has ignored us as a dynamic force in the history of Major League Baseball.

The bad rap many Latin players have had over the years has been unfair. Try to imagine a kid in the 1950s, a teenage boy in a new country. He hopes to compete against the best baseball players in the world, but he can't communicate in his new country's language. And if you were black during that time, the problems were amplified many times over.

When I first came to the United States, almost all the Latin ballplayers in the major leagues had been white Cubans. And no one was better than Dolf Luque, who made his major league debut with the Boston Braves in 1914. Called "The Prince of Havana," Dolf Luque pitched twenty years in the majors, winning 194 games and twice leading the National League in ERA. His best season was with the Cincinnati Reds in 1923, when he went 27–8 with an ERA of 1.93.

I was very disappointed when Ken Burns's PBS baseball special barely mentioned Major League Baseball's Latin connection. I'm not sure the name Minnie Minoso was even mentioned once. Minnie was as important to the Latin player major league aspirations as Jackie Robinson was to the black player.

Minnie, baseball's only six-decade player, had his first major league turn at bat in 1949, just two years after Jackie broke the color barrier. By 1951 he had become one of baseball's most exciting players. Just take a look at his record. However, outside Chicago, where he is a Windy City icon, he is barely recognized as Major League Baseball's black Latin pioneer.

From 1951 through 1961, Minnie led the American League in triples three times, in stolen bases three times, doubles once, base hits once, and total bases once. He batted over .300 eight times, was among the American League's top five hitters five different times, and won three Gold Gloves.

Just ask guys like Tony Oliva or Jose Cardenal what Minnie Minoso meant to them when they were growing up, and what a true inspiration he was to them during their own struggles.

Minnie became the first black Cuban to be a big-league star. He suffered a lot of pain along the way, though he doesn't discuss it publicly. He had one of the best rookie seasons ever in 1951, yet the Baseball Writers of America named Gil McDougald of the New York Yankees the American League Rookie of the Year. But to complain is not Minnie's way. It never has been. He let his ability and his accomplishments speak for themselves.

We Latin players, both black and white, had it rough. Talk to Chico Carresquel, who came to this country from Venezuela at age twenty-two to star for the Chicago White Sox in the early 1950s. Chico became the first Latin American to start an All-Star Game when he took the field for the American League at shortstop in 1951.

He arrived in the United States almost penniless. What little money he had he used to buy his baseball mitt and other equipment. In fact, Chico's language problems were so great at the time that Luis Aloma, the Cuban-born White Sox pitcher, became Chico's full-time translator while he accumulated a 13–2 record as the team's top relief pitcher in 1950 and 1951.

Chico was considered the best shortstop in baseball in the early 1950s, and he was a four-time American League All-Star. But today's Latin athletes most likely have never heard of Chico Carresquel. He paved the way for the great Latin shortstops of the future, but he's barely a footnote in the history of the game today.

That's just the tip of the iceberg. We paved the way, and today the major leagues are full of outstanding young Latin stars—and the list is growing longer. It's been a long, hard journey from Minnie Minoso in the 1950s to Livan Hernandez in the 1990s.

As one friend recently said to me, it's getting so you can't tell your Gonzalezes from your Rodriguezes. Then mix in a few Martinezes and Hernandezes and see what you get: talented and outstanding players such as the Texas Rangers' young All-Stars Juan Gonzalez and Ivan Rodriguez; Seattle's Alex Rodriguez; Boston's Pedro Martinez; and Atlanta's Nicaragua-born Dennis Martinez, who at age forty-three broke Juan Marichal's record for major league wins by a Latin pitcher.

Of all the Latin countries, Cuba had a head start in delivering ballplayers to the major leagues, although until the breakthrough of Minnie Minoso all were at least nominally white.

The Cincinnati Reds signed two Cuban ballplayers as early as 1911: infielder Rafael Almeida and outfielder Armondo Marsons. Almeida played three years with the Reds and hit .270. Marsons, a speedy outfielder, hit .317 for the Reds in 1912 and played until 1918.

From Cuba, pitchers Sandy Consuegra, Pedro Ramos, and Camilo Pascual, catcher Ray Noble, infielder Tony Taylor, and shortstop Zoilo Versalles followed Minnie to the majors in the 1950s. Tony Oliva, Luis Tiant, Tony Perez, and Jose Cardenal became great Cuban ballplayers of the 1960s. Luis Tiant's father, like mine, was a great Latin ballplayer. Often called the "Cuban Carl Hubbell," even the "Black Lefty Grove," Luis Tiant Sr. was a star in the Negro Leagues as well.

Jose Cardenal's story in an interesting one. He was a fine ballplayer and is now a coach with the New York Yankees. Jose came to the United States in 1961, the year of the Bay of Pigs invasion. Knowing that it would be difficult to get him out of Cuba, as Castro made it very hard for youngsters like Jose to leave the country, the Giants placed him with a family in El Paso, Texas, even before they signed him to a contract. Jose made his big league debut with the Giants in 1963.

Tony Oliva also has an interesting story. In 1964 Tony became the first rookie in major league history to win a batting championship. It was the first of three he would win. Tony also led the American League in hits five different times.

He was originally brought to this country by the Minnesota Twins. But they released him, and he was at the airport waiting for a return flight home when the Bay of Pigs invasion occurred. All flights to Cuba were canceled, and Tony was stranded. Two Latin scouts told the Twins they might as well keep Tony since he had a six-month visa. Two years later Tony won the American League batting championship as a rookie, leading the league in base hits and runs scored as well. The next year he won a second batting championship.

Tony's story is a happy one. Far sadder is that of shortstop Zoilo Versalles, who came up with the Washington Senators in 1959. Zoilo was the American League MVP in 1965, preceding both Roberto Clemente (1966) and me (1967) as the first Latin player to win an MVP Award. But soon after he was not allowed to see his family in Cuba because of the break in US-Cuban relations. He succumbed to a destructive lifestyle after that. Soon he was ruined financially, and he hit the streets. He died a short time ago.

Venezuela has produced a steady stream of outstanding major league shortstops. Just look at the Chicago White Sox. Chico Carrasquel started their Venezuelan connection in 1950. When he was traded to the Cleveland Indians in 1956, he was replaced by fellow countryman Luis Aparicio, a future Hall of Famer and American League Rookie of the Year. Then in 1985, the connection continued when the White Sox obtained Ozzie Guillen in a trade with the San Diego Padres.

Venezuela-born Dave Concepcion became the Cincinnati Reds shortstop in 1970, and he was an integral part of the famous Big Red Machine that decade. Pitcher Ramon Monzant, one of the original 1958 Giants like me, came from Venezuela. So did such stars Vic Davalillo and Cesar Tovar.

The Dominican Republic gave us the Alou brothers, Felipe, Matty, and Jesus, as well as Julian Javier, Juan Marichal, Manny Mota, and Rico Carty. Many people think that Felipe was the first Dominican to play in the big leagues in 1958. That honor goes, instead, to Ozzie Virgil, who came up as an infielder with the New York Giants in 1956. And Bobby Avila, the Cleveland

Indians' All-Star second baseman and 1954 American League batting champ, was born in Mexico.

I truly believe that Puerto Rico has the world's largest pool of baseball talent. But until the 1950s the market had not been discovered, and even after that the young talent was not very well organized. I always loved working with kids, and as early as 1961, Roberto Clemente and I would travel around the islands in the offseason working with Little Leaguers.

We came on the major league scene rather late. Hiram Bithorn and Luis Olmo had major league careers in the 1940s. By comparison, Cuba had sent over forty ballplayers to the major leagues by 1950. I was the thirteenth native-born Puerto Rican to make his major league debut in the 1950s when I joined the Giants, and only the fifteenth overall.

Those who preceded me include Ruben Gomez (New York Giants, 1953), Vic Power (Philadelphia Athletics, 1954), Roberto Clemente (Pittsburgh Pirates, 1955), Felix Mantilla (Milwaukee Braves, 1956), and Juan Pizarro (Milwaukee Braves, 1957).

The greatest of the lot, of course, was Roberto Clemente. He could do it all—hit, run, field, throw, hit in the clutch. In fact, with the possible exception of Rocky Colavito in the American League, I don't think I've ever seen a stronger right-field arm that Roberto's. Carl Furillo of the Dodgers may have had an arm like that, but I only got to see him at the end of his career.

Roberto did it day in and day out without the fanfare some other ballplayers got. He kept a lot inside of him. But his record alone tells so much: a .317 lifetime average, four-time National League batting champion, National League MVP in 1966, and twelve-time National League All-Star.

Roberto won 12 straight Gold Glove Awards. He led the National League for a record five times in assists, throwing out 22 runners in 1958. He accumulated 3,000 hits and batted over .300 thirteen times. He was a World Series star as well, leading the Pirates in batting in 1960 and 1971, and he hit safely in every World Series game he played. And all this while being plagued by back pain that was the result of an arthritic spine caused by an automobile accident.

I was shocked and saddened when I learned of his tragic death in an airplane crash on New Year's Eve 1972. Actually, I thought it was all a dream. I had spent New Year's Eve with my mother and brother. I was home asleep when a friend called my brother to ask if I was all right. He had heard reports that a plane went down with a famous Puerto Rican baseball player on it. Until Roberto's identity was released, some people assumed it was me.

Pedro set him straight. But when the news was verified, UPI called me at five in the morning. The reporter asked me to comment on the death of Roberto Clemente. When I awoke in the morning, I thought I was dreaming, that I had dreamt the whole thing. Unfortunately, it was true. Roberto had died in a plane crash. The plane was carrying medical supplies and food to earthquake victims in Nicaragua.

I loved Roberto and his wife, Vera. Roberto and I went back such a long time. I caught his throws from the outfield while he was being tutored by Willie Mays at Santurce in 1954, when I was the team's sixteen-year-old batboy.

I remember when he bought his first car, a 1955 Chevy Bel Air. Since I didn't have a car of my own, Roberto would pick me up and let me drive him to the ballpark. He would also let me take the car to run errands for him while he was at the ballpark. Then on the weekends we would double date. And Roberto was our twenty-year-old chaperone when a bunch of scared teenagers flew from San Juan to Florida together in 1955.

Roberto Clemente has rightfully remained a baseball icon in Puerto Rico, and one of major league baseball's all-time greats. I still keep in touch with Vera Clemente, and I saw her recently at an All-Star Game in Denver. She was the honorary captain of the National League squad.

Their son, Luis, is doing much to keep the memory of his father alive. Roberto left a powerful and inspirational legacy. There's a large sports complex in San Juan called Sports City. It stands as a monument to the great Roberto Clemente. Yet the facility has never fully become what it was originally intended to be. Politics has gotten in the way, and some of the money allocated to the complex has been used for other purposes.

Roberto did so much for our people, and so much for the game of baseball. He became the first Hispanic member of the Hall of Fame in 1973, when the customary five-year waiting period was waived. Later he became only the second baseball player, after Jackie Robinson, to be featured on a US postage stamp.

By 1992 the number of Latin players to have reached the major leagues neared 600. And of all the Latin countries, only the Dominican Republic has produced more major leaguers than Puerto Rico.

Puerto Rico has a great baseball tradition. The game is often passed down from father to son. Look at the Alomars. Sandy Alomar Sr. signed with the Milwaukee Braves in 1964 and enjoyed a fifteen-year career in the majors. His two sons, Roberto and Sandy Jr., are now major league All-Stars. Ozzie Virgil Jr. followed his father to the big leagues in 1980 and became an All-Star catcher with the Philadelphia Phillies and the Atlanta Braves.

One of my proudest moments came in 1993 when I was elected to the Puerto Rican Hall of Fame, thus joining my father. What an honor. Two generations of Cepedas, father and son. There are only about thirty members in the Puerto Rican Hall of Fame, including major leaguers like Luis Arroyo, Carlos Bernier, Roberto Clemente, Nino Escalara, Luis Olmo, Vic Power, and Jose Santiago.

But even after my induction, there remained a noticeable hostility toward me in Puerto Rico. This was especially true in the city of Ponce.

Two more people than anyone else got the ball rolling on my behalf. One was Marco Rivera, a well-known attorney and president of the committee to put me in the Hall of Fame. The other was a journalist by the name of Harry Rexach. My half sister Hilda helped too. She worked in public relations and did a fine job of greasing the wheels. But much more was going on behind the scenes than I was aware of. Tato Rojas, a friend of mine who was on the Puerto Rican Hall of Fame committee and now lives nearby in Vallejo, California, remembers how it went:

> Marco Rivera and Harry Rexach put together a committee with the sole purpose of getting Orlando into the Puerto Rican Hall of Fame, where he rightfully belonged. But some people were still angry at him.

We began sending out lots of letters on Orlando's behalf. Here we had a situation where he could well be elected to the Hall of Fame in Cooperstown and still not be in the Puerto Rican Hall of Fame. We strongly felt that he should be selected here in Puerto Rico before the Cooperstown vote.

All the numbers indicted that Orlando should have been in the Hall of Fame a long time ago. Unfortunately for him, he had served some time and was being penalized beyond measure. Some people couldn't understand that after serving time and getting his life together, there was another Orlando Cepeda who grew out of that experience.

We came along at a time when there wasn't big money in baseball. We were not given huge bonuses. While we were climbing the major league ladder in hopes of achieving major league status, we were usually just about the poverty level. I never had a telephone. Calls to Puerto Rico were very expensive, and at times I didn't talk to my mother for as long as six months.

We also battled our way to the top with a different heritage and a different language. We were young and at times had no idea of what was really happening. When we fought back and got angry, we were labeled troublemakers, lazy, moody, undisciplined. The rap against Latin players has not totally vanished either. Many of the younger players will tell you this today.

Last summer I ran into a guy from Texas. We were talking about baseball and ballplayers. I mentioned Juan Gonzalez and his remarkable feats, including driving in over 100 runs by the All-Star break, and his chance at breaking Hack Wilson's all-time RBI record. "Well, he doesn't work too hard," the guy replied. He said the same thing when I mentioned Ivan Rodriguez. By the end of the 1998 season Juan had driven in more runs (157) in a single season than any American League player since 1959, when Ted Williams and Vern Stephens drove in 159 runs apiece for the Boston Red Sox.

I told Juan and Ivan recently to just go out and play baseball. Do what you have to do on the ball field and forget everything else. The label on Sammy Sosa for years was that he was a dumb ballplayer. Now he's making lots of pitchers look pretty dumb.

In Puerto Rico, the line between the races is very thin, and racial discrimination was not a part of our everyday life. Unlike Cuba, where racial differences were far more pronounced, we hadn't faced the bigotry that American blacks and Cuban blacks endured at home.

With the renewed interest in the Negro Leagues today, there is another factor that I rarely hear mentioned. The Puerto Rican Leagues and the Cuban Leagues used to support the Negro League players. Without winter ball, these guys would have starved to death. Yet most baseball documentaries completely ignore this fact.

I've been lucky. These kids who are in the big leagues today respond to me and seem to respect me. They do so because they know I feel the same way about them and that they can always talk to me and I will listen. I've known Moises Alou and Stan Javier since they were born. What a credit to their fathers, Felipe Alou and Julian Javier. Moises and Stan have strong baseball traditions bred into them. But a working knowledge of baseball history is lost among many of the younger players and has been for some time. George Bell, for one, didn't know who I was when we met, and he was born in the Dominican Republic in 1959. A young pitcher I talked to during a recent spring training was so enamored by today's hitters that he told me Juan Marichal couldn't get anyone out if he was pitching today.

If he'd known the accomplishments of Latin players in the major leagues before 1980, he would've thought twice before he said something as foolish as that. Just take a look at the following facts.

Between 1965 and 1980 Zoilo Versalles (1965), Roberto Clemente (1966), Rod Carew (1977), and I (1967) won MVP Awards.

A Latin American was named Rookie of the Year five times between 1956 and 1980: Luis Aparicio, Chicago White Sox (1956); myself, San Francisco Giants (1958); Tony Oliva, Minnesota Twins (1964); Rod Carew, Minnesota Twins (1967);

and Alfredo Griffin, Toronto Blue Jays (1979). Then, between 1981 and 1990, add Fernando Valenzuela (1981), Ozzie Guillen (1985), Jose Canseco (1986), Benito Santiago (1987), and Sandy Alomar Jr. (1990).

From 1951 through 1979 Latin Americans led their respective leagues in stolen bases twenty-two different times. Luis Aparicio led the American League nine straight years (1956 through 1964). Bert Campaneris of the Oakland A's led the American League six times, and Minnie Minoso three times—1951–1953, his first three major league seasons.

Before 1980 Latins had already captured seventeen batting titles: Rod Carew won seven titles; Roberto Clemente won four; Tony Oliva won three; and Bobby Avila, Matty Alou, and Rico Carty had one each.

I became the first Latin player to lead either league in home runs when I hit 46 for the Giants in 1961. No other Latin would lead either league until Ben Oglivie hit 41 for the Milwaukee Brewers in 1980. My 142 RBIs in 1961 and 111 with the Cardinals in 1967 make me one of five major league players (the other four being Babe Ruth, Jimmy Foxx, Vern Stephens, and Johnny Mize) to lead a league in RBIs with two different clubs. No Latin player would lead either league in RBIs again until Tony Armas drove in 123 runs for the Boston Red Sox in 1984.

I am proud to be considered one of the Latin pioneers on the major league scene. But the baseball public is getting younger, and we pioneers are getting older. Time is catching up with all of us. I get a kick when I think of how David Garcia and Hank Sauer called me a "nice kid." That was a long time ago, and the "nice kid" they mentored back then is now over sixty years old.

For a Latin ballplayer in the US, there is still a great cultural gap to overcome. I can understand what some of these younger players must be feeling because I have been there. With the expanding role of Latin Americans in Major League Baseball today and the expanding fan base, a hard-hitting look at the problems of past and present Latin players is a story just waiting to be told. I hope it will be told soon.

Needless to say, I am very proud of Sammy Sosa. This is not just because of his outstanding season and his 66 home runs but because of the very genuine and appealing way he handled himself all season.

When the Cubs played the Giants here in San Francisco late in the year, I congratulated him on his hitting and home runs. But even more importantly, I congratulated him on how well he was dealing with the press. Sammy showed people that he wasn't just a great baseball player but a decent human being.

Sammy is a real credit to baseball and to Latin ballplayers. A lot of fans probably don't realize that with 158 runs batted in, Sammy had more RBIs in 1998 than any major league player in nearly half a century. In fact, Sammy drove in more runs than any National League player since Hack Wilson's record-setting 190 RBIs in 1930.

⋄18⋄

The Beat Goes On

The past few years have been among the best of my life, and they're just getting better. I have a wonderful wife and partner in Mirian.

My sons were all outstanding athletes, but they did not become professional baseball players like their father and grandfather. And that may have been for the best. I am very proud of Orlando Jr. and Carl. Both are very successful in sales, enjoy fine business reputations in the sports attire field, and are doing extremely well. My son Malcolm and his wife have given me a beautiful grandson, Malcolm Orlando, whom I adore. My youngest son, Ali, is still in school.

I'm involved in baseball on many levels, and I work for the greatest baseball organization in the world, the San Francisco Giants. As an integral part of the Giants Community Relations Staff, I have the opportunity to work with kids—lots of kids. I don't pretend that my words alone will change anyone's behavior. But the kids I talk to seem to listen. They ask questions. If just one or two choose a more positive pattern of behavior and change the direction of their lives, I will be very happy and proud. In all instances, I tell the truth. I tell them the way it is. For example, in Philadelphia a few years ago I told a group of youngsters what can happen if you follow the wrong path.

"That's why I'm here today," I said. "To tell you the dangers of dealing with the wrong people. I went to jail for marijuana. I made a big mistake. You know why? Because I was hanging with the wrong people."

I have a message for kids, a good message. And the San Francisco Giants keep me busy these days. I visit homeless shelters, and I work for Athletes Against AIDS. I visit hospitals and schools, speaking out against drug abuse and telling kids that they don't need drugs to get through life. I figure that a baseball player owes it to the kids to give them what he's learned.

I'm very active in youth and community services organizations throughout Northern California. I serve as a liaison between the San Francisco Giants and the Latin American community. And my work takes me beyond the state of California. I spend lots of time in New York, with the Puerto Rican communities in the Bronx and Manhattan.

Each December during the holiday season the Giants make dozens of visits to various hospital and youth group holiday gatherings. I personally visit the University of California and the San Francisco Medical Centers, and I visit with the kids at the Pediatric Center Ward's annual Santa Party.

I spend several hours at the annual Giants Fan Fair, greeting fans and signing autographs. As a member of the Soka Gakkai International, I adhere to the organization's goals for world peace and brotherhood. I am committed to helping young people keep themselves on the right track.

The number-one goal in my life today is to be a better person. The second is to get in the Hall of Fame. In recent years, that's become a major issue. I'd be less than honest if I didn't say that selection to Cooperstown means very much to me. It will be one of the greatest days of my life if and when I am elected to the Hall of Fame. I hope and pray that day will come in 1999. I barely missed by seven votes in 1994, my last year of eligibility by the Baseball Writers of America. My name is now before the Veterans Committee.

But I never wanted to get to the Hall of Fame on sympathy. I've got the numbers. I feel that I should be there on merit. I don't blame not being selected on being black, or Latin, or both, nor do I blame my marijuana conviction twenty years ago. Too many media people try to push you into that corner, and I won't bite.

In my first year of eligibility in 1980, I received a scant forty-three votes. By 1984, I received 124 votes. In 1990, I was up to 221. The San Francisco Giants organization could not have done more to bring me to the attention of the baseball public and media. Words just can't express my gratitude to Peter Magowan, Pat Gallagher, Larry Baer, and Bob Rose in the Giants' front office for all they did on my behalf.

By 1993 the vote total had climbed to over 250. I was just sixty-six votes shy, and my hopes began to soar as my last year of eligibility loomed ahead. Many writers across the country took up my cause, writers such as Tom Weir of *USA Today*, Stan Hockman of the *Philadelphia Daily News*, Jim Murray of the *Los Angeles Times*, and George Vecsey of *The New York Times*. So did Jerome Holtzman, the dean of Chicago sportswriters. Before the Hall of Fame vote in 1994, Hal Brock of the Associated Press pointed out, "There are 18 retired players who have hit more than 300 home runs and batted over .295. Seventeen of them are in the Hall of Fame." I was the odd man out.

But of all my media boosters, what Bernie Miklasz wrote in the *St. Louis Post Dispatch* touched me the most. In a September 1993 piece he wrote:

> Character? Integrity? Okay, what about the rejuvenation of a man who crawled back from a plunge so deep and bleak that he contemplated suicide? What about a man who attacked his demons head-on and became a better person? Cepeda's one mistake was ultimately valuable in that it led to a thousand visits to the schools and the playgrounds. Put it this way: Is any living enshrined member of the Hall of Fame doing as much to touch the lives around him? Cepeda is more than some vague platitude; he is character and integrity at work.
>
> This is important work, valuable work, work worth more than all the museum pieces in Cooperstown. See, this is what the voters don't understand: Orlando Cepeda already has won. He is just waiting to give the speech.

And I was waiting. But everything was out of my hands. The night of the voting we booked a suite at the Park 55 Hotel in San Francisco. Mirian and I and a few close friends like Tato Rojas and his wife, Ruth; boxer Mike Gallo and his family;

Laurence Hyman; and Tony Dorsey of SGI were there. Gary Hentbroth donated the suite and provided us with champagne and sandwiches. The curtains were open so we could see the Bay. The TV was on. At a certain hour the phone was going to ring. We were calm while we all anticipated the call. But the phone didn't ring.

Five or six minutes later it finally did. Someone answered. The voice at the other end identified himself as Bob Rose. "Hi, I'm calling for Orlando," he said. I took the receiver and listened carefully. The room was utterly silent. Then I covered the receiver. I looked at Mirian, looked at my friends who were waiting anxiously, and told them the result, "Missed by seven votes."

I talked with Bob for a few more minutes and hung up. Mirian was very stoic. Nobody knew quite what to say. Finally Tato Rojas broke the silence. He simply said, "Everything in its place and time."

At first I was shocked. Then I told myself, there's a reason for this. I just had to go forward now. In the meantime Bob had told me to come down to the ballpark. But with all the excitement I had forgotten. So we headed to Laurence Hyman's house instead. Earlier Laurence had planned a get-together at his house after the voting, no matter what the result.

When I didn't arrive at the ballpark, Bob Rose called a friend who knew the number to my car phone. My friends Omar and Maria quickly called me to say that everyone was waiting at the ballpark for me. The TV and radio stations, the press, everyone.

So we turned around and headed to the ballpark. When I got there I found a huge gathering. Hundreds of media people. It looked like I was the guy who would be inducted into the Hall of Fame, not the fellow who just missed. I'll never forget what happened next. I was introduced, and instead of being nervous, I have never felt so calm in my life.

That's when I really felt the power of my practice, the power of Buddhism. I was in control. They kept asking me if the reason I didn't make it was because I was Puerto Rican. Maybe because I was black. Or was it because I was busted for marijuana? But I avoided all those questions. I wanted no part of them. It was just meant to be that way, I told them.

I felt no bitterness, and that was true victory—my greatest victory, in fact, because I won over myself that day. I was tested big time, and I had won. In the old days I would have lapsed into blaming others. I might have said, as I had in the past, "The hell with the Hall of Fame! I couldn't care less."

At that moment, that crucial moment, I remained calm and controlled. I had prevailed over anger and bitterness. I felt at peace with myself and the world around me.

Later I received a number of letters from writers and fans alike saying I'd shown a lot of class and dignity. Peter Magowan, Pat Gallagher, Bob Rose, and others in the organization had given me the opportunity to show to the world the person I had become, and I hadn't let them down.

I may have rehearsed my acceptance speech, the speech I would have given had I been elected to the Hall of Fame. But I never rehearsed my response if I wasn't elected. It came naturally. My wife had tears in her eyes. I squeezed her hand knowing that I had won my greatest victory ever. The angry man was gone.

Many things have changed over the years. During my baseball career there were good days and bad. There were home runs and strikeouts, RBIs and errors. I tasted fame and degradation. I heard cheers and scorn.

But one thing never wavered, and one thing never changed. Music has always been the one constant in my life. I was "Cha Cha, the Dancing Master." With music I could somehow survive.

Music makes me happy. I grew up with music. It's been with me all my life. My father loved music—besides being a baseball player, Perucho played the marimba. My uncle, Raphael Cepeda, was one of the best trumpet players in Puerto Rico and played with the big Puerto Rican bands. We didn't have a record player when I was growing up, but my brother, Pedro, who also loved music, would tune in Cuba on the radio every Saturday night to get the best of the Latin sounds.

During the tough times music was all I had. It pulled me through. When I was in prison they wouldn't allow record players in the cells. Yet somebody from New York, knowing how much music meant to me, sent me some albums. On Saturdays the prison authorities would let me go to a special room and listen to these albums. It really sustained me. I had something to look forward to.

For many years now I have played the conga drums. I never took lessons. You don't need lessons to play conga. It's just inside you. It's like playing baseball—you learn by trial and error.

Anyone in the know is aware that Tito Puente is my great hero. When my brother, Pedro, was in the army in 1952 he saw Tito at the Paladium in New York City. When Pedro returned to Puerto Rico, he was so excited. "I saw Tito Puente! Wow!" I never saw him more thrilled.

Four years later, when I finished C ball at St. Cloud, I went to New York. I took the $50 that Louisville Slugger had given me to use my name on a bat, and I bought a new suit especially to see Tito Puente at the Paladium.

What a thrill! What an evening! What music! Tito Puente, Tito Rodriguez, and Machito—they were all there, three of the all time greats under one roof. Tito Puente is still tops. Whenever he performs in the Bay Area I always see him. We are great friends now.

So music means everything to me. I go to bed with music, I get up with music. I listen to music in my car, and I relax at home with music.

Writer Richard Keller recently did a piece on me for *Giants* magazine. It wasn't about baseball statistics, but rather it was a look at the city that I know and love. We revisited some of the old haunts. We drove around the Sunset, and so much flashed before my eyes. I remembered the gray apartment atop PJ's Oyster restaurant, which was my first San Francisco residence.

Next came a real surprise. I walked up 9th Avenue and found myself in front of the Ballpark Sports Card Shop. The proprietors, Renee and Jim Towan, had arranged a surprise for me there. There was a display window out front with autographed photographs, bats, balls, and assorted memorabilia from my playing days.

Inside the store there were videotaped highlights from my career running continuously on an overhead television screen. There was a chocolate cake with white frosting and nine white candles, one for each season I played for the Giants. Finally Renee Towan read from a scroll proclaiming April 21 as Orlando Cepeda Day in the Sunset District "for the many years he lived here during his All-Star career with the Giants." I was deeply touched.

Then we made our way toward Ocean Beach. Again the old times flashed so vividly. Opening Day 1958; the Giants and the Dodgers; the debut of Major League Baseball on the West Coast; my big-league debut at Seals Stadium; signing my first major league contract five minutes before game time for $7,000.

I remembered my disbelief when looking across the field and seeing the likes of Pee Wee Reese, Gil Hodges, and Duke Snider; the thrill of playing on the same ballclub as Willie Mays; the outside changeup that Don Bessent threw me in the third, which I connected with for the first of my 379 major league home runs. I lined that one over the right-field fence.

There was the pink house on 19th Avenue and Pacheco Avenue where I moved in 1960 and where I once lived when I was a young baseball star with the world in front of me. I thought it would go on forever.

Then we stopped the car in front of a two-story duplex at 48th and Pacheco—a short distance from the Pacific Ocean. It was the building I bought in 1961, right next to Willie McCovey's. I lived upstairs and rented the downstairs. Willie Mac and I were just a couple of happy-go-lucky kids back then.

Living in San Francisco in the late fifties and early sixties was heaven. The novelty of each new and exciting day: Cal Tjader at the Blackhawk, such great jazz; Mongo Santamaria and Willie Bobo, the giants of Latin jazz, at the Copacabana; Wes Montgomery at the Jazz Workshop. No, it was better than heaven.

Those nights out with Felipe, Willie Mac, and Juan. That special night at the Blackhawk with Miles Davis, John Coltrane, and Cannonball Adderley when they surprised me with a new song, "Cepeda, Cepeda, Viva Cepeda," improvising it as they went along.

Keller and I reached the top of Diamond Heights. I took a look at the house I bought in 1965, where I lived until I was traded to the St. Louis Cardinals a short time later. By that time the city, the ballclub, and the fans were like a second family. I hated to leave. But sometimes you just have to.

But I came back. It's more than thirty years later, and I'm still here. I consider myself a fortunate man. Life gave me another chance, a wonderful new opportunity, and Buddhism gave me the tools to turn things around.

On September 17, 1997, I turned sixty years old. The Giants allowed me the opportunity and the honor of throwing out the first pitch that day. That was the very day the Giants clinched the National League West by beating the Los Angeles Dodgers. The win put the Giants into the postseason for the first time since 1989. Birthday wishes flashed beautifully from the scoreboard at Candlestick Park:

"Happy Birthday, Orlando Cepeda! Happy 60th, Baby Bull!"

Epilogue

My Northern California home has been called a baseball museum of sorts. It gives me enormous pleasure to sit in my study or workroom and look at more than half a century of baseball history both here in the United States and in the Caribbean.

I have photographs of my father, both alone and with greats such as Satchel Paige, Josh Gibson, and Silvio Garcia. One particular favorite shows my father in a group called "The Most Perfect Team." It was a dream team organized and sponsored by the President of the Dominican Republic in 1937. He wanted to put together a team that could rival the New York Yankees. He assembled the best Negro League players, the best Cuban players, the best Puerto Rican players, and the best from the rest of the Caribbean.

Photographs, memorabilia, and mementos adorn my walls. How very fortunate I was to be able to play Major League Baseball with and against some of the greatest names ever: Willie Mays, Roberto Clemente, Roger Maris, Hank Aaron, Felipe Alou, Curt Flood, Mickey Mantle . . . I have photographs and mementos of all the great ones who shared a baseball diamond with me.

There is an enlarged photograph of the 1968 St. Louis Cardinals team, which first appeared on the cover of *Sports*

Illustrated. I never tire of looking at it. Was there ever a better all-around baseball team or a better bunch of teammates? Certainly not on any other team I played on.

I'm glad to see that there is a renewed interest in Roger Maris today. Roger was always shortchanged by the baseball establishment. The 1998 breaking of Roger's record by Mark McGwire and Sammy Sosa meant a re-evaluation of Roger. It was a long overdue appreciation of a fine ballplayer.

Another favorite portrait I hold extremely dear is a beautiful painting of my son Orlando Jr. at age two painted by Curt Flood. When I look at it hanging in my front hall, I recall the beautiful and artistic human being Curt was. He was an outstanding ballplayer who happened to feel things too deeply for his own good at times.

I especially value an autographed picture of Muhammad Ali in the ring. My third son, Ali, was named after the Champ. Other pictures in full view include jockey Angel Cordero, a good friend, and Michael Jordan, my idea of what a superstar athlete should be both on and off the field. There are photos of Dizzy Gillespie, Danny Glover, Al Pacino. Parts of my life in and out of baseball stand as visible reminders of how fortunate I have been.

And it has been a good life. Sure, there were some bad times. I made more than my share of mistakes. But I feel I paid my debts, emotional and otherwise. And I managed to survive and become a better person. And as I bettered myself, better people entered my life.

◆ ◆ ◆

As a baseball player I am often asked to name my All-Time Team. Remember, I played in one of the greatest baseball eras ever. To reduce the number of great ballplayers to an All-Star team of ten or twelve players is imperfect at best. But I played in the big leagues for seventeen seasons, and I saw so many great ones come and go . . . well, here are the best I saw:

Catchers	Johnny Bench
First Base	Willie McCovey
Second Base	Julian Javier
Third Base	Clete Boyer

Shortstop	Luis Aparicio and Jose Pagan
Outfield	Hank Aaron, Roberto Clemente, Willie Mays
Pitchers (R)	Juan Marichal and Bob Gibson
Pitchers (L)	Sandy Koufax and Warren Spahn
Reserves	Richie Allen, Frank Robinson, Ernie Banks, Eddie Mathews, Carl Yastrzemski, Al Kaline
Manager	Bill Rigney
Best Pure Hitters	Rico Carty and Tony Oliva

Nineteen ninety-eight marked the fortieth anniversary of the original San Francisco Giants. It's a special anniversary for me as well, because it marked my major league debut. I'm glad that with the passing years Willie Mays and I have come to terms. We've both mellowed with age and are proud to be a part of the great baseball tradition in San Francisco. Former Giants team-mates Willie Mac, Mike McCormick, and Eddie Bressoud live in the Bay Area, and we get together often for Giant reunions.

Today I can particularly enjoy the influx of Latin players. There are so many talented youngsters out there to propel base-ball into the twenty-first century. My dedication and commit-ment to the Latin baseball experience remains forever firm.

Some of my closest friends are Tony Oliva and his wife, Gordell; Juan Marichal and his wife, Alma; and Tony Perez and his wife, Pituca. All three men are fine family men. They are real gentlemen in addition to having been outstanding ballplayers.

In fact, I am the godfather of Tony Perez's son Eduardo, who is currently with the Cincinnati Reds. If he has any baseball-related problems, he knows to call me. We need help at times from those who came before us. The kids today need the same guidance from those of us who came before them.

If I have learned any lesson in life, it's that human decency and goodness do not begin and end with any particular race or group of people. As a general rule, people who respect them-selves and respect others will find respect in return. It doesn't matter if you're black or white, Anglo or Hispanic, respect is a two-way street.

That's where I have been so fortunate. Even during the

toughest times, goodness managed to surface, and for that gift I am forever grateful.

A friend of mine has a fixture on his wall. On a wooden plaque are the words "About People." The verse that follows says it as well as anything I have seen or read:

> If you really love 'em
> Tell 'em!
> If you're thinkin' of 'em
> Tell 'em!
> If they're good 'n' true
> And dear to you
> The thing to do
> Is tell 'em!

Appendix A

Significant Factors

Rookie of the Year—San Francisco Giants (1958)

Comeback Player of the Year—St. Louis Cardinals (1966)

National League Most Valuable Player—St. Louis Cardinals (1967)

Designated Hitter of the Year—Boston Red Sox (1973)

Seven-time National League All-Star, nine All-Star Games total

379 home runs

1,365 runs batted in

Nine seasons batting over .300

Three World Series appearances—San Francisco Giants (1962), St. Louis Cardinals (1967 and 1968)

One League Championship Series—Atlanta Braves (1969)

First player to hit more than 20 home runs with four different teams— San Francisco Giants, St. Louis Cardinals, Atlanta Braves, Boston Red Sox

Led the National League with 46 home runs and 142 RBIs in 1961; 142 RBIs remains a San Francisco Giants record

Only player in major league history to be unanimously chosen both Rookie of the Year and League MVP

Appendix B

Career Major League Statistics

Year	Team	Games	At-bats	Runs	Hits	Dbls	Trpls	HR	RBIs	Batting Avg	Bases on Balls	Strike-outs	Stolen Bases
1958	SF	148	603	88	188	38	4	25	96	.312	29	84	15
1959	SF	151	605	92	192	35	4	27	105	.317	33	100	23
1960	SF	151	569	81	169	36	3	24	96	.297	34	91	15
1961	SF	152	585	185	182	28	4	46	142	.311	39	91	12
1962	SF	162	625	105	191	26	1	35	114	.306	37	97	10
1963	SF	156	579	100	183	33	4	34	97	.316	37	70	8
1964	SF	142	529	75	161	27	2	31	97	.304	31	43	9
1965	SF	33	34	1	6	1	0	1	5	.176	3	9	0
1966	SF/ STL	142	501	70	151	26	0	20	73	.301	38	79	9
1967	STL	151	563	91	183	37	0	25	111	.325	62	75	11
1968	STL	157	600	71	149	26	2	16	73	.248	43	96	8
1969	ATL	154	573	74	147	28	2	22	88	.257	55	76	12
1970	ATL	148	567	87	173	33	0	34	111	.305	47	75	6
1971	ATL	71	250	31	69	10	1	14	44	.276	22	29	3
1972	ATL/ OAK	31	87	6	25	3	0	4	9	.287	7	17	0
1973	BOS	142	550	51	159	25	0	20	86	.209	50	81	0
1974	KC	33	107	3	23	5	0	1	18	.215	9	16	1
TTLS 17 yrs.		2,124	7,927	1,131	2,351	417	27	379	1,365	.297	588	1,169	142

Appendix C

The thirteen pitchers who surrendered the most home runs to Orlando Cepeda.

10	Lew Burdette	(TR)		
10	Warren Spahn	(TL)	(HOF)	
9	Curt Simmons	(TL)		
6	Bob Purkey	(TR)		
6	Ray Sadecki	(TL)		
6	Claud Osteen	(TL)		
5	Bob Friend	(TR)		
5	Sandy Koufax	(TL)	(HOF)	

5	Vern Law	(TR)
5	Johnny Podres	(TL)
5	Roger Craig	(TR)
5	Tony Cloninger	(TR)
5	Ken Holtzman	(TR)

(TR) Right-hander
(TL) Left-hander
(HOF) Hall of Famer

(Information provided by the Society of American Baseball Research.)

Appendix D

Home Runs

Career Home Runs
#1	April 15, 1958	Don Bessent, Los Angeles Dodgers
#100	July 9, 1961	Ray Sadecki, St. Louis Cardinals
#200	June 20, 1964	Mike Cuellar, St. Louis Cardinals
#300	August 4, 1969	Jerry Robertson, Montreal Expos
#379	August 14, 1974	Luke Walker, Detroit Tigers

Home Runs by City, Top Ten
117	San Francisco	National League
43	St. Louis	National League
39	Atlanta	National League
29	Chicago	National League
24	Cincinnati	National League
22	Philadelphia	National League
21	Los Angeles	National League
18	Milwaukee	National League
16	Pittsburgh	National League
12	Houston	National League

Total Number of Ballparks Homered In
26

(Information provided by the Society of American Baseball Research.)

Acknowledgments

I had wonderful people come into my life at the right time. My wife Mirian soon found out that I wasn't a rich baseball player, but she loved me, cared for me, and gave to me regardless of where I was at the time. Most importantly, she believed in me.

Mirian's late father, Kuikue, was a real friend and surrogate father to me. My uncles Ubaldo and Alejandro Pennes always looked after me and were wonderful role models—whether I was a young boy in danger of going astray or an adult experiencing troubled times. How I miss them both. My brother, Pedro, and my sisters, aunts, cousins, and nephew were with me always.

There were always loyal and good friends as well. Angel Cordero and his mother were there for me through the tough times. When I needed money for an airline ticket to New York, it was there.

Joe Trout, who I met at Elgin over twenty years ago, is still a good friend. Joe; his wife, Pat; and his mother, Jane, were like family to me during the hard times in Philadelphia. Joe and I are like brothers.

My good friends in Puerto Rico, Mariano and Angie Diaz and Pedro and Angie Rosario, never stopped supporting me through periods of pain, sorrow, and humiliation. Emilio Montanez, an attorney in Puerto Rico, represented me in court when I didn't have the money to pay a lawyer.

Harry Rexach, a journalist and friend for forty-five years;

George Colon, a sports collector; and David Albarran, another good friend, all worked hard against the public tide to convince people that I belonged in the Puerto Rican Hall of Fame. Eddie Millan, a good friend and Las Vegas hotel executive, always found the time to put me up when I needed some rest and recreation.

Vincent Donahue, my dear friend of forty-five years, and actor Tony Martinez supported me one hundred percent during my bad times in Puerto Rico. Tato Cruz bought my airline ticket to Eglin when I was broke and hired me to coach an amateur team in Juncos when everyone was against me.

Manny Gonzales flew to Puerto Rico after I was busted and was a good friend and supporter. Ben and Nellie Fernandez, Clark and Janette Parker, and Ruben and Martha Rodreguez have always welcomed me in their homes. David, Jeanie, and Dean Blackman and the whole Blackman family were always there for me. How honored I was to participate in Allison Blackman's *bat mitzvah* ceremony this year—the only person not of the Jewish faith to have been asked.

Baseball players are special people. The talent required to play the game is enormous. Many of us are still in touch. Two of my closest friends, Felipe Alou and Juan Marichal, are still very involved in the game. How far back we go!

It's always fun to be around my old batting coach and teammate Hank Sauer. In my younger days with the Giants, I don't know what I would have done without him. And they don't come any finer than Bill Rigney, my first manager. He gave me the opportunity I needed as a twenty-year-old kid. And to former major league coach and manager Dave Garcia, thanks for caring so much and helping me when I was just a scared kid from Puerto Rico trying to make it as a baseball player in this country.

These are some of my unsung heroes. Like that Beatles song from the sixties says, "In my life I've loved them all."

No list of acknowledgments would be complete without a special debt of gratitude to my former St. Louis Cardinals teammate and New York Mets announcer Tim McCarver for writing the introduction. The same for Peter Magowan, President and

Managing General Partner of the San Francisco Giants, for writing the foreword.

Equally to Larry Baer, Executive Vice President and Chief Operations Officer of the San Francisco Giants; Pat Gallagher, Vice President of the San Francisco Giants; Bob Rose, Vice President of Communications; and Maria Jacinto in the Giants' Public Relations Division. Thanks for all your enormous help and assistance.

The same to Rebecca, Kerry, and Sue, my able assistants in the Community Relations Department, for making my job so much easier. Likewise to my good friends Russ, Amy, Bob Bisio, and everyone else in the Giants' Ticket Office.

Thanks you Brian David, my attorney and business manager, and to good friends Jon Gilmore and John Taylor, who have helped me with legal advice. And to Max Shapiro and Laurence Hyman, how much I thank you for bringing me back to baseball at a time when I felt all was lost.

To Al Albergate and Tony Dorsey of SGI and to the Soka Gakkai in Los Angeles, Sacramento, and Suison, your friendship and spiritual help know no limits.

Friends Bill Diaz and Gary Disien have been great and caring neighbors. To photographer Frank Hadfield, thanks for the Golden Gate photographs. There is no city like San Francisco.

Ten months ago Herb Fagen approached me with an idea: to tell the true and honest story of my life. I had been reluctant till then, but he convinced me that the right time was now. We spent many long hours together and became good friends. He heard my words, took his notes, and made me think. My life unfolded before my very eyes with memories that had long been hidden. The result is our book, *Baby Bull: From Hardball to Hard Time and Back*. I am very proud.

Orlando Cepeda

◆ ◆ ◆

The Society of American Baseball Research (SABR), as usual, provided a multitude of information. They are the true custodians of the baseball flames. And a rousing thanks to SABR member Dick Beverage for his expertise in proofing the manuscript for factual and statistical accuracy.

Two former baseball greats are also deserving. Many thanks

to my very good friend and two-time American League batting champion Ferris Fain for his help in selecting a title for the book—a real on-target job. And to Minnie Minoso, one of my boyhood heroes growing up in Chicago, who five years ago took a chance on a former history teacher turned middle-aged writer and chose me from among many to co-author the story of his life, *Just Call Me Minnie: My Six Decades in Baseball*, and who in the process first brought baseball's Baby Bull, Orlando Cepeda, to my attention.

A million thanks to those baseball people who granted interviews and helped with the project: Tim McCarver, Peter Magowan, Bill Rigney, Dave Garcia, Hank Sauer, Stanley Javier, Juan Gonzalez, Ivan Rodriguez, Pat Gallagher, and Tony LaRussa. The same to Al Albergate, Laurence Hyman, Brian David, and Tato Rojas. Your comments and remembrances are invaluable.

To my mom, Gert Fagen, and my sister, Ruth Phillips— family love and support is everything. To Sally Landis, "My Gal Sal", thanks for your patience and understanding. To my pal Irving Katzman, thanks for being the best friend a guy could have.

Thanks to my agent, Jake Elwell of Wieser and Wieser, for another job well done. The same to Mike Emmerich, Senior Editor at Taylor Publishing, and to Stacey Sexton, Assistant Editor at Taylor, for seeing the project through to completion.

Finally, to Orlando Cepeda, baseball's Baby Bull, a true Hall of Famer in every possible way. It's been a real privilege and a genuine pleasure.

Herb Fagen

Index